The Politics of Spain

Spain's evolution from authoritarian dictatorship to modern democracy
was a remarkable achievement, and it created a model that has since
been emulated by other countries undergoing similar transitions. Yet
its success raised a question that perplexes experts to this day: how and
why did a successful democracy emerge in the absence of any tradition
of democratic stability? This landmark textbook examines the causes
and conditions that explain modern Spain's political development, and
analyzes the basic characteristics of Spanish democracy today – its core
political institutions, its political parties and party systems (both
regional and national), and patterns of electoral behavior. Written by
two leading experts in the field, this is a truly indispensable guide for
all undergraduate students of Spanish politics, history, society, and
culture.

RICHARD GUNTHER is a professor in the Department of Political Science
at Ohio State University.

JOSÉ RAMÓN MONTERO is a professor in the Department of Political
Science and International Relations at the Universidad Autonóma de
Madrid.

CAMBRIDGE TEXTBOOKS IN COMPARATIVE POLITICS

Series Editors:
Jan W. van Deth, *Universität Mannheim, Germany*
Ken Newton, *University of Southampton, United Kingdom*

Comparative research is central to the study of politics. This series offers accessible but sophisticated materials for students of comparative politics at the introductory level and beyond. It comprises an authoritative introductory textbook, *Foundations of Comparative Politics*, accompanied by volumes devoted to the politics of individual countries, and an introduction to methodology in comparative politics. The books share a common structure and approach, allowing teachers to choose combinations of volumes to suit their particular course. The volumes are also suitable for use independent of one another. Attractively designed and accessibly written, this series provides an up-to-date and flexible teaching resource.

The Politics of Spain

RICHARD GUNTHER and JOSÉ RAMÓN MONTERO

CAMBRIDGE
UNIVERSITY PRESS

CAMBRIDGE UNIVERSITY PRESS
Cambridge, New York, Melbourne, Madrid, Cape Town, Singapore, São Paulo, Delhi

Cambridge University Press
The Edinburgh Building, Cambridge CB2 8RU, UK

Published in the United States of America by Cambridge University Press, New York

www.cambridge.org
Information on this title: www.cambridge.org/9780521604000

First published 2009

Printed in the United Kingdom at the University Press, Cambridge

A catalogue record for this publication is available from the British Library

Library of Congress Cataloguing in Publication data
Gunther, Richard.
The politics of Spain / Richard Gunther, José Ramón Montero.
    p.   cm. – (Cambridge textbooks in comparative politics)
Includes index.
ISBN 978-0-521-84333-1
1. Spain – Politics and government.   2. Public administration – Spain.   3. Democracy – Spain.
I. Montero, José R., 1948–   II. Title.   III. Series.
JN8221.G86   2008
320.946 – dc22   2008042409

ISBN 978-0-521-84333-1 hardback
ISBN 978-0-521-60400-0 paperback

Contents

Figures

Maps

Tables

Acknowledgments

The series of Cambridge Textbooks in Comparative Politics is the product of a unique combination of personal talents and institutional support. Without this leadership and support, the overall project, and this book in particular, would not have been possible. For that, we wish to express our deep gratitude to Jan van Deth and Ken Newton. We appreciate their invitation to participate in this ambitious initiative to publish an innovative, high-quality series of books that can be used in undergraduate political science courses throughout the world. Ken, in particular, went to great efforts to strengthen the quality of this book through his tireless and rigorous editing of each individual chapter. Since neither of us had previously written for an audience of undergraduate students, we had a lot to learn about adapting our writing style to make this work accessible to a broader audience. In the final product, as a result of his efforts, it is, indeed, much easier to see the forest for the trees.

Over the course of writing this book, several institutions played key roles in providing us with the resources and assistance necessary to carry it to fruition. The Political Science departments of the Ohio State University and the Universidad Autónoma de Madrid, as well as OSU's Mershon Center, provided financial support and infrastructural resources that made it possible to carry out the analysis and writing of this book. We are particularly grateful for the research assistance of Héctor Cebolla, the editorial suggestions of Adriana LaMonte, and, especially, the important contributions to our analysis of public policy by Ignacio Molina. In Madrid, the Centro de Estudios Avanzados in Ciencias Sociales (CEACS) of the Instituto Juan March provided superb facilities in which much of this collaborative work took place, and its splendid library, created and maintained by Martha Peach, Almudena Knecht, and Paz Fernández, was an invaluable resource. We are also grateful for additional financial assistance provided by the Spanish Ministerio de Educación y Ciencia (SEJ2006-10073 CPOL) and the Comunidad de Madrid (CCG06-UAM/HUM-1598).

Cambridge University Press's editor, John Haslam, provided constant encouragement, and we appreciate his patience in the face of delays at certain stages of the writing process. We are also most grateful to assistant editor Carrie Cheek, who provided invaluable help and guidance in bringing this book into print, and to Jo Bramwell, for her excellent work in copy-editing the manuscript.

We must, of course, conclude with the usual disclaimer: we alone are responsible for any shortcomings or deficiencies in this book. The support, assistance, and advice that we received from the persons and institutions cited above helped to make this book a much better product. We hope that readers will benefit from these efforts, and will come away from this book knowing a bit more about comparative politics and politics in Spain.

Abbreviations

AP	Alianza Popular (conservative; became Partido Popular in 1989)
BNG	Bloque Nacionalista Galego (left-wing regional-nationalist party in Galicia; once anti-system, now catch-all left-wing party)
CCAA	Comunidades autónomas (regional governments)
CCOO	Comisiones Obreras (formerly Communist-dominated trade union, now one of the two major unions in Spain)
CDC	Convergència Democràtica de Catalunya (Catalan nationalist party, one of two parties making up the CiU coalition)
CDS	Centro Democrático y Social (centrist party, 1982–93)
CEDA	Confederación Española de Derechas Autónomas (right-wing Catholic party, Second Republic, 1931–6)
CEOE	Confederación Española de Organizaciones Empresariales (Spanish Confederation of Business Organizations; "umbrella" association for big business)
CEPYME	Confederación Española de la Pequeña y Mediana Empresa (Spanish Confederation of Small and Medium Businesses)
CGPJ	Consejo General del Poder Judicial (national council overseeing the judicial system and the appointment of judges)
CIS	Centro de Investigaciones Sociológicas, Madrid
CiU	Convergència i Unió (coalition of two center-right Catalan nationalist parties; was Pacte Demòcratic per Catalunya in 1977)
CNEP	Comparative National Elections Project
CNT	Confederación Nacional del Trabajo (anarcho-syndicalist union, Second Republic)
COREPER	Permanent Committee of Representatives of the European Union
EC	European Community (officially the European Communities), from 1967 until 1993 the commonly used name for what is now the European Union
EA	Eusko Alkartasuna (Basque Solidarity) (Basque nationalist party; split from PNV in 1986; center-left)
EBB	Euskadi Buru Batzar (executive committee of PNV)
EE	Euskadiko Ezkerra (Basque Left) (Basque nationalist leftist party once tied to ETA; became fully "loyal" competitor in Spanish politics in 1981 and merged with the Basque regional branch of the PSOE in 1993)

EH	Euskal Herritarrok (Basque Citizens) (one of the new names of HB after Batasuna was banned)
EHAK	Euskal Herrietako Alderdi Komunista (Communist Party of the Basque Peoples), an extreme-left, ultra-nationalist, anti-system party (one of several successors to Herri Batasuna, following its banning by the courts)
ERC	Esquerra Republicana de Catalunya (left-wing Catalan nationalist party)
ETA	Euskadi ta Askatasuna (Basque Homeland and Freedom) (Basque separatist terrorist organization)
EU	European Union
GDP	Gross domestic product (the standard measure of all economic activity within a country)
HB	Herri Batasuna (Popular Unity) (ultra-nationalist Basque party tied to ETA; anti-system, extreme-left)
IC	Iniciativa per Catalunya (Catalan branch of leftist IU)
IU	Izquierda Unida (United Left) (coalition including PCE and various left-wing and post-materialist groups)
NATO	North Atlantic Treaty Organization
OECD	Organisation for Economic Co-operation and Development
PA	Partido Andaluz (center-left, formerly Partido Socialista de Andalucía)
PCE	Partido Comunista de España (Spanish Communist Party)
PDC	Pacte Democràtic per Catalunya; see CiU
PNV	Partido Nacionalista Vasco (Basque Nationalist Party) (center-right)
PP	Partido Popular (was Alianza Popular 1977–89)
PR	Proportional representation
PRC	Partido Regionalista de Cantabria
PRP	Partido Riojano Progresista (conservative, regionalist party in La Rioja)
PSC	Partit dels Socialistes de Catalunya (Catalan branch of PSOE)
PSOE	Partido Socialista Obrero Español (Spanish Socialist Worker Party)
PSP	Partido Socialista Popular
PSUC	Partit Socialista Unificat de Catalunya (Unified Socialist Party of Catalonia) (Catalan branch of Communist Party)
UA	Unidad Alavesa (center-right regional party in Alava; opposed to Basque nationalism)
UCD	Unión de Centro Democrático (center-right party)
UDC	Unió Democràtica de Catalunya (Democratic Union of Catalonia) (Christian democratic party in CiU coalition)
UGT	Unión General de Trabajadores (formerly socialist trade union, now one of the two major unions in Spain)
UPN	Unión del Pueblo Navarro (center-right, regionalist party in Navarra)
VAT	Value-added tax

1 The state and democracy in Spain: a historical overview

Spain's democratic regime today is a stable, consolidated system that fits well within the mainstream of West European **democracies**. As we will see in the following chapters, it does have some distinguishing characteristics, but several of these (such as its high level of cabinet stability) represent achievements that have enhanced the quality and performance of democracy in Spain.

This success story is not to be taken for granted. Prior to 1977, Spain had never experienced governance within a stable and fully democratic system. The Restoration Monarchy of 1875–1931 was not fully democratic, and while the Second Republic (1931–36) was a democratic system it was so polarized and unstable that it came to an end with the outbreak of a devastating civil war (1936–39). Over the course of the following four decades, Spain was governed by an authoritarian dictatorship under Generalísimo Francisco Franco. When he died in 1975, it was not at all clear that a **consolidated democracy** would emerge within a country that completely lacked a tradition of stable democratic rule, and which was still divided

Democracy A democracy is a political system whose leaders are elected in competitive multi-party and multi-candidate processes in which opposition parties have a fair chance of electing representatives to legislative bodies and attaining executive power. These elections must be held at regular intervals, and must allow all members of the political community to express their preferences through the use of basic freedoms of association, information, and communication.

Consolidated democracy A consolidated democracy is a political regime which is fully democratic (see Key Term 1.1), whose key political institutions are regarded as legitimate by all politically significant groups, which accept and adhere to democratic "rules of the game."

Map 1.1 The regions of Spain since 1980

Social cleavages are deep and persistent differences in society where (1) objective social differences (class, religion, race, language, or region) are aligned with (2) subjective awareness of these differences (different cultures, ideologies, and orientations), and are (3) organized by political parties, groups, or movements. Cleavages are often the basis of political conflict.

along the lines of historically disruptive **social** and political **cleavages**.

In this chapter, we will analyze the successful democratic transition in Spain initiated by Franco's death and largely completed with the ratification of a democratic constitution in December 1978. In order to appreciate the significance of this successful democratization process, however, we will briefly examine Spain's political history, beginning with the very founding of the Spanish state. This historical overview is particularly important insofar as it will enable us to understand the origins of several divisive cleavages that have contributed to conflict and political instability over several centuries, including the outbreak of six civil wars. These cleavages include:

- **Center–periphery conflicts**. Throughout Spanish history (including the present democratic era) there have been tensions over the proper structure of the state. Particularly following the instauration of the Borbón dynasty in the eighteenth century, some political leaders favored a centralized state governed from Madrid, while others have demanded the preservation or restoration of regional self-government rights. These conflicts were most intense where nationalist movements sought to preserve regional languages and cultural traditions, and to defend historic self-government rights.
- **Regionalist or regional-nationalist identities**. Most of the population of Spain speaks Castilian Spanish as a first language, but in Catalonia, Valencia, the Balearic Islands, Galicia, Navarra, and the Basque Country people also speak different languages, and have their own distinctive cultural traditions. Many residents of these regions have strong regionalist identities (in Galicia, Valencia, the Balearic Islands, and Navarra) or regard themselves as constituting a nation (in Catalonia and the Basque Country).
- **Conflicts over religion**. Since the early nineteenth century, Spaniards have been divided into one camp which strongly identifies with traditional or conservative Roman Catholicism, which favors close ties between Church and state, and a second camp that includes more secularist individuals who favor a separation between Church and state. These conflicts originated in the mid eighteenth century as disputes within the intellectual and political elite over the proper role of the Church in society, but by the 1830s they had spread to the mass level and involved considerable violence.
- **Class conflicts**. While all societies are characterized by varying degrees of socioeconomic inequality, class conflict was particularly intense in Spain in the late nineteenth and early twentieth centuries due to extreme inequality (especially in the agrarian south) and to the embrace of extremist ideologies in several regions (including anarchism, anarcho-syndicalism, and revolutionary socialism).
- **Monarchy vs. republic**. The monarchy served as a stable, unifying force in Spanish politics throughout the first several centuries of the country's history, but the restoration of a reactionary king (Fernando VII) following the War of Independence (1808–14) against the Napoleonic occupation (during which the **liberal** 1812 constitution was written) triggered see-saw struggles pitting supporters of the legitimate, Borbón dynasty against a rival royal line, and ultimately pitting those favoring the monarchy against republican forms of government. In this historical context, the restoration of the

Borbón monarchy in 1975 and the overwhelming and virtually universal support for King Juan Carlos I since then must be regarded as a remarkable achievement.

Liberalism emerged in the late eighteenth century in reaction against several aspects of Western European society during the era of absolutism. It stressed the autonomy and dignity of the individual in several domains of social and political life. It demanded more equal civil liberties in contrast with aristocratic privilege, religious freedom rather than subservience to an established state religion, and individual initiative and the free market instead of state-dominated mercantilist economies, and, eventually, it led to democracy in lieu of monarchical authoritarianism. In Spain and some other Western European countries (e.g., France), protracted conflict with the Church infused anticlerical sentiments into "continental" versions of liberalism, but American and English liberalism was largely devoid of hostility toward the Church or religion in general. It should be noted that in the United States the term "liberalism" took on entirely new meanings in the twentieth century.

As we shall see in this chapter, some of these sources of political conflict emerged in the earliest stages of Spain's history as a single country and as a state. These divisions became particularly disruptive in the early twentieth century and contributed to the collapse of its only truly democratic political regime, the Second Republic. But in establishing the current democratic system, some of them were laid to rest as sources of political conflict, others were satisfactorily "regulated," while the center–periphery cleavage remains an ongoing source of political conflict.

Spain's success in navigating over or around these historically disruptive social and political cleavages on its way to a consolidated, democratic political system is, to some extent, the product of social changes, some of which we will examine in this chapter. But to a considerable degree, it is also the product of the particular way that the founding elites of this new democracy interacted with one another during the crucial stages of the transition. These patterns of behavior have been referred to by Spaniards as "the politics of consensus." Outside observers have called them "the Spanish model" of democratic transitions. This model has helped to guide other democratizing political leaders in their respective regime transitions (e.g., in Poland, Hungary, and Korea). In the concluding section of this chapter, we will analyze "the politics of consensus" in some detail.

Box 1.1

The Cortes of Cádiz and the first constitution

During the occupation of Spain by Napoleon's forces – ostensibly ruled by Napoleon's brother, Joseph Bonaparte, who had been installed as King of Spain – there was incessant Spanish resistance in the form of guerrilla warfare (with occasional intervention by units of the British army), and not all parts of the country were effectively under the control of the French. A heterogeneous assembly of aristocrats, clergy, and the bourgeoisie met in Cádiz in 1808 and wrote what was the first liberal constitution in Europe. While it was initially respected by Fernando VII following his restoration to the throne after the defeat of Napoleon, his subsequent embrace of reactionary absolutism in 1823 led to its suppression.

■ State-building in Spain

The Spanish **state** is one of the oldest in the world. The Hispanic Monarchy established control over almost all of the present country of Spain by 1492, under King Ferdinand and Queen Isabella (*los Reyes Católicos*, Fernando V and Isabel I) with the last piece (Navarra) falling into place just two decades later. Only the neighboring country of Portugal preceded Spain in establishing governmental authority throughout its current mainland territories, and most other European countries – let

> **The state** is a set of sovereign governmental institutions which controls a well-defined, contiguous territory, which imposes a single legal code over all persons residing in that territory, and which ultimately or potentially possesses a monopoly over the right to use force to implement that legal code.

alone almost all of those in other world regions – achieved this status centuries later: Great Britain and France, for example, in the eighteenth century, Germany and Italy in the mid nineteenth century, and most Central and East European countries following World War I.

Nonetheless, the Spanish **state-building** process was incomplete, and no fewer than six civil wars erupted over differing views regarding the proper form of the state, the most recent in 1936–39. As we will see in the following chapter, disagreements over the proper structure of the state continue to serve as the basis of political conflict in Spain, and since the late 1960s have culminated in over 800 deaths resulting from acts of terrorist violence. These political struggles have pitted proponents of a centralized governmental structure against those demanding that certain regions retain or regain considerable self-government rights and privileges.

> **State-building** in the Middle Ages involved two processes. One is the acquisition of territory (typically by war or marriage), and the other involves the establishment of a common set of government institutions and laws.

Reinforcing these incompatibilities, and further contributing to their capacity to serve as bases of conflict, was linguistic and cultural diversity. Over 10 million people (about a quarter of Spain's population) speak languages other than Spanish as either a first or second tongue. These differences in language, culture, and political tradition are the long-term product of the way the Spanish state was created.

A proper understanding of this important characteristic of politics in Spain today therefore requires a brief overview of that state-building process.

■ The creation and evolution of the Spanish state

The political evolution of **Iberia** following the collapse of the Roman Empire (which converted most of the population to Christianity following its proclamation as the official religion of the Empire in AD 312) was similar to that of most other parts of continental Western Europe. The conquering Visigoths (a Germanic tribe that terminated Roman control of Iberia in AD 476)

> **Iberia** includes the mainland parts of Spain (that is, all except the North African territories of Ceuta and Melilla) and Portugal (except for the Azores and Madeira islands). It is bounded on the north by the Bay of Biscay and the Pyrenees, on the west by the Atlantic Ocean, on the east by the Mediterranean, and on the south by the Straits of Gibraltar.

Table 1.1 Timeline: Spain, from the Romans to 1808

<hr>

From the Romans to the Moorish invasion
(210 BC–AD 711)

Roman governance of Iberia (218 BC–AD 409)

Roman Senate declares Hispania a Roman province (218 BC)
Division of Hispania into three provinces, Tarraconense, Betica and Lusitania (27 BC)
Pacification of Hispania completed under Augustus (19 BC)
Arrival of Christianity (AD 58)
Hispanic emperors of Rome: Trajan (98), Hadrian (117), Marcus Aurelius (161), and Theodosius (364)
Roman control of Hispania ends (409)

Invasion by "Barbarian" tribes (fifth century)

The *Suevi* (from the Elba and Oder regions) occupy Galicia, the *Vandals* (East Germania) reach Betica
  (now Andalucía), and the *Alans* (Caspian Sea) occupy the rest of Hispania
King Recaredo imposes Catholicism as an official religion in the 3rd Toledo Concillium (589)
Moorish invasion (711)
Rodrigo, last Visigoth king, defeated at Guadalete by Tarik (711)

Middle Ages
(AD 711–1500)

Evolution of Al-Andalus

Emirate dependent on Damascus (711–56)
Ummayyad Emirate (758–912)
Independent Caliphate of Córdoba (912–1031)
Taifas kingdoms (1031–90)
The Almoravid dynasty (1090–1172)
The Almohad dynasty (1172–1224)
Kingdom of Granada (1238–1492)

Reconquest

Reconquista begins in Asturias led by King Pelayo I, founder of the Kingdom of Asturias (718)
Count of Barcelona establishes Christian kingdom (873–98)
The County of Castilla established (850)
Conquest of Toledo (1085)
El Cid conquers Valencia (1094)
Portugal officially independent (1143)
Alfonso III inflicts serious defeat on Moors at Battle of Las Navas de Tolosa (1212)
King Fernando III conquers Córdoba (1236), Jaén (1246), Sevilla (1248), Jerez, and Cádiz (1250)
Isabel wins Granada (1492) for Castile. End of the Reconquista

Isabella and Ferdinand, the Catholic Kings (1474–1517)

Royal marriage between the kingdoms of Castilla and Aragón (1469)
Creation of the Spanish Inquisition (1478)
Colombus reaches America (1492)

Table 1.1 (*cont.*)

Modern age
(1500–1808)

The expansion of the Spanish Empire in America

Mexico (1519–21) administered by the Virreinato de la Nueva España (1535)
Peru (1531–3) administered by the Virreinato del Perú (1543)
The Philippines (1569)

The Spanish Habsburgs

Carlos I King of Spain and Charles V Emperor of Habsburg Empire (1517–56)
Felipe II (1556–98)
The *Armada Invencible* is defeated by England (1558)
Portugal inherited by Felipe II and becomes part of Spain (1580–1640)
Felipe III (1598–1621)
Felipe IV (1621–65)
Carlos II (1665–1700), leaves no direct heir

The War of Succession (1701–13), and arrival of the French Borbón dynasty

Spain loses its Italian provinces
Gibraltar occupied by England (1704)

The Borbón monarchs

Felipe V (1700–46)
Luis I (1724)
Fernando VI (1746–59)
Carlos III (1759–88)
Carlos IV (1788–1808)

---

embraced Christianity and established a monarchy and an aristocracy that appeared to be drifting towards the same kinds of **feudal** social, economic, and political control as was emerging elsewhere in Europe.

In 711, however, social and political developments took a decidedly different turn. Iberia was invaded and quickly conquered by the Moors, an ethnically mixed group of Muslims who surged across the Straits of Gibraltar from North Africa. In the prosperous Moorish kingdoms that ruled various parts of Iberia over the next seven centuries there were considerable advances in science, technology, economic activity, and philosophy. Among other things, they preserved and analyzed the works of Aristotle and other classical Greek philosophers at a time when most of Europe was mired in the depths of the Middle Ages. Moreover, Christians and a sizable Jewish population were allowed to practice their own religions, although there were some periods of repression and intolerance.

> **Feudalism** is a geographically decentralized sociopolitical order in which the strongest political authority is possessed by aristocrats who own massive tracts of land (and, in the case of serfdom, the peasants residing on it) and function as the principal law-makers, law-enforcers, and law-adjudicators. While they are nominally subservient to a monarch, the king's authority is sharply limited, most commonly consisting of the right to call upon the aristocracy to provide military services temporarily in time of war.

Figure 1.1 The cathedral of Sevilla (the largest Gothic cathedral in Europe) was once a mosque, whose minaret was converted into the bell tower, now called La Giralda

The Reconquista *and the origins of linguistic and cultural diversity*

Beginning in the mid eighth century, a *Reconquista* (reconquest) led to the expulsion of the Moors from Iberia by linguistically, culturally, and politically diverse groups of Christians, who swept from the north to the south over the course of seven centuries (see map 1.2). This was the territorial-acquisition phase of the Spanish state-building process. It began with the proclamation of the Christian Kingdom of Asturias in 739, and the last step in the *Reconquista* was the defeat and absorption of the Kingdom of Granada in 1492.

What made the population of Spain so diverse was that the *Reconquista* was not undertaken by one homogeneous people, but rather by several distinct groups, each with its own language, culture, and political traditions. One wave of the reconquest pushed south along the Atlantic coast, beginning in Galicia.

Map 1.2 Evolution of the Reconquest, 1000–1492

This particular thrust culminated in the establishment of present-day Portugal. Accordingly, the language of Galicia is Galego, a dialect of Portuguese, and the population of the region shares many cultural traits with that of northern Portugal. Somewhat surprisingly, Galicia remained an integral part of the Kingdom of Castilla-León, even after the establishment of an independent Portuguese state in the twelfth century, and the region lacks a tradition of political autonomy that might have served as the basis of a nationalist movement challenging the Spanish state.

Elsewhere throughout the territories conquered by the Kingdom of Castilla-León (Cantabria, Castilla-La Mancha, Extremadura, Andalucía, Murcia, and

> ## Box 1.2
>
> *Use of regional languages in Spain*
> In the mid 1990s, virtually everybody in Spain was able to understand and speak Castilian Spanish, but in several regions distinctly different languages are also used extensively. In the far northwest region of Galicia, about 2.5 million persons (89% of the region's total population) speak Galego, a dialect of Portuguese. In the northeast corner of the country, just under 5 million residents of Catalonia (79% of the total population) speak Catalan, whose origins can be traced back to medieval Occitan, a regional French dialect. Closely related to Catalan are the languages spoken in the Balearic Islands (by 72% of the population, or about 0.5 million persons) and the Valencian region (55%, or just over 2 million persons). The Basque language, Euskera – which is not an Indo-European language – is spoken by about a quarter of those residing in the Basque Country and by 16% of the population of Navarra.

Madrid) a language was spread that developed into present-day Castilian Spanish. Linguistic and cultural homogeneity across these interior regions facilitated the emergence of a centralized form of governance.

The reconquest of the northeastern territories that became the Kingdom of Aragón (Catalonia, Aragón, Valencia, and the Balearic Islands) originated in the Languedoc region of France, pushing down the Mediterranean coast as far as Alicante, and on to the Balearic Islands. Thus, the languages and dialects of the northeastern quarter of Spain (Catalan, Valenciano, Alicantino, Mallorquín, etc.) had their roots in the regional medieval dialect of French, Occitan (the "*langue d'Oc*"), mixed with some local dialects. And the cultural values of these regions were more cosmopolitan and linked to the rest of Western Europe than were those of the more isolated regions of Castilla-León.

The linguistic and cultural diversity that characterizes Spain today, and clashes over the proper structure of the state that have spanned over four centuries, were the result of the merger of the two kingdoms of Castilla-León and Aragón. In 1469, the Castilian Crown Princess Isabel (Isabella in English) married Fernando (Ferdinand), then Prince of Aragón. Their two kingdoms were quite different from each other, particularly in their dissimilar institutional structures and decision-making processes.

Differing political traditions

The Castilian monarchy ruled territories that make up the present regions of Cantabria, Canary Islands, Asturias, Galicia, Castilla-León, Madrid, Castilla-La Mancha, Extremadura, Murcia, and Andalucía (see map 1.3). It had a tradition of centralized government and comparatively strong monarchical powers over

Map 1.3 The kingdoms of Castilla-León and Aragón in the late fourteenth and early fifteenth centuries

the aristocracy. The Kingdom of Aragón (which included present-day Catalonia, Aragón, Valencia, and the Balearic Islands), in contrast, was presided over by a king whose powers and governmental authority were quite limited. First, **the Cortes** of Aragón retained far greater powers than its Castilian counterpart. More importantly, and of great relevance for present-day politics, the Kingdom

> ## Box 1.3
>
> *The Carlist Wars*
>
> Large parts of the Basque region and the former Kingdom of Aragón rose in revolt against the Spanish Government in the 1830s, 1840s, and 1870s. Traditionalist conservatives in those regions refused to acknowledge the accession to the throne of a female head of state (Queen Isabel II), and supported the rival claim of the late King Fernando's younger brother, Carlos María Isidro. These wars involved much more than struggles over the dynastic succession. They pitted religious traditionalists against liberals (many of whom were anticlerical), and they were violent struggles between defenders of regional self-government rights and those favoring a more centralized state.

The Cortes. The two houses of Spain's present-day parliament (the Congress of Deputies and the Senate) are collectively referred to as the Cortes Generales. The historical origins of this representative body can be traced back to chambers of medieval "estates" (including the aristocracy, clergy, and local notables) which claimed varying levels of authority *vis-à-vis* the Crown. The two most important of these were the Cortes of Castile and the Cortes of Aragón.

Fueros were charters of privileges and some self-government rights that were granted to regions, towns, and medieval corporate entities (e.g., the Church). The expansion of the powers of the centralized Castilian state over the following centuries involved the weakening and (in several instances) abrogation of *fueros* in all regions except Navarra and the Basque province of Álava.

of Aragón was a loose, quasi-confederal entity that gave many of its regions a broad array of self-government rights enshrined in ***fueros***.

The status of the Basque region was even more unusual. Ostensibly within the Kingdom of Castilla-León, it possessed considerable self-government rights until its *fueros* were revoked following defeat in the nineteenth-century Carlist wars. Moreover, since the affiliation of the Basque region with Castilla-León was initially based on the "election" of the Castilian monarch by the Basque aristocracy as their sovereign, some Basque nationalists even today describe this relationship as a *pacto con la Corona* (pact with the Crown), rather than as reflecting full integration within the Spanish state. And since this claim seems to imply a right of self-determination and potential secession, this characterization is strongly challenged by those who would oppose the disintegration of the Spanish state.

With the integration of the Kingdom of Navarra in 1512, all of the mainland Iberian territories of present-day Spain were united within a single state, but important structural and political-cultural differences continued to divide the country for centuries, resulting in six civil wars which pitted proponents of a centralized state structure against those demanding the preservation or restoration of traditional self-government rights.

■ Spain's Golden Century

During the sixteenth and seventeenth centuries, Spain was the richest and most powerful country in the world. Following the discovery of the "New World" by

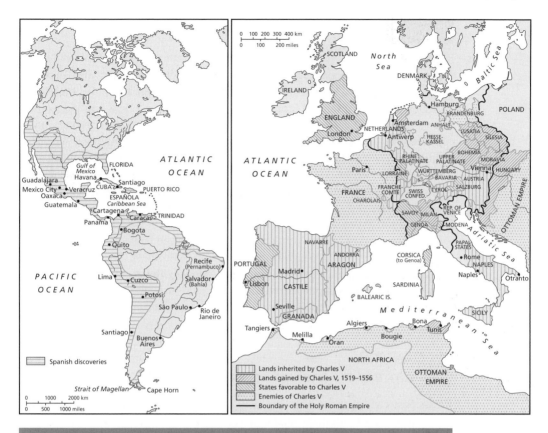

Map 1.4 The European and American territories of the Hapsburg Empire under Charles V

Christopher Columbus [Cristóbal Colón, in Spanish], an empire was established that included all of what is today referred to Latin America except Brazil, as well as the Philippines, southern Italy and Sicily. And when the Spanish King Charles I (grandson of Ferdinand and Isabella) was elected Holy Roman Emperor (Charles V), these territories expanded to include the Low Countries (now Belgium and the Netherlands), parts of Germany, and much of Central Europe (see map 1.4). In the world of literature, theatre, art, and architecture, Spanish artists and writers were preeminent from the period from about 1550 to about 1650 – commonly referred to as "The Golden Century" (*el Siglo de Oro*). Following the defeat of Felipe II's Invincible Armada in 1588, some signs of decadence and decline began to appear. And with the coming to power of the physically deformed and mentally retarded King Charles II in 1665, Spain's leadership position in world affairs began to crumble. With the death of Charles II in 1700, the royal position of the Habsburg dynasty came to an end in Spain.

> ## Box 1.4
>
> *Felipe II*
>
> One of the most noteworthy of the Habsburg monarchs of Spain was Felipe II, who ruled from 1556 to 1598. Following the successive abdications of his father Charles V, the Holy Roman Empire was divided between Felipe (who inherited Spain and its overseas colonies, the Low Countries, and the Italian territories) and his illegitimate brother Fernando (who would govern the German and Austrian territories). While Spain's role in world affairs reached its high point during his reign, numerous destructive conflicts also erupted, particularly as a result of his claim to other kingdoms. In 1580, he inherited the crown of Portugal, but over the following sixty years the Portuguese resented their absorption into the Spanish Empire. Portugal regained its independence following a war that broke out in 1640. Felipe's most famous conflict of this kind involved England. Having married Mary Tudor (the eldest daughter of Henry VIII), who ruled England as Mary I, he asserted his claim to the English throne following the accession of Elizabeth I, a Protestant. Felipe's attempt to invade England and take the crown by force culminated in the disastrous sinking of the "Spanish Armada" (officially named the "Invincible Armada") in 1588.

Civil wars and the triumph of centralism

In the first two of these wars (in 1640 and 1702–13), Catalans fought against the centralizing tendencies of the Spanish state. Their defeat and the coming to power of a new Borbón dynasty in Madrid led to the abrogation of their self-government rights and the first major advance towards the imposition of a single model of the state, based on the highly centralized French government system imported by the new Borbón King Felipe V (1683–1743), grandson of the absolute Bourbon King Louis XIV of France. Both the centralized state and the absolutist conception of the monarchy imported from France were deeply resented by those favoring the preservation of the traditional *fueros*. This dynastic change was also accompanied by efforts to centralize and "castilianize" government, and to impose the Spanish language on the Catalan population that not only failed to eradicate Catalan but ultimately (in the 1890s) contributed to the emergence of Catalan nationalism.

Since the Basques and Navarrese had joined the victorious Borbón side in the War of the Spanish Succession (1702–13), they were allowed to retain their *fueros* over the following century. Upon the death of Fernando VII in 1833, however, they refused to accept the crowning of the late king's infant daughter, Isabel II, as his successor. Instead, they supported the claim to the throne of Fernando's younger brother, Carlos María Isidro. The three Carlist wars (1833–40, 1846–48 and 1872–75) were much more than dynastic conflicts: they were a reaction against steps towards the creation of a modern, centralized liberal state. Carlism was an ultra-religious, anti-modernizing movement which took up the defense of the *fueros* of Navarra and the Basque region against the state-centralizing and anticlerical policies of the Liberal governments in Madrid, who supported Isabel II. The Liberals won all three wars, culminating in a reduction (in 1839) and then virtual elimination (in 1876) of Basque self-government. Thus, by the final quarter of the nineteenth century, the tensions and inconsistencies inherent in two rival models of the state were resolved (albeit temporarily) in favor of a French-style centralized state structure. In the 1890s, however, a major political development that was spreading throughout Europe had a powerful political impact in Spain. This was the spread of nationalism, and demands for the creation of self-governing Basque and Catalan "nation-states."

To this point in our historical overview, we have examined the origins of tensions and conflicts over the structure of the state, pitting Castilian centralizers against defenders of regional self-government rights. We have also seen the first instances (the Carlist Wars) of conflict over the role of religion in social and political life. In the following section, we will see how the emergence of conflicting nationalist movements further reinforced some of these historical sources of present-day political conflict.

■ The origins of peripheral nationalism

Nationalism can contribute to a sense of community and enhance the political authority of the state in homogeneous societies in which the territorial boundaries of the state correspond with those of the nation. But in "**plurinational states**," where the two sets of boundaries are incompatible with each other, it can give rise to serious political conflict. In the case of Spain, this was manifested in conflict between Spanish nationalism, on the one hand, and Basque and Catalan nationalist movements, on the other, all of which emerged in the 1890s.

Plurinational states are those that include populations identifying themselves as belonging to more than one national group. In some instances, the minority-national group will identify with both the majority-national group (in this case, Spanish) and the regional-national group (e.g., Catalan). In other instances, however, the two national identities are regarded as incompatible with each other. The latter situation may culminate in an effort to secede from the plurinational state and form a separate, homogeneous nation-state.

Spanish nationalism, rooted in the language and traditional culture of Castilian Spain, emerged as a significant force following the War of Independence against Napoleon in 1808–14, given its status as a war of national liberation against a foreign invader. Subsequently, however, the chronic instability of the new liberal regime, punctuated by numerous military **pronunciamientos**, several different constitutions, the three Carlist Wars, and the failure of the industrial revolution gave Spanish nationalism a somewhat defensive and pessimistic tone. The humiliating defeat in the 1898 Spanish-American War and subsequent loss of the last Spanish colonies (Cuba, Puerto Rico, and the Philippines) reinforced these

Pronunciamientos are rebellions against the national government by military officers. In some instances they may take the form of a *coup d'état*, although in most instances the rebellion is not followed by an attempt by the rebel officers to form a national government of their own; instead, they may be limited to demands for a change of the government, policies, or even constitutions of the national government.

Box 1.5

The nation and nationalism

As classically defined by John Stuart Mill (1806–73, in *Considerations on Representative Government*), a people can be considered as constituting a nation "if they are united among themselves by common sympathies, which do not exist between them and others – which make them to cooperate with each other more willingly than with other people, desire to be under the same government, and desire that it should be government by themselves, or a portion of them exclusively." While typically this sense of shared group identity and destiny is based upon some cultural common denominator (most frequently language), it is not the shared objective social characteristic that defines the group, but, rather, the subjective belief itself. A people (whatever social characteristics they may or may not share) must be considered a "nation" if they regard themselves as constituting a nation and demand a nation-state of their own, in which all of their self-identified people would reside and govern themselves.

tendencies. Given this traumatic, triggering event, Spanish nationalism took on a self-critical tone. Its recurring themes involved the irreversible decline of Spain from its grand imperial past as a result of *los males de la patria* (the afflictions of the country). Under the Restoration Monarchy (1875–1923 – see Box 1.6), the most durable regime since the beginning of the nineteenth century, criticisms were focused upon the weaknesses and inefficiencies of the state, fraudulent elections under a semi- or quasi-democratic regime, clientelistic and factional political parties, retarded economic development, and a pre-industrial social structure. These were some of the objects of struggle between the "two Spains" – pitting the *official* Spain of the political elite against the *real* Spain of ordinary citizens, as well as Liberals and progressive social forces against conservatives, who supported the continuing hegemony of traditional Spanish institutions. Spanish nationalism was not manifested in a single political party, but, rather, was diffused across a number of parties, particularly those towards the right side of the political spectrum. It was also strongly rooted in the Church and the military, where it was further inflamed by Spain's costly, frustrating, and occasionally humiliating efforts to maintain a colonial presence in large enclaves in northwest Africa.

Basque nationalism was first prominently manifested in the founding of the Partido Nacionalista Vasco (PNV [Basque Nationalist Party]) in 1895. Its founder, Sabino Arana Goiri (1865–1903), wrote its first political text (*Bizcaia por su independencia*), invented the nation's new name (Euzkadi), created the Basque flag (the *ikurriña*), and established a standard grammar for the Basque language (Euskera). Arana had supported Carlism, and the central themes of his nationalist ideology and the party's motto, *God and the Old Laws* (i.e., *fueros*), were a product of this traditionalist background. But his conception of the Basque nation went well beyond the reactionary anti-modernism and anti-liberalism of Carlism by

Table 1.2 Timeline: Spain, 1808–2008

Monarchy and the liberal state

Napoleonic occupation of Spain (1808–14)
Independence of American colonies (1810–24)
The Liberal Constitution (1812)
Fernando VII King of Spain (1814–33)
Regency of Queen María Cristina of Naples (1833–40)
First Carlist War (1833–40)
Isabel II de Borbón (1843–68)
Second Carlist War (1845–9)
Concordat with Vatican (1851) stabilizes relations between Church and state
Third Carlist War (1868–76)
Amadeo of Savoy new King of Spain (1871–3).
First Republic, extreme political instability (1873–4)
The Restoration of the Borbón Dynasty under Alfonso XII (1875–85)
Regency of María Cristina of Habsburg (1885–1902)
Loss of Cuba, Philippines, and Puerto Rico, and defeat in Spanish-American War (1898)
Alfonso XIII (1902–31)
Second Rif War in North Africa
Dictatorship of General Miguel Primo de Rivera (1923–30)

Second Republic (1931–6)
Civil War (1936–9)
The Franco dictatorship (1939–75)

International isolation (1946–51)
Concordat with Vatican (1953)
American military bases in Spain (1953)
Spain becomes member of UN (1955)
Juan Carlos is appointed successor of Francisco Franco (1969)
ETA assassinates President of Government, Luis Carrero Blanco (1973)
Franco dies (1975)

Juan Carlos I (1975)

First post-Franco democratic election (June 1977)
Adolfo Suárez prime minister (1977–81)
Constitution ratified in referendum (1978)
Leopoldo Calvo-Sotelo prime minister (1981–2)
Attempted *coup d'état* (February 23, 1981)
Felipe González prime minister (1982–96)
Spain joins NATO, and accedes to the European Union (1986)
José María Aznar prime minister (1996–2004)
José Luis Rodríguez Zapatero prime minister (2004–)

Box 1.6

The Restoration Monarchy

The regime that was established with the restoration of the Borbón monarchy in 1875 regularly convened elections to the national parliament, but it was not democratic. It fell short of a fully democratic system in several ways. First, for the first two decades, the right to vote was sharply restricted to males who had considerable property and met certain educational requirements (about 6% of the population). Second, when "universal" male suffrage was declared in 1890 (to include about 27% of the population) it was accompanied by the introduction of procedures that guaranteed that electoral outcomes could be determined by the leaders of the two major parties, the Liberals and Conservatives, through the use of a number of manipulative techniques, including coercion and outright fraud. In rural areas, illiterate peasants voted in accord with instructions from local notables, or *caciques* (taken from an Indian word for "chief"), who often provided services to their "clients," but in return for unquestioning political support. These electoral irregularities were so extreme as to enable the two parties regularly to alternate in power with each other in accord with specific agreements negotiated prior to the elections. Violations of democratic norms are so significant as to preclude categorization of the Restoration Monarchy as a democratic regime. They seriously hindered the development of mass parties, such as the socialist PSOE (Partido Socialista Obrero Español, founded in 1879). This regime came to an end following the establishment of a dictatorship under General Miguel Primo de Rivera in 1923, although King Alfonso XIII did not abdicate as head of state until 1931.

including an ethnic definition of the national community. Accordingly, Euzkadi was portrayed as besieged by a centralizing state and by waves of immigrants attracted from other parts of Spain by the region's industrialization. Arana argued that there was a separate Basque "race," which was being threatened by the invasion of the Basque country by *maketos* – that is, workers from other parts of Spain and their families who migrated to this rapidly industrializing region in search of work. Given its ethnic definition of the nation and its objective of protecting the purity of the Basque race from "contamination" by mixing with these foreigners, admission to the PNV was initially limited according to the "rule of the eight family names" – that is, it was restricted to those who could prove that all four of their grandparents were ethnically Basque. More importantly, the party demanded the restoration of the region's historic *fueros*. This led to repeated demands for the granting of autonomy to the region, although this objective was not fulfilled until after the outbreak of the Spanish Civil War in 1936.

In sharp contrast, Catalan nationalism was oriented toward the creation of a supra-party movement that would attract support from all social classes. Although the first Catalan nationalist party to emerge (the conservative *Lliga Regionalista* (Regionalist League), founded in 1901) also had roots in Carlism, it was from the beginning a much broader alliance of political forces. Rather

Box 1.7

Sabino Arana on the differences between Basque and Catalan nationalism
Following a period of residence in Catalonia, the founder of Basque nationalism, Sabino Arana, described the difference between Basque and Catalan nationalism, especially regarding their attitudes towards immigration and the role of language, as follows: "Catalan politics consists in attracting to it other Spaniards, whereas the Vizcayan [Basque] program is to reject from itself all Spaniards as foreigners. In Catalonia every element coming from the rest of Spain is Catalanized, and it pleases them that urban immigrants from Aragón and Castilla speak Catalan in Barcelona. It is not to speak this or the other language, but rather the difference between languages which is the great means of preserving ourselves from the contagion of Spaniards and avoiding the mixing of the two races. If our invaders were to learn Euskera, we would have to abandon it, carefully archiving its grammar and dictionary, and dedicate ourselves to speaking Russian, Norwegian or some other language, as long as we are subject to their domination" (Sabino Arana Goiri, *Obras Completas* [Buenos Aires: Sabindia-Batza, 1965], p. 404, cited in Antonio Elorza, *Ideologías del nacionalismo vasco* [San Sebastián: Haranburu, 1978], p. 129). While more recent conceptualizations of Basque nationalism have abandoned Arana's original ethnic definition and have sought to attract migrants from other parts of Spain to the Basque nationalist cause, the two nationalist movements continue to differ from each other with regard to the importance of language as a central feature of national identity: for Catalans, it is the *sine qua non*, while many committed Basque nationalists do not even speak Euskera.

than defining national identity in ethnic terms, it was oriented towards the diffusion of Catalan language and culture, and the creation of regional political institutions. This broad, assimilationist notion of Catalan nationalism stood in sharp contrast with the more exclusionary and ethnic conception of the Basque nation set forth by Sabino Arana. These differences were further accentuated when Catalan nationalist aspirations were partially achieved in 1917 with the creation of the *Mancomunitat*, an association among the four Catalan provinces under the presidency of Enric Prat de la Riba (1870–1917). However, this regional government institution lacked much authority to legislate and implement public policies.

Small regionalist (but not nationalist) movements also began to emerge in Galicia and Valencia towards the end of the nineteenth century, although they never had as much political impact as in the Basque Country or Catalonia. Their initial orientation was strongly cultural, and based upon the languages and cultures of those regions. The fact that these movements never expressed the same demands for autonomy or outright independence as their Basque and Catalan counterparts – despite the widespread use of distinctive regional languages in both Galicia and Valencia – clearly illustrates the point that nationalism cannot be understood as a manifestation of social or cultural factors alone.

The first three decades of the twentieth century were marked by increasing conflicts between, on the one hand, Basque and Catalan nationalist parties that demanded the restoration of regional self-government rights, and, on the other hand, Spanish nationalists who opposed what they perceived as the "disintegration of the Spanish nation." These regional conflicts also involved issues related to economic interests and development. The rapid expansion of the heavy industrial sector (especially the steel and shipbuilding industries) of the Basque region led to massive migration into the region by individuals from other parts of Spain. This triggered the xenophobic reaction described above. In the case of Catalonia, differences between the economic self-interests of Catalan industrialists and the agrarian interests of the interior of Spain triggered the emergence of the first Catalan nationalist party, the bourgeois-dominated Lliga Regionalista. Tensions between regional nationalists and the Spanish state were polarized during the 1920s, under the dictatorship of Miguel Primo de Rivera (1923–29), when he abolished the Catalan *Mancomunitat* in 1923 and adopted an oppressive policy toward peripheral nationalisms.

The 1931 constitution of the Second Republic (1931–36) attempted to reconcile these conflicting preferences by including articles intended to insure the continuing unity of Spain, while at the same time making possible the devolution of self-government rights to some (but not all) regions. Under the constitutional provisions for the so-called *Estado integral*, Catalans successfully secured an autonomy statute in 1932 that made possible the formation of a regional government with its own president and parliament, budget, and policy jurisdictions. However, a farcical declaration of independence in 1934 initiated by the Catalan nationalist Lluís Companys (1882–1940), led the Spanish government to declare a state of emergency and suspend **the Generalitat**, thereby recentralizing the state. This decision was reversed in 1936 by the left-wing Popular Front government, and a Catalan regional government was reestablished.

The Generalitat is the name of the regional government of Catalonia both today and in the 1930s.

These struggles came to a head with the outbreak of civil war in 1936, pitting conservative Catholic Spanish nationalists and the army under the leadership of General Francisco Franco (1892–1975) against Basque and Catalan nationalists and various left-wing groups that supported the government (as will be discussed in the following section). The Spanish Nationalist victory in 1939 led to the establishment of a dictatorship that implemented a complete recentralization of the state, as well as decades of vicious repression of Basque and Catalan nationalism. While cultural repression was relaxed somewhat in the mid 1960s, this state of affairs remained largely unchanged throughout the four decades of the authoritarian Franco regime (1939–75).

■ The Second Republic (1931–1936)

The short-lived Second Republic (1931–36) was the only period of democratic rule prior to the current democracy founded in 1977. Elections were conducted on the basis of universal suffrage (since women acquired the right to vote in 1931) and without excessive manipulation or fraud, unlike what had occurred under the Restoration Monarchy. And unlike that earlier period of parliamentary (but not fully democratic) governance, when there was a carefully orchestrated alternation in power between the two dominant political parties, elections under the Second Republic effectively determined which parties would form a government, and real turnover resulted. Unfortunately, the Second Republic exhibited every conceivable manifestation of instability, and was destroyed as a product of the Civil War that erupted in July 1936.

The Second Republic suffered from extremely high levels of cabinet instability, party-system fragmentation, and ideological polarization. The average government remained in office just 101 days, making this democratic system the most unstable in inter-war Europe. In part, this resulted from extreme fragmentation of the parliamentary party system. In each of the three legislative sessions (1931, 1933, and 1936), over 20 parties had parliamentary representation, and the largest party never had more than 24% of the seats. This party-system fragmentation was, in turn, largely a product of Spain's electoral law (see table 1.3).

The electoral system of the Second Republic allowed voters in each multi-member district to cast several votes for candidates (always fewer than the number of candidates to be elected from that district), and included provisions designed to "manufacture" a majority. It did this by giving the party or coalition receiving a plurality in each district up to 75% of that district's seats. The second-place party or coalition received the remaining 25% of the seats, and other parties received no parliamentary representation at all. While substantial regional differences in partisan support allowed for a high level of fragmentation, these majoritarian provisions of the electoral system also drastically magnified pluralities of popular votes for each electoral coalition into huge majorities in the allocation of parliamentary seats. This produced huge pendular swings in

Box 1.8

Majoritarianism

As defined by Arend Lijphart, majoritarian procedures and institutions of government tend to concentrate power in the hands of the political executive. This includes such features as the fusion of executive and legislative powers, a unicameral legislature, unitary government, government control over central banks, and courts with no special powers to review constitutional matters or legislation. With regard to electoral systems, majoritarianism involves electoral district structures and seat-allocation procedures that translate pluralities (sometimes small pluralities, as in the Spanish Second Republic) into parliamentary majorities. The conceptual opposites are purely proportional systems that allocate parliamentary seats strictly in accord with the percentages of the popular vote received by each party.

Table 1.3 Election results and parliamentary representation in the Second Republic

Parties	1931 Votes (%)	1931 Seats	1931 Seats (%)	1933 Votes (%)	1933 Seats	1933 Seats (%)	1936 Vote (%)	1936 Seats	1936 Seats (%)
National parties									
PCE (Communist)	0.8	–	–	1.9	–	–	2.5	12	2.4
Other extreme left	–	–	–	–	–	–	2.3	12	0.4
PSOE (Socialist)	21.4	120	24.6	19.4	57	12.3	16.4	91	18.4
Alianza Republicana	4.1	22	4.5	2.6	5	1.1	–	–	–
Radical-Socialist	11.8	61	12.5	1.4	1	0.2	–	–	–
Izquierda Republicana	0.2	1	0.2	–	–	–	13.7	81	16.4
Other republicans	13.6	69	14.2	6.5	22	4.7	7.1	43	8.7
Liberals	2.5	13	2.6	2.9	22	4.7	1.3	1	0.2
Radicals	13.2	72	14.8	14.3	84	18.1	3.6	9	1.8
Conservative republicans	8.9	27	5.5	3.9	16	3.5	0.8	5	1.0
Other conservatives	4.4	27	4.5	10.3	63	13.6	5.7	24	4.8
CEDA (religious right)	1.9	5	1.0	14.5	99	21.0	23.2	108	21.8
Monarchists	0.2	1	0.2	3.0	16	3.4	4.5	14	2.8
Traditionalists	1.0	4	0.8	4.3	19	4.1	3.4	16	3.2
Fascists	–	–	–	–	1	0.2	0.1	–	–
Regionalist parties									
Esquerra Republicana de Catalunya	6.7	31	6.4	3.7	17	3.7	4.5	25	5.1
Lliga Catalana	1.8	3	0.6	3.8	22	4.8	2.7	12	2.4
Partido Nacionalista Vasco	1.5	7	1.4	2.2	12	2.6	1.4	11	2.2
Other	3.6	24	4.9	1.0	5	1.0	0.9	17	1.2
Total	100	487	100	100	463	100	100	495	100
Total population (in thousands; 1930 census)	24,026			24,026			24,026		
Eligible electorate (in thousands)	6,199[a]			12,901			13,338		
Voters (in thousands)	4,349			8,683			9,729		
Voters as % of eligible electorate	70.13			67.31			72.95		

[a] It should be noted that women did not have the right to vote at the time of the 1931 elections.

parliamentary control and government formation from one election to the next. And those massive shifts, in turn, led to substantial reversals of government policies relating to important and divisive issues, and to "social cleavages." Some of these cleavages have deep historical roots, contributed substantially to the instability and polarization of the Second Republic, and remain politically relevant today.

■ The religious cleavage

Perhaps the most pervasive and politically divisive of social cleavages in Spain pitted defenders of an established Church (often distinguished by its reactionary social and political stands and by its intolerance) against anticlericals (who occasionally resorted to extreme violence in their assaults on the Church and the clergy). While Spain is uniformly Roman Catholic, and the Church had served as a unifying symbol and social force throughout the first several centuries of Spain's existence, by the early nineteenth century it had become a source of deep political and social division. In part, this resulted from the same kinds of tensions between nineteenth-century liberals and traditionalist-conservative Catholics that can be found in other West European countries. But in Spain, conflicts over the role of the Church in politics and society were often quite violent. The three Carlist Wars not only involved a rebellion by those demanding the preservation of regional self-government rights against what they perceived as the centralizing tendencies of the Spanish state, but also were rooted in a deep resentment on the part of liberals against the repression of individual liberties and the intolerance often exhibited by the Spanish Church. A period of stability and moderation of these tensions accompanied the signing of a concordat with the Vatican (a formal treaty specifying the Church's rights and privileges in Spain) in 1851, but by the end of the nineteenth century a sharp polarization reappeared, as the Church drifted towards the reactionary right and was opposed by increasingly militant anticlericals.

The founding of the Second Republic in 1931 was linked closely with the triumph of anticlericalism over the Catholic Restoration Monarchy and the established Church. It was accompanied by an outbreak of anticlerical violence. The first government was formed by a coalition of centrist and center-left anticlerical parties who used their parliamentary majority to enact a constitution that was regarded as deeply offensive by the Church and devout religious believers, who also tended to be strong supporters of the monarchy. While some of its clauses did little more than separate Church and state, others (such as those abolishing religious schools) were regarded as objectionable and were even regarded by some as a declaration of war against Catholics. The anticlerical tone of the constitution led the largest party of the Catholic right (the CEDA [Confederación Española de Derechas Autónomas]) to adopt a "semi-loyal" if not "anti-system" stance, which combined a radical defense of the Church with a rejection of the social reforms of the center-left Republican governments, as well as with a challenge to the regime's legitimacy and fundamental democratic "rules of the game." Tensions and conflict over religious issues remained unresolved throughout the life of the Second Republic, eventually culminating in the outbreak of Spain's most devastating civil war in July of 1936.

■ Monarchy vs. republic

The very founding of the Second Republic activated a deep political cleavage that divided Spaniards. The exile of King Alfonso XIII in 1931 alienated from the new regime some Spaniards with durable loyalties to the monarchy. While the King recognized that the victory of republican parties in the 1931 municipal elections spelled the end of his legitimate authority, he never formally abdicated, and instead made it clear that he opposed the new regime. Accordingly, monarchist parties and elites denied the legitimacy of the Second Republic from the beginning.

Political conflicts over the monarchy may have been intensified by the events of the 1930s, but they had deep historical roots. To be sure, hostility towards Spanish monarchs was the product of their behavior concerning short-term political issues (such as the King's meddling in the disastrous colonial wars in North Africa), but the most severe polarization resulted from the linkage of the monarchy with long-standing social and political cleavages. This was most clearly the case with the reactionary reign of Fernando VII following his restoration to the Spanish throne by an invading French army in 1823. Throughout his reign, Fernando was committed to the suppression of liberalism, the restoration of absolutism, and the purging of reformers from the church. He even restored the Inquisition, and crushed the last vestiges of civil and political rights secured before and during the Napoleonic era. In short, he inextricably linked the monarchy with the divisive struggle between liberalism and reactionary clericalism.

While these tensions were alleviated somewhat by the 1850 concordat with the Vatican and governance by the so-called *Moderados* (moderate liberals) during the reign of Isabel II, her abdication in 1868 was followed by a period of unprecedented political chaos. A new monarchical line was briefly installed in 1871 under Amadeo of Savoy (Duke of Aosta and son of the Italian king Vittorio Emmanuele I), but he lasted only two years and resigned in disgust as head of state, proclaiming the country to be "ungovernable." His abdication led to the establishment of the First Republic – which lasted just eleven months (February 1873 through January 1874). During that short period, Spain had four different governments and experienced considerable mass-level instability as well, mostly related to a frenzy of cantonalism that pushed Spain to the brink of disintegration.

The political peace that prevailed in Spain during the first three decades of the Restoration Monarchy seemed to suggest that this source of political conflict might have been resolved. But the premature death of the popular king Alfonso XII and the coronation of the child-king Alfonso XIII under the regency of his mother, María Cristina of Habsburg-Lorraine (1858–1929), again revived tensions over the form of the state. Alfonso frivolously intervened in politics and the conduct of the North African wars, supported the dictatorship of Primo de Rivera, and allied himself with reactionary sectors of the Church. His removal from office in 1931 was the ultimate consequence both of the collapse of the Restoration monarchy and the inexorable rise of republican parties during the first three decades of the twentieth century.

■ Class and left–right ideological cleavages

Politics in all Western democracies involves conflict over economic issues rooted in social class differences. Spain is no exception to this rule. But as a result of two factors, this economic-based conflict was more intense and disruptive in Spain than is typically found in consolidated democratic systems. These polarizing factors involve: (1) land-ownership patterns and regional differences in economic inequality; and (2) radical, extremist ideologies that increased antagonism between social classes.

Extreme inequality of land ownership in the south of the country contrasted sharply with the medium-sized family farms predominant in the north. Throughout Andalucía, Extremadura, and Castilla-La Mancha, huge estates (**latifundia**) prevailed, often the possessions of absentee, aristocratic landowners, and invariably worked by extremely impoverished day-laborers. The landless, rural working class enjoyed no job security (and were unemployed for much of the year), received no social welfare protection from the state or from paternalistic landowners, worked for pitifully low wages, and lived in "agrotowns" rather than on the lands where they worked. Thus, it is not surprising that they were attracted to radical revolutionary appeals, especially those disseminated by **anarchist** political activists in the final third of the nineteenth century. In accord with the tenets of anarchism, they preferred violent direct action – such as in the form of strikes, land seizures, and assassinations – over parliamentary political action.

> **Latifundia** (a Latin term meaning "broad estates") are huge agricultural properties. The term was first used to describe the slave-worked estates that characterized southern Italy under the Roman Empire, but is now commonly used in reference to such properties in Southern Europe and Latin America.

> **Anarchism,** of the variety which most strongly influenced European politics in the late nineteenth and early twentieth centuries, is a political ideology that rejects all forms of authority, especially that of the state, but also the authority of religious leaders and property-owning elites. As classically stated by the Russian Mikhail Bakunin (1814–76), "all exercise of authority perverts; all submission to authority humiliates." Accordingly, anarchists were strongly anticlerical, favored abolition of the state, and demanded replacement of private ownership of the means of production with communal ownership.

Similarly, **anarcho-syndicalist** sectors of the working class in the industrial and mining areas of Catalonia, Asturias, Aragón, and elsewhere also gravitated towards direct and sometimes violent action. In Catalonia, the largest "trade union" was the CNT (Confederación Nacional del Trabajo), which rejected the very notion of representative parliamentary democracy, and called for direct revolutionary action. Its uncompromising militancy contributed to the outbreak

Anarcho-syndicalism Anarcho-syndicalists shared with anarchists a hostility towards the state, organized religion, and private ownership of the means of production. They differed, however, in that they believed that the abolition of these forms of authority relationships could be brought about only through the organized efforts of workers under the leadership of an anarcho-syndicalist trade union, and through polarization of politics and labor relations which would bring about a "general strike" that would paralyze the economy and bring the state to its knees.

in 1918 of a "war of *pistoleros*" against their employers, who, in turn, hired thugs and gunmen in their struggle against workers. In the 1930s, they fomented numerous acts of social and political violence. Even the trade union linked to the relatively moderate Spanish socialist party (Partido Socialista Obrero Español [PSOE]), the UGT (Unión General de Trabajadores), often employed strategies of violent confrontation against their adversaries. In Asturias and other parts of the industrialized north coast, the UGT, under the leadership of the self-styled Spanish Lenin, Francisco Largo Caballero (1869–1946), participated in an attempted revolutionary overthrow in 1934 of the right-wing government in Madrid.

■ A polarized party system

As a product of the incentives of the electoral system and the depth of divisive social cleavages, partisan politics was characterized by a high level of ideological polarization. The parliamentary party system was both atomized and polarized, with a great and increasing ideological distance separating the principal parties of the left (PSOE) and right (CEDA), and with anti-system parties present on both ends of the political spectrum. Accordingly, partisan conflict was both "bilateral" (where almost every party was attacked from both its left and its right) and irresponsible. Support for fundamental principles of democracy declined over time, and "democratic rules of the game" were increasingly violated. Indeed, both the PSOE and CEDA adopted "semi-loyal" if not disloyal stands *vis-à-vis* the Republic, and many Spaniards were increasingly attracted by the non-democratic models of Soviet communism and German national socialism.

Given these sharply contrasting ideologies, it is not surprising that shifts in the composition of the government – from the center-left, to the right, and then back to the left, with the formation of the Popular Front government of 1936 – were accompanied by drastic policy reversals that only served to polarize political relations further. The anticlerical stance of the center-left governments of 1931–33 was reversed by the extremely conservative and religious-dominated coalition governments of 1933–35, which was reversed yet again by the sharply anticlerical and radical position of the Popular Front government. Similarly, the moderate land-reform policies adopted by the first center-left governments were stopped and reversed by the right-wing governments of 1933–35, and then were revived and expanded in 1936. These polarizing policy reversals also affected relations between Catalan nationalists and the Spanish government: as noted earlier, a Catalan regional government, the Generalitat, was established in 1932, and then abolished in 1934 following a disloyal, unilateral declaration of independence by the Catalan president. The Popular Front government not only restored the

Generalitat in 1936, but also hastily granted regional autonomy to the Basque Country following the outbreak of civil war.

A marked polarization of politics could be noted with each successive election. The share of the votes received by extremist parties increased between 1931 and 1936 by 15.4% of the total, while electoral support for more moderate parties declined by an equivalent amount. Thus, with the passage of time, the more moderate, centrist parties and elites were progressively displaced by more extremist political forces at both ends of the political spectrum. In 1936, the legitimacy of the regime was increasingly called into question by most parties, including the two largest.

■ The Franco regime

Divided by deep social and cultural cleavages, polarized at both the mass and elite levels by sharply opposed political ideologies and antagonistic behavioral styles, the Second Republic collapsed in July 1936. Right-wing Spanish-nationalist conspirators in the military had hoped to seize power quickly through their *pronunciamiento* and purge the country of what they regarded as the corrosive influences of godless socialists, communists, anarchists, and Freemasons, and to impose order on an increasingly tumultuous country. Instead, the Spanish nationalist military uprising plunged Spain into nearly three years of bloody civil war, in which they enjoyed the support of Italian and German Fascist regimes. While the inter-war period in Europe witnessed the breakdown of numerous democratic regimes, this was the only one that was terminated by the outbreak of a full-scale civil war – called a "Crusade" by the rebels, but regarded by others as a dress rehearsal for World War II.

In 1939, the victorious Nationalist forces, by this time under the unquestioned leadership of Generalísimo Francisco Franco (see Box 1.9), established a new regime throughout Spain whose characteristics were a mirror image of those of the Second Republic. The Franco regime was:

- **Authoritarian:** Rejecting the very notion of democracy, the regime was (following an initially totalitarian phase) authoritarian. The ultimate source of political authority was the dictator, Francisco Franco. Throughout the period from 1939 to the dictator's death in November 1975, it successfully repressed efforts to reestablish competitive political parties and trade unions, and crushed out basic political liberties. Initially, Franco sought to mobilize political support following his cooptation of the fascist Falange Española, but over the first decade of his regime he repeatedly watered down its ideological commitments through forced mergers with a variety of groups, such as the Carlist Traditionalists, and various Catholic and monarchist groups. By the end of this process, the lack of coherence of this "single party" was reflected in the cumbersome hodgepodge that was its official name: the Falange Española Tradicionalista y de las Juntas de Ofensiva Nacional Sindicalista – a mix of fascists, Carlists, Catholics, and populist trade-unionists. In 1958, it was

Box 1.9

Francisco Franco

Francisco Franco (1892–1975) was born in Galicia, but was a staunch Spanish Nationalist throughout his life. At the age of fifteen he entered a military academy, and two years later he became an officer. His initial military experience was in Morocco, in the campaign to suppress Arab and Berber resistance against Spanish colonial occupation. The youngest general in Europe, he was given responsibility for repressing the working-class rebellion in Asturias in 1934 – in some respects a "dress rehearsal" for the Civil War that followed less than two years later. On July 18, 1936, he launched a *coup d'état* against the government of the Republic in Madrid, initiating a destructive civil war that lasted nearly three years. Following the victory of the Spanish Nationalist forces in 1939, he established an authoritarian regime that he headed (officially described as "Head of State, Generalísimo of the Army, and by the Grace of God, Caudillo of Spain and of the Crusade") until his death in November 1975.

Box 1.10

Corporatism

Corporatism was initially seen (as in the papal encyclical *Rerum novarum*, 1891) as a "third way" between capitalism (rooted in liberalism and pluralism) and socialism. It was most extensively developed in Benito Mussolini's fascist Italy (1922–43), and involved the state very heavily in the management of labor relations and in "industrial policy." In lieu of institutionalized conflict between workers and employers, the state played a dominant role in setting wage and benefit levels, and regulating conditions of employment. Strikes were illegal, but at the same time workers were given substantial job security, and employers' rights to reassign workers were sharply curtailed. The state also became a substantial owner of, or granted heavy subsidies to, industrial firms, as part of an effort to regulate the economy.

re-christened the Movimiento Nacional (National Movement). While its name may have become less unwieldy, it was a party in name only, functioning in the end as nothing but a powerless propaganda machine and patronage-dispensing organization. By the 1970s, it had even ceased to play a significant role in the recruitment of government ministers.

- **Half-heartedly corporatist:** In lieu of "horizontal" (class-based) trade unions, the regime forced both workers and management personnel into "vertical" corporate syndicates that were dominated by the Government. At the same time, in its ideological orientation and elite recruitment patterns, the regime allowed for a certain "limited pluralism" among groups making up the victorious Civil War coalition, including Catholics, monarchists, and traditionalists, as well as members of the Church, the army and the Falange. And many secondary associations (such as business associations, neighborhood and women's groups, sports clubs, and all organizations affiliated with the Catholic Church) were tolerated and allowed to function independently of state intervention or control as long as they were considered to be supportive or non-threatening by the regime. Representation of the people in government was supposed to be through their indirect representation in a corporatist version of the Cortes, composed of representatives of so-called "organic" units of society, including the syndicates, the family, and a variety of government institutions. Only after 1967 were any members of this supposedly representative chamber elected, and that involved only one third of the members of the Cortes.

- **Confessional:** Reversing the anticlerical stance of the Second Republic, Franco reestablished Roman Catholicism as the official state religion, and restored to it virtually all of those powers and financial resources that had been eroded away over the previous century and a half. In return, the Church gave crucial support to Franco's uprising (calling the struggle a "crusade"), and provided much-needed legitimacy to the new political regime. The Church played a powerful role in Spanish society, especially in the educational system. Some have called the relationship between Church and state under the Franco regime "National Catholicism" (echoing Hitler's "National Socialism"), since it represented an attempt to impose on Spanish society a version of traditionalist religious beliefs and values that had largely vanished by the end of the Restoration Monarchy.

- **Conservative:** Since the outcome of the war represented the defeat of leftist, working-class parties, the regime was most conservative in its socioeconomic and political outlook. The governing elite of the country was drawn overwhelmingly from the upper socioeconomic strata, and its public policies distinctly favored the "haves" over the "have-nots."

- **Spanish Nationalist:** In sharp contrast with the self-government powers that the Second Republic's governments had devolved to Catalonia and the Basque Country, the state structure was rigidly centralized. Reflecting the triumph of intolerant and reactionary Spanish nationalism in the Civil War, the state crudely repressed the Basque and Catalan languages and cultures, even to the extent of prohibiting the speaking of those languages in public and the dancing of the Catalan *sardana*.

The Franco regime, and the Salazar/Caetano regime (1932–74) in neighboring Portugal, were the most durable authoritarian systems in twentieth-century Western Europe. Over the course of nearly four decades, the regime evolved in some significant ways. Following the vicious repression of those who had supported the Second Republic and a brief flirtation with the fascist totalitarian model in the early 1940s, the regime underwent a protracted but uneven process of relaxation. What might have been established as a coherent official ideology was repeatedly watered down and made more heterogeneous (if not

Figure 1.2 Francisco Franco and religious officials, Santiago de Compostela, 1938

incoherent). A conservative, religious, Spanish-nationalist, and anti-liberal "men-tality" was widely shared by the governing elite, but by the end of this process of dilution, the head of the renamed National Movement concluded that what the regime stood for could be summarized in one simple sentence: "We believe in God, Spain, and Franco." Accompanying this was a demilitarization and, to some extent, depoliticization of the state apparatus itself. Even though its head of state was Generalísimo Franco, and the regime was established by a military seizure of power, military officers were progressively replaced by civilians as government ministers for all departments except the three military ministries. And the state administration was increasingly dominated by apolitical technocrats, as well as a new generation of individuals who secretly harbored pro-democratic sentiments.

■ The first signs of change

In the 1960s and early 1970s, a number of changes occurred that altered Spanish society and even some aspects of the regime's political characteristics. Many of these transformations were triggered by an economic Stabilization Plan, adopted in 1959 in response to an economic crisis and pressures from the International Monetary Fund. These neoliberal policies were intended to convert Spain's stagnant, state-dominated "corporatist" economy into a more flexible and efficient market economy. They were also designed to end Spain's economic and social isolation from the rest of Europe.

Economic change

Over the following decade and a half, Spain's economy developed rapidly. In contrast with the economic stagnation of the 1940s and 1950s, the real rate of economic growth (that is, after controlling for inflation) averaged 7.3% between 1961 and 1973 (see figure 1.3). Rapid economic development transformed the class structure of Spain in a manner that helped to reduce some of the extreme inequality and economic deprivation of earlier years. Between 1960 and 1975 the portion of the labor force engaged in agriculture declined from 37% to 22%, and between 1960 and 1977 the country's gross domestic product per capita rose from $300 to $3,260 – a figure just short of Italy's $3,530, but exceeding Portugal's $1,840, Greece's $2,950, and even Ireland's GDP per capita of $3,060. This socioeconomic transformation also involved massive migration from rural areas (especially in Andalucía and Extremadura) to rapidly expanding urban areas (particularly those near the industrial zones of Catalonia, the Basque Country, and Madrid). Lagging somewhat behind these other manifestations of socioeconomic modernization (largely because of inadequate state support for public education), only about 90% of Spain's adult population were literate by the beginning of the 1970s.

Partial political liberalization

In the late 1960s, some limited steps towards relaxing harsh authoritarian controls were taken. Prior censorship of the press was eliminated, although periodic crackdowns established poorly defined limits on the extent to which criticism

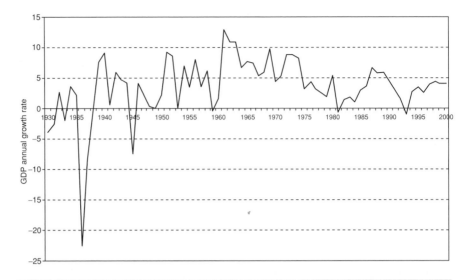

Figure 1.3 Annual growth rates in Spain, 1930–2000
Source: Carles Boix, "Spain: Development, Democracy, and Equity," prepared for the World Development Report Background Papers (2006), 48

or other departures from authoritarian practices would be tolerated. The public use of the Basque and Catalan languages was tolerated. Shop stewards (the lowest-level officials) of the corporatist labor syndicates were directly elected after 1966.

However, rather than achieving the intended objective of "letting the steam out of the pressure-cooker," this partial liberalization helped to open the door for more radical demands for change, Demands for broader political freedoms became more widespread, and the "workers' committees" (*comisiones obreras*) formed by the elected shop stewards were infiltrated by the clandestine Communist Party, culminating in the emergence of the Comisiones Obreras (CCOO) as Spain's Communist-dominated and largest trade union. Basque and Catalan nationalist aspirations were revived. And most importantly for the transition to democracy to follow, political parties began to reemerge: the clandestine Spanish Communist Party (Partido Comunista de España [PCE]) and the PSOE increased in membership and organizational activities (particularly following a misleading speech by Franco's prime minister Carlos Arias Navarro [1908–89] in early 1974 that seemed to promise increased tolerance of political pluralism), while more moderate Christian democratic, social democratic, and liberal factions began to organize as embryonic political parties.

Other sectors of Spanish society also underwent considerable change. Some branches of the Workers' Brotherhood of Catholic Action (exempted from state supervision and control by the concordat of 1953) began to function as a *de facto* trade union. Following the Second Vatican Council (1962–65), the Church progressively distanced itself from the regime, going so far as to apologize formally for the sectarian and polarizing role it had played in the 1930s. As we shall see, the political neutrality adopted in the early 1970s by the Episcopal Conference under the presidency of Cardinal Vicente Enrique Tarancón (1907–74) contributed substantially to the success of the transition to democracy and to the generally satisfactory regulation of the traditionally divisive religious cleavage in Spanish society.

But still authoritarian

While some of the socioeconomic prerequisites for successful democratization appear to have been met, the prospects for success of regime democratization could not be taken for granted. Heavy-handed crackdowns by the regime – on workers' strike activities in the early 1960s, on students demanding political change in the late 1960s, on Basque nationalist demonstrations on several occasions, and on some political parties that were emerging or reviving in 1974 and 1975 – made it clear that Franco's inner circle had no intention of allowing a transition to democracy to unfold, at least as long as the Generalísimo was in control. Franco, himself, had bragged that he would leave Spain "well tied up" (*atado y bien atado*) following his death, and had created an institutional structure that seemed to offer little hope for democratization by legal means. Among these key institutional features were the instauration of a monarchy under a king hand-picked by Franco, a reactionary Council of the Realm (which controlled the nomination of the three candidates for prime minister that were to be presented to the king for his consideration), and a largely unelected, corporatist Cortes, most of whose members were extremely conservative in their political orientations. Not only would the traditionally divisive religious, class, nationalistic, and republican–monarchical cleavages have to be addressed in adopting a new constitution, but the heavy-handed crackdown on the Basques (including the suspension of civil liberties under two declared states of emergency) had culminated in a substantial radicalization of nationalist demands. More radical Basque nationalists now demanded outright independence from Spain, and various factions of ETA ("Basque Homeland and Liberty" or, in the Basque language, *Euskadi ta Askatasuna*, founded in 1959) launched a campaign

Box 1.11

Franco's Law of Succession
The *Ley de Sucesión* was passed in 1947 and remained as one of the most important of the Franco regime's Fundamental Laws. According to this law, the successor head of state to Franco was to be appointed by the dictator and approved by the Cortes. The current King Juan Carlos, descendant of the Borbón dynasty, was officially proclaimed successor and Prince of Spain in 1969, and became king after Franco's death, in 1975.

of terrorist violence in support of those demands that, over the following three decades, claimed the lives of over 800 persons. Perhaps the most dramatic of these terrorist acts at that time was the assassination of Franco's prime minister, Luis Carrero Blanco (born in 1903), in December, 1973. Two years later, Franco died, setting in motion an uncertain process of political change.

■ The transition to democracy

There were four distinct phases in Spain's transition to democracy.

(1) The first phase began in November 1975 with the death of Franco and the instauration of Juan Carlos I, grandson of Alfonso XIII, as King of Spain, and ended with the July 1976 dismissal of the ultra-conservative prime minister Arias Navarro and his replacement by the aggressively reformist Adolfo Suárez (born in 1932). During this period, there was no substantial progress towards democratization. This provoked frequent and massive demonstrations organized by the Communist and Socialist opposition nationwide, and by Basque and Catalan nationalists in their respective regions. On occasion, these demonstrations were put down by heavy-handed police efforts to restore law and order. A marked polarization of public opinion and increasing concerns over political instability were the result.

(2) The second phase lasted from July 1976 until Spain's first democratic election in over four decades, which took place in June 1977 (see table 1.4). It was characterized by rapid political liberalization (for instance, the Partido Comunista de España [PCE] was legalized in April 1977) and decisive progress towards the convening of the June election. Most of the key decisions were made unilaterally by Adolfo Suárez, but he took great pains to consult extensively with representatives of both the former Francoist *familias* and particularly opposition parties and social groups with regard to such major decisions as the legalization of parties and class-based trade unions, the design of an electoral system, and the convening of the first democratic election.

(3) The third phase began in the summer of 1977 and ended with the ratification of the new democratic constitution in a referendum held in December 1978. In the course of this constituent process, all but one of the traditionally divisive cleavages discussed above – concerning the structure of the state – were satisfactorily regulated or definitively laid to rest.

(4) The fourth and final phase of the transition to a new democratic regime involved decentralization of the state and the establishment of regional governments. This process began with separate rounds of negotiations between the Spanish government and Basque or Catalan representatives over charters of autonomy for their respective regions. Following the ratification of autonomy statutes for these two regions in 1979, self-governing rights and institutions were negotiated with all of the other regions of Spain,

Table 1.4 Votes and seats in the Congress of Deputies, 1977

Votes per party	Votes received	% of votes	Seats received	% of seats	Votes per seat
Nationwide					
UCD	6,309,991	34.0%	165	47.1%	38,242
PSOE	5,371,466	28.9	118	33.7	45,521
PCE-PSUC	1,709,870	9.2	20	5.7	85,494
AP	1,488,001	8.0	16	4.6	93,000
PSP-US[a]	816,582	4.4	6	1.7	136,097
DC[b]	257,152	1.4	0	0	–
Regional					
PDC	514,647	2.8	11	3.1	46,786
PNV	314,272	1.7	8	2.3	39,284
UCDCC[c]	172,791	0.9	2	0.6	86,396
EC	143,954	0.8	1	0.3	143,954
EE	64,039	0.3	1	0.3	64,039
Others	1,423,505	7.6	2[d]	0.6	711,525

[a] Partido Socialista Popular-Unidad Socialista

[b] Equipo de la Democracia Cristiana, Federación de la Democracia Cristiana, Democracia Cristiana Vasca-Euskal Kristan Demokrasia, Equipo Demócrata Cristiana e Social Democracia Galega, Partido Popular Gallego, Unión Democrática Cristiana, Unión Democrática del País Valenciá, Democracia Cristiana Aragonesa, Democracia Social Cristiana de Catalunya

[c] Unió del Centre i la Democràcia Cristiana de Catalunya.

[d] Note that "others" includes two tiny regional slates of candidates which elected deputies: the Candidatura Aragonesa Independiente de Centro and the Candidatura Independiente de Centro in Castellón

Source: Ministerio de la Gobernación, Dirección General de la Política Interior, *Elecciones Generales 1977: Resultados Congreso por provincias* (Madrid, 1977).

culminating in the creation of the highly decentralized ***Estado de las autonomías***. In the end, this process was overwhelmingly successful. Even many Basque nationalists who had harbored reservations about the constitution became more supportive of the new regime. However, hard-core supporters of ETA and Herri Batasuna (its allied political party) maintained their anti-system stance, while the PNV (which wholeheartedly endorsed the region's autonomy statute) nonetheless generally maintained its semi-loyal orientation towards the constitution and the new regime.

The ***Estado de las autonomías***. Spain's quasi-federal system, called the *Estado de las autonomías* (state of the autonomies), was established in a piecemeal fashion through the granting of autonomy statutes to each of seventeen Spanish regions, called *comunidades autónomas* (autonomous communities). These give somewhat differing levels of autonomy to each region, representing a departure from the more uniform devolution of political authority to states in most federal systems. (Chapter 3 of this book presents an extensive analysis of Spain's *Estado de las autonomías*.)

Successful democratic consolidation

Spain's new democracy was consolidated by about 1982, with the partial regional exception of the Basque Country. The new constitution was overwhelmingly supported in the 1978 referendum, and at the national level there are no anti-system parties that receive any significant political support. Only lingering (but clearly diminishing) support for Basque independence and related terrorist agitation remain as an incomplete facet of this otherwise successful transition to democracy.

The success of this process, particularly impressive in light of the depth of potentially divisive cleavages and Spain's lack of a tradition of stable democratic rule, has led many observers to refer to it as "the Spanish model" of democratic transition – a model that has been studied and emulated in some other countries (e.g., Poland and Hungary) in their efforts to create stable democratic regimes.

■ The Spanish model

The so-called "Spanish model" of democratic transition includes several key features: negotiations between reformist sectors of the outgoing non-democratic regime and representatives of opposition groups; the use of the institutions and procedures of the Franco regime to initiate the regime-transformation process; moderate but sustained pace of progress towards democratization; inclusion in the decision-making process of representatives of all key political forces; private, face-to-face deliberations at crucial stages; and limiting the number of participants in face-to-face negotiations to a manageable few.

Institutional continuity

Initiating the dismantling of *franquismo* within the institutional framework of the Franco regime itself helped to legitimize the process of change. In accord with the Fundamental Laws of the regime, a "Law for Political Reform" was passed by the quasi-representative quasi-legislature, the Cortes, and ratified by a referendum in December 1976. The entire transition unfolded under the legitimate authority of a head of state selected by Franco himself, King Juan Carlos. Accordingly, the legitimacy of the process of dismantling the second most durable authoritarian regime in Europe (behind only that of Portugal) could not be challenged by Franco loyalists, and acceptance of the new regime by those on the right was facilitated.

Unequivocal commitment to and consistent progress towards democratization

Several procedural variables appear to have been of considerable significance in making possible the successful transition. One of these involved the pace and deliberateness of progress towards the convening of democratic elections. Beginning in July 1976, Prime Minister Adolfo Suárez was unequivocal in stating his commitment to full democratization immediately after his appointment as prime minister. Lacking such an explicit commitment, opposition groups might have continued to agitate in the streets to push the process forward, possibly with polarizing consequences (which was vividly apparent in the tumultuous revolution that was occurring in neighboring Portugal at nearly the same time). Steady progress towards the convening of the first democratic elections was evident throughout the second stage of the transition, and this made possible the demobilization of opposition groups and the depolarization of the political climate.

Demobilization

While protests in the streets during the first six months after the death of Franco (during which time the Council of the Realm gave Juan Carlos no alternative but to allow the ultra-conservative Carlos Arias Navarro to serve as prime minister) certainly helped to maintain pressure for political change, and gave additional support to the King in his decision to dismiss the do-nothing Arias government, once serious discussions between Adolfo Suárez and representatives of the opposition began, the anti-Franco opposition suspended their campaign of massive demonstrations. This helped to defuse a polarizing political atmosphere, and initiated a period characterized by mutual restraint on behalf of both the government and the opposition. It also gave subsequent inter-party negotiations over a new constitution better prospects for success.

Inclusiveness

Secondly, as a result of certain features of the electoral law of 1977 (to be discussed later in this book), the Congress of Deputies – the lower house in the currently bicameral Cortes Españolas – included representatives of all politically significant groups. As can be seen in table 1.4, each of the major sectors of the Spanish polity was present in the constituent assembly elected in June 1977. The two principal parties of the left – the socialist PSOE (which absorbed the smaller Popular Socialist Party in 1978) and the communist PCE – held over 40% of the seats, while a slight majority was held by the two nationwide parties to the right of center, the Alianza Popular (AP, created by seven prominent figures from the Franco regime) and the Unión de Centro Democrático (UCD, the heterogeneous product of a merger among liberal, social-democratic, and Christian democratic groups from the so-called "moderate opposition," and reformists with origins in the Franco regime). Moreover, the principal Catalan nationalist group (the Pacte Democràtic per Catalunya, which later became Convergència i Unió [CiU]) and the Basque Nationalist Party (PNV) were also fairly represented in this crucial legislative session. Perhaps more importantly, the crucial private negotiations over

Table 1.5 Stands on divisive issues among supporters of selected parties (in %)

Issue	Party supported in 1979 election						
	PCE	PSOE	UCD	AP	PNV	CiU (PDC)	All respondents
Monarchy							
Prefers the term "republic"	65	37	6	7	35	21	22
Prefers the term "monarchy"	14	30	63	68	18	47	48
Religion							
Church "a harmful influence"	63	35	9	12	25	16	23
Church "a beneficial influence"	13	29	64	61	46	56	49
Class/ideology							
Preferred the term "socialism"	87	73	19	10	44	31	26
Preferred "private property"	5	10	46	69	27	44	56
Structure of the state							
Continue centralized state	7	18	45	62	12	13	30
Some autonomy for regions	57	64	43	29	47	66	47
Much autonomy for regions	22	9	3	3	13	11	9
Independence for region	10	4	1	1	19	5	6
(N)	(317)	(1064)	(1313)	(129)	(194)	(101)	(5439)

Source: 1979 DATA survey

the constitution included all of those groups except the Basques – interestingly, the only political force that did not fully embrace the newly established regime.

Inclusion of all politically significant groups allows for the **articulation of demands** reflecting all relevant viewpoints regarding controversial issues. Conversely, exclusion of any important group may artificially shift the decision away from the true center of gravity of preferences on important issues. As can be seen from the public-opinion data presented in table 1.5, the historically divisive cleavages over the monarchy, religion, and class/ideology were perfectly reflected in the bases of support for the major political parties. Those who voted for the two principal parties of the left, the communist PCE and the socialist PSOE, were republicans, preferred "socialism" over "private property," and had negative views of the Church. Supporters of the two parties to the right of center were mirror opposites in their stands regarding these traditionally divisive issues. And the regional cleavage clearly differentiated the Basque and Catalan nationalist parties from the two Spanish parties to the right of center, one of which (the UCD) governed Spain throughout the transition period.

Inclusion within group negotiations also serves to convince representatives of the relevant groups that **a compromise solution is the only way** to attain even some of their initial demands without incurring significant long-term costs. Moreover, direct involvement in face-to-face negotiations that are even partially successful may help to socialize the participants into adopting more favorable attitudes towards the group and the outcome of the group process. Active participation in the group process predisposes individuals to defend more vigorously the agreement reached by the group, thus making more likely its endorsement by their respective followers. Perhaps most importantly, the inclusion of all significant elites in the decision-making process disposes them to believe that they have **a stake in the new political system**. Conversely, exclusion can, by itself, lead groups to deny the legitimacy of the system and to reject its decisions.

Small number of participants

At the same time, the Spanish model suggests that these negotiations should not include an excessively large number of individuals. As studies in social psychology have demonstrated, large groups tend to dissolve into debating societies and reach decisions only with great difficulty. Thus, another feature of the 1977 electoral system contributed to this successful outcome. As we shall later see, the electoral law substantially reduced the potential fragmentation of the party system, culminating in a "two-plus" party system. This made inter-party negotiations much more manageable than they otherwise might have been. At the same time, the crucial Basque and Catalan nationalist parties were given a fair level of representation in this constituent assembly.

Privacy

The crucial phases of inter-party deliberations over the constitution and the Basque and Catalan autonomy statutes took place behind closed doors. Other things being equal, discussion in public rather than private contributes to the unwillingness of participants to make concessions. Indeed, deliberations in public may provide incentives for individuals to engage in demagogic posturing as a means of attracting supporters or advancing their own personal careers. Over the course of the Spanish transition, whenever private negotiations were conducted great progress was made, and compromise resolutions of divisive issues were secured; conversely, public deliberations often led to polarizing stands that threatened to undo previously agreed compromises.

■ A regional exception: the Basque Country

It is important to note that the partial failure of the democratic consolidation process in the Basque Country is "the exception that proves the rule." That is, several of the norms that helped to define "the politics of consensus" (*la política del consenso*), as summarized above, were not followed. Accordingly, instead of depolarization and mutual accommodation, the processes of political change in the Basque Country involved increasing political violence and, in the end, a failure to achieve consensual support for the new constitutional order.

Exclusion

The only "politically significant" set of party elites not included in the crucial subcommittee deliberations over the constitution were the Basque nationalists. They were supposed to be represented in the early stages of negotiations over the constitution by a Catalan Deputy, but that proved to be unworkable. Accordingly, despite the fact that subsequent negotiations conceded to the PNV almost everything that they had requested ("over 90%," in the words of Xavier Arzalluz, its parliamentary leader), the party refused to endorse the 1978 constitution.

Continuing mobilization and polarization

While mass-level demobilization occurred in most parts of the country beginning in the second stage of the transition, extraordinarily high levels of mass mobilization continued in the Basque Country over an extended period of time. A 1979 survey data revealed that an astounding 40% of Basque respondents (more than double the level in other parts of the country) had personally participated in protest demonstrations. Thus, in contrast with the behind-closed-doors elite negotiations taking place in Madrid, the principal arena for "dialogue" between government and opposition in the Basque country was the streets. In marked contrast with the "politics of consensus" among cordial, mutually respectful political elites in Madrid, the ultimate consequence of the dialectic of rocks, clubs, and tear gas that dominated the transition process in the Basque Country was extreme polarization.

In short, the political dynamics of the post-Franco transition in the Basque Country were markedly different from those that led to the consolidation of democracy in the rest of the country, in this otherwise successful process of democratization. It is likely that exclusion of Basque elected representatives from the crucial early stages of negotiation over the constitution, coupled with continual mobilization and street confrontations in the Basque country – both representing significant departures from "the Spanish model" – contributed to the partial failure of the democratic consolidation process in that region.

■ The successful transition to democracy

In the end, "the politics of consensus" – the centerpiece of the Spanish model of democratic transition – culminated in the consolidation of a stable democratic regime by about 1982. The constitution that was overwhelmingly approved in the December 1978 referendum was strongly supported by all nationwide parties, from the Communist Party on the left to the Alianza Popular on the right, as well as by Catalan nationalist parties. That document embodied a definitive resolution of the historically divisive cleavage over the monarchy, and provided for satisfactory regulation of the religious and class/ideology cleavages, neither of which posed a credible threat to regime legitimacy or stability. Only the "stateness problem" resisted definitive resolution: although most regionalist and nationalist groups were fully satisfied by the substantial decentralization of the state which the constitution made possible, the status of the Basque Country remained an object of serious contention. We shall further explore the extent of support for the current democratic regime among Basques in a later chapter.

Overall, however, the Spanish transition to democracy must be regarded as a remarkable success. And the stable, typically European democracy firmly set in place represents a marked departure from the absence of a tradition of stable democratic politics that had characterized Spain over the preceding two centuries.

Summary

This chapter has examined the difficulties that Spain has experienced in its previous attempts to establish and sustain democratic government.

- It has shown how destabilizing polarization toppled the Second Republic (1931–36), leading to a civil war (1931–36) and the emergence of an authoritarian dictatorship under Francisco Franco (1939–75).
- It has explored the historical origins of traditionally divisive cleavages (over religion, the degree of centralization of the state, over conflicting national identities, over social class differences, and over the monarchy) and concluded that many of these sources of political conflict had their roots in the state-building process.
- It has shown how social and political changes during the 1960s and 1970s transformed Spanish society and helped to pave the way towards democratization of a more affluent and developed country.
- And it has analyzed aspects of the transition to democracy that contributed to its success (apart from the partial exception of the Basque Country).

We next turn our attention to the type of democratic regime that was established through this process.

Further reading

Brenan, Gerald, *The Spanish Labyrinth* (New York: Cambridge University Press, 1974)

Carr, Raymond, *Spain, 1808–1939* (Oxford: Clarendon Press, 1966)

Carr, Raymond, and Juan Pablo Fusi, *Spain: From Dictatorship to Democracy* (London: George Allen & Unwin)

Cotarelo, Ramón, ed., *Transición política y consolidación democrática: España 1975–1986* (Madrid: CIS, 1992)

Elliot, John H., *Imperial Spain* (London: Penguin, 2002 [1967])

Encarnación, Omar, *The Myth of Civil Society: Social Capital and Democratic Consolidation in Spain and Brazil* (New York: Palgrave Macmillan, 2003)

Gibson, Heather D., ed., *Economic Transformation, Democratization, and Integration into the European Union* (Houndmills: Palgrave, 2001)

Giner, Salvador, ed., *España: sociedad y política* (Madrid: Espasa Calpe, 1990)

González, Juan Jesús, and Miguel Requena, *Tres décadas de cambio social* (Madrid: Alianza, 2005)

Gunther, Richard, "The Very Model of the Modern Elite Settlement," in Richard Gunther and John Higley, eds., *Elites and Democratic Consolidation in Latin America and Southern Europe* (Cambridge: Cambridge University Press, 1992)

Gunther, Richard, Giacomo Sani, and Goldie Shabad, *Spain After Franco* (University of California Press, 1986)

Gunther, Richard, P. Nikiforos Diamandouros, and Hans-Jürgen Puhle, eds., *The Politics of Democratic Consolidation* (Baltimore: Johns Hopkins University Press, 1995)

Juliá, Santos, Javier Pradera, and Joaquín Prieto, eds., *Memoria de la transición* (Madrid: Editorial Taurus, 1996)

Linz, Juan, "Early State-Building and Late Peripheral Nationalisms Against the State," in S. N. Eisenstadt and Stein Rokkan, eds., *Building States and Nations* (Beverly Hills: Sage, 1973)

"From Great Hopes to Civil War," in Juan J. Linz and Alfred Stepan, eds., *The Breakdown of Democratic Regimes* (Baltimore: Johns Hopkins University Press, 1978)

"From Primordialism to Nationalism," in Edward A. Tiryakian and Ronald Rogowski, eds., *New Nationalisms of the Developed West* (Hemel Hempstead: George Allen & Unwin, 1985)

"Innovative Leadership in the Transition to Democracy in Spain," in Gabriel Sheffer, ed., *Innovative Leadership in International Politics* (Albany: State University of New York Press, 1993)

Linz, Juan J., and Alfred Stepan, "The Paradigmatic Case of *Reforma Pactada – Ruptura Pactada*: Spain," in Linz and Stepan, *Problems of Democratic Transition and Consolidation: Southern Europe, South America and Post-Communist Europe* (Baltimore: Johns Hopkins University Press, 2006)

Maravall, José María, *The Transition to Democracy in Spain* (New York: St. Martin's Press, 1982)

Payne, Stanley, *The Franco Regime: 1936–1975* (Madison: University of Wisconsin Press, 1987

The Spanish Revolution (New York: Norton, 1970)

Pérez Díaz, Victor, *The Return of Civil Society: The Emergence of Democratic Spain* (Cambridge, Mass.: Harvard University Press, 1993)

Preston, Paul, *The Coming of the Civil War* (London: Macmillan, 1978)

Franco: A Biography (New York: Basic Books, 1994)

Tarrow, Sidney, *Mass Mobilization and Regime Change* (Baltimore: Johns Hopkins University Press, 1995)

Tezanos, José Félix, Ramón Cotarelo, and Andrés de Blas, eds., *La transición democrática española*, 2nd edn. (Madrid: Editorial Sistema, 1993)

Vicens Vives, Jaime, *Approaches to the History of Spain* (Berkeley: University of California Press, 1967)

Zaldívar, Carlos Alonso, and Manuel Castells, *España: fin de siglo* (Madrid: Alianza Editorial, 1992)

2   The constitutional framework

The constitution ratified by a referendum in December 1978 established a democratic parliamentary monarchy. **The Congress of Deputies** is supreme with regard to the election of the prime minister, the oversight of government, and the formulation of policy at the national level.

The role of the monarch is sharply restricted by specific terms of the constitution. Nonetheless, as we shall see, the symbolic role played by King Juan Carlos has on occasion been exceptionally important. The Spanish constitution also paved the way for the decentralization of the state, creating regional governments and giving them greater responsibility for the formulation and implementation of public policies. Finally, it includes numerous commitments to the establishment of social justice and the social rights of citizenship.

> **The Congress of Deputies** The Congreso de los Diputados is the "lower house" of the Spanish parliament (Cortes Generales). The Senate is the "upper house," but is quite weak.

This chapter examines the main institutions of the Spanish political system. These include:

*   The formal powers and political role of the monarch;
*   The asymmetrical nature of the bicameral legislature;
*   The institutional characteristics of the Congress of Deputies;
*   The composition and powers of the prime minister and the government;
*   The dynamics of executive–legislative relations;
*   Other important political institutions (such as the Constitutional Court).

Box 2.1

Majoritarian and consensual democracies

The "executives–parties" dimension of Lijphart's majoritarianism/consensualism consists of several sub-dimensions, including the formation of minimum-winning/oversized coalition governments, cabinet durability, the effective number of parliamentary parties, and electoral disproportionality (all of which will be defined later in this chapter or in chapter 4), as well as the number of issue dimensions that divide parties from one another (discussed in chapter 6). Majoritarian systems include institutions and practices that facilitate the formation of parliamentary majorities in support of powerful and durable single-party governments. Carried to an extreme, it may lead to "winner-take-all" behavior by a governing party that receives only a plurality (rather than an absolute majority) of the vote. At the other end of the executives–parties dimension are consensual institutions that result in parliamentary party systems and governments that accurately reflect the diversity of the electorate's political preferences, sometimes at the expense of government stability. The "federal–unitary" dimension of majoritarianism vs. consensualism includes measures of centralization of government power and resources (vs. territorial decentralization), the existence of a "rigid" constitution that explicitly guarantees civil and political liberties of citizens, and a unicameral legislature vs. balanced bicameralism (with the latter strengthening "checks and balances" against the power of the executive).

An important theme of this chapter is the majoritarian nature of legislative–executive relations. Despite the fact that consensual practices played a key role in the transition to and consolidation of democracy in Spain, after the transition it has functioned as a predominantly majoritarian system. But several counter-majoritarian institutions also play important political roles in Spanish politics.

■ A predominantly majoritarian democracy with several consensual features

In the introductory volume of this series, Ken Newton and Jan van Deth introduced Arend Lijphart's useful distinction between majoritarian and consensual democracies. Political institutions and decision-making processes in Spain include strong elements of both types.

(1) **Majoritarian:** With regard to the executive–legislative dimension, Spain is clearly majoritarian.
  • Ever since the first democratic elections of 1977, the national-level executive has consisted of single-party governments, oscillating between

governments enjoying the support of absolute majorities of parliamentary seats, and minority governments supported through agreements with regional parties.

- Moreover, all ministerial and many high-ranking sub-ministerial appointments have been partisan.

(2) **Mostly consensual:** Most institutions relating to the federal–unitary dimension, however, are predominantly consensual.

- Spain is clearly "federal" with regard to the degree of geographical centralization of power and resources. Beginning with the enactment of Basque and Catalan autonomy statutes in 1979, there has been a profound and continuing process of decentralization: the institutional geography has been radically altered from a unitary and rigidly centralist state to the so-called ***Estado de las autonomías***, with seventeen regional governments in control of a broad range of policy jurisdictions and resources.

> The ***Estado de las autonomías.*** Spain's quasi-federal system, called the *Estado de las autonomías* (state of the autonomies), was established in a piecemeal fashion through the granting of autonomy statutes to each of seventeen Spanish regions, called *comunidades autónomas* (autonomous communities). These give somewhat differing levels of autonomy to each region, representing a departure from the more uniform devolution of political authority to states in most federal systems. (Chapter 3 of this book presents an extensive analysis of Spain's *Estado de las autonomías*.)

- Also consistent with the consensual model, the constitution is relatively explicit in its defense of civil and political rights, and particularly rigid regarding its modification; it has been amended only once (and that was dictated by a European Union mandate in 1992 to allow citizens from other EU countries to vote in and stand as candidates in local elections).
- Similarly, there is an independent central bank that sets monetary policy and oversees the banking system, as well as a powerful Constitutional Court that frequently intervenes to rule on the constitutionality of new legislation and to protect fundamental rights. Both institutions have markedly "counter-majoritarian" elements.
- Only with regard to a strongly asymmetric bicameralism does Spain's democracy depart from the consensual model on the federal–unitary dimension: the Senate is extraordinarily weak, leaving the Congress of Deputies in virtually full control of the legislative process at the national level.

In this chapter, we will examine in some detail the most important political institutions of Spanish government at the national level. In Chapter 3 we will turn our attention to center–periphery relations within the *Estado de las autonomías* – that is, between the central Spanish government and the seventeen regional governments or *comunidades autónomas*.

> ## Box 2.2
>
> *The main institutions of the Spanish central government*
>
> - The **head of state** is the monarch, currently King Juan Carlos I.
> - The **President of the Government** (prime minister) is very powerful within this parliamentary system. The prime minister has complete control over the appointment of government ministers, and has (typically in collaboration with Vice-Presidents of Government whom he/she designates) a dominant policy-making role within the **Council of Ministers**.
> - The **Congress of Deputies** is the "lower house" of the asymmetric bicameral Cortes Generales, but by constitutional design it is the dominant legislative body. Most of the daily work in that chamber is conducted within specialized committees.
> - **The Senate.** The "upper house" of the legislature is the **Senate**, but it is quite weak.
> - The **Constitutional Court** (Tribunal Constitucional, which is institutionally separate from the Supreme Court [Tribunal Supremo]) is at the top of the hierarchy of judicial institutions, and plays an extremely powerful role in its independent review of the constitutionality of legislation.
> - Counter-majoritarian **arbiter institutions** were established to guarantee "fair play" in those sectors of democratic political life that should be insulated from partisan influences, such as with regard to the judiciary, public broadcasting networks, the university system, oversight of elections, and regulation of the banking system.

■ The role of the monarch

As discussed in the previous chapter, Juan Carlos I played an extremely important role in the transition to democracy. The fact that he had been selected as head of state by Francisco Franco meant that his authority would be regarded as legitimate by those on the right, who otherwise might have opposed the dismantling of the Franco regime. But that also meant that he would initially be regarded by opposition groups as an inheritance from Franco. Juan Carlos addressed these latter concerns by quickly making it clear that he favored the establishment of a new democracy, and by playing a crucial role in moving that process forward. While his appointment by Franco gave him "backward legitimacy" in the eyes of potential opponents of democratization, his contributions to the transition generated "forward legitimacy" that led many on the left (including the traditionally republican Spanish Communist Party) to support him as well. Thus, the new democratic system benefited considerably from complementary support coming from both sides in this potentially difficult and conflictual process.

Nonetheless, the powers given to the king by the constitution are sharply limited. Consistent with the notion that "the monarch reigns but doesn't govern," the monarch's political role is restricted.

- As head of state, he formally possesses authority as commander-in-chief of the armed forces, with the power to declare war or peace. He also has the power to convene referendum elections and sign international treaties. But all of these formal powers require prior authorization by the government or parliament.
- His participation in ratifying legislation and dissolving parliament is constrained by the requirement of the *refrendo* – a countersignature by the prime minister or by the government minister relevant to the specific piece of legislation.
- Similarly, the nomination and designation of the prime minister have to be countersigned (*refrendado*) by the president of the Congress of Deputies.

Thus the king's actual involvement in the daily affairs of government is tightly constrained both by the constitution and by Juan Carlos's firm determination not to become embroiled in potentially divisive political matters (in sharp contrast with the behavior of both his grandfather, the exiled Alfonso XIII, and his brother-in-law, the deposed King Constantine of Greece).

His symbolic position as a unifying and stabilizing force, however, should not be underestimated. He played a key role in the transition to democracy, which would have been most difficult had he not boldly intervened to appoint Adolfo Suárez as prime minister, and provide legitimacy and support for the entire process. Moreover, on February 23, 1981, he was single-handedly responsible for the defense and restoration of Spain's new democracy in the face of a military coup. A small group of rebellious civil guards, in collusion with a significant number of captain generals (regional commanders) of the army, initially succeeded in storming into the Congress of Deputies (during a special session debating the investiture of Leopoldo Calvo Sotelo as prime minister following the resignation of Adolfo Suárez) and holding hostage at gunpoint all of the government ministers and virtually the entire elected political elite of Spain. Wearing his military uniform, symbolic of his authority as commander-in-chief of the armed forces, Juan Carlos broadcast over television a call for all Spaniards to remain firm in their support of democracy and its constitution, and to resist appeals by the rebels. Even more decisively, he exercised his role as commander-in-chief by personally telephoning all of the captain generals and ordering them to remain in their barracks. As a result, the coup collapsed in less than twenty-four hours, and Spanish democracy was quickly consolidated over the following year. Since then, his public performance and that of the royal family have been impeccable. It is not surprising that Juan Carlos is by far the most popular public figure in Spain, and that the monarchy remains as one of the most valued political institutions.

Figure 2.1 Colonel Antonio Tejero and rebellious civil guards invading the Congress of Deputies

Figure 2.2 King Juan Carlos I on television calling on all Spaniards to support the democratic regime in the face of the attempted coup

Parliamentary governance at the national level

Spain has an asymmetric bicameral legislature in which the Senate is extraordinarily weak. Cabinet ministers sit as members of the Congress of Deputies (whether they had been previously elected to parliament or not), and it is that chamber which completely dominates the parliamentary processes. In actual practice, however, the real center of decision-making authority lies with the Council of Ministers, and predominantly with the President of the Government (prime minister). The ability of individual members of the Congress to introduce legislation is sharply restricted by parliamentary regulations and by the concentration of power and resources in the hands of the leaders of the various parliamentary groups. And dominating the deliberations in the Congress is the government, which is the source of over 90% of all legislation.

The Senate

At best, the Senate plays a secondary and subordinate role in the legislative process.

- The Constitution (article 90.2) enables the Senate to reject or amend legislation approved by the Congress of Deputies, but the Congress can overrule the Senate's veto by **absolute-majority** vote, or delete any of its amendments by a **plurality** vote.
- While the Congress occasionally accepts amendments introduced by the Senate (particularly when they represent technical improvements in the bill or reflect agreements between parties concluded after the legislation has been passed by the Congress), only on one occasion has the Senate effectively overridden a policy decision reached in the Congress of Deputies.

Absolute majority vs. plurality Some parliamentary decisions require an "absolute majority" for passage, that is, the bill must be supported by at least 50% + 1 of all members of the Congress of Deputies. Others can be enacted only by "qualified majorities" of two-thirds or three-fifths, particularly for the appointment of some counter-majoritarian bodies. And still other bills or policy decisions need only a simple majority of those voting, even though that would amount to only a plurality of members rather than an absolute majority.

The parliamentary session that began in March 2004 provided an opportunity to test these propositions, since, for the first time in the life of the new democracy, the Congress and Senate were dominated by different parties. And in this legislature, aside from this single instance of Senate intervention, it was clear that the Congress of Deputies controlled the legislative process.

The Senate is designated by the constitution as "the chamber of territorial representation" (article 69.1). In actual practice, however, it is not only weak, but an institution whose fundamental role has always been in question. In large measure this is the result of the substantial decentralization of the state that unfolded in a manner that could not have been clearly anticipated in 1978, when the constitution was written. It is also a consequence of the politics of various stands taken by the authors of the constitution. While they agreed that they did not want to create a balanced bicameral system in which the "upper house" would have the same powers as the Congress of Deputies, they disagreed about exactly what kind of parliamentary body it should be. In the end, they created a Senate that would not have the same legislative powers as the Congress of Deputies, would not be clearly given responsibility for making purely technical refinements in legislation, and would not function adequately as a chamber of territorial representation.

> **Comunidades autónomas (CCAA)** The autonomy statutes enacted over the 5 years following ratification of the constitution established regional governments for each of the 17 "autonomous communities" thereby created. CCAA are the most powerful government bodies below the national level, followed by municipal government institutions (*ayuntamientos*). Provincial governments (*diputaciones provinciales*) have sharply limited authority.

The institutional characteristics of the Senate are so inconsistent with the basic nature of the decentralized Spanish state (*Estado de las autonomías*) and with the preferences and demands of powerful regional nationalist parties that it is not generally regarded as a legitimate representative of Spain's regions. To begin with, decentralization has taken the form of devolving political power to Spain's 17 **comunidades autónomas (CCAA)**, or regions, while 208 of the Senate's 256 seats are allocated through *provincial-level* elections, with four senators elected from each of Spain's 50 provinces, and the remainder from scattered territories (Ceuta, Melilla, and the Balearic and Canary Islands) not connected to the Iberian Peninsula (see map 2.1). The appointment of an additional 48 senators by regional parliaments is insufficient to offset the resulting representational biases.

This lack of fit between the predominantly regional decentralization of power and the provincial basis of representation destroys the effectiveness of the Senate as a chamber of territorial representation in several ways.

- The underpopulated rural provinces of Castilla-León and Castilla-La Mancha are vastly over-represented, particularly in contrast with populous Catalonia.
- The partisan composition of the Senate is unrepresentative of the various regional governments. In all but one legislative session, its powerfully majoritarian electoral system has manufactured a Senate majority for the party of government in Madrid while, at the same time, the major regional governments (especially those of Catalonia and the Basque country) are often controlled by opposition parties.

For these reasons, the Senate has not been regarded as a legitimate arena for the representation and articulation of regional interests, and numerous proposals have been made for its radical restructuring. Given that its *raison d'être* has been so frequently questioned, there have been few protests over its powerlessness and general irrelevance to the Spanish political process.

The Congress of Deputies

In contrast with the Senate, where each province has equal representation, deputies are elected to serve in the Congress in rough proportion to the

Map 2.1 The distribution of provinces in Spain[a]
[a] Provinces are shaded according to their belonging to different *comunidades autónomas* (see Map 1.1).

population of each province. Accordingly, populous Barcelona sends 31 representatives to the Congress, Madrid elects 35 deputies, etc. However, one focus of criticism has been that sparsely populated rural provinces are systematically over-represented. This is the net result of the small size of the Congress of Deputies (350, making it one of the smallest representative chambers in Western Europe) in combination with the electoral law's guarantee that even the least populated province (excluding the North African territories of Ceuta and Melilla) will have three representatives in the Congress. On average, each province has about seven deputies – whose political significance will be discussed when we explore Spain's electoral system in chapter 4.

In terms of its internal structure, there are two types of institution that are of considerable significance. These are "parliamentary groups" and standing committees within the Congress of Deputies.

Figure 2.3 The Congress of Deputies

Parliamentary groups

In order to form a parliamentary group, it is necessary for nationwide parties to have at least 15 deputies, or for regional parties to have at least 5 deputies. As described in the website of the Congress of Deputies (www.congreso.es, 2007),

> [parliamentary] groups have great importance in the internal functioning of the Congress and are the principal actors which participate in its decision-making processes. Accordingly, seats on [parliamentary] committees...are proportionally allocated among them...Their representatives constitute the *Junta de Portavoces* [committee of spokespersons], the body which determines the daily agenda of the house. Deputies are seated by parliamentary group. The right to propose initiatives – such as private members' bills (*proposiciones de ley*), amendments in opposition to government bills (*enmiendas a la totalidad*), and resolutions (*proposiciones no de ley*) – is reserved for parliamentary groups [exclusively]. Participation in parliamentary debate is structured by spokespersons of parliamentary groups.

Moreover, virtually all of the staff support and other resources needed by individual members for informed involvement in the legislative process are under the control of the heads of the parliamentary groups. The regulations of the Congress of Deputies clearly subordinate the individual member to the parliamentary group, in which the leaders of the parliamentary parties play by far the dominant roles. Control of these essential support services and proceedings of the Congress of Deputies by the leaders of the parliamentary groups gives parties considerable ability to control the behavior of their individual members, at least with regard to their capacity for legislative initiatives.

Even the ability of deputies to intervene in parliamentary debate is sharply restricted by regulations, deadlines, and prior-authorization requirements. As we shall see in chapter 6, this does not mean that parliament is irrelevant to the policy process, even in those legislatures when the PSOE or the PP holds an absolute majority. While government bills are rarely modified through votes in committee or plenary sessions, representatives of the government party take opposition stands into account either through negotiations or unilateral concessions when drafting bills. Moreover, government parties enjoying a parliamentary majority do not need the votes of opposition groups to pass their legislation, but they often seek to maintain a positive public image by garnering opposition support when possible.

Standing committees

Most of the daily work of the Congress of Deputies concerning both the enactment of legislation and the oversight of government is conducted within specialized standing committees. In the legislative session that began in 2008, there were a total of 32 committees, of which 28 are permanent, and most of them are linked to the work and policies of specific government ministries. As in most Western European parliaments where party discipline is strictly enforced in parliament, the ability of these committees to modify legislation effectively is substantially restricted. Indeed, only the seven-member subcommittee designated by the Constitutional Committee with responsibility for drafting a new constitution in 1977 enjoyed considerable autonomy in performing that crucial task, and this reflected the explicit abandonment of partisanship by the major parties in the course of the *política del consenso* that made possible the consolidation of Spanish democracy (as described in the preceding chapter).

Various indicators of parliamentary activity are reflective of an increasing electoral and parliamentary competition between the two major parties, the Socialist PSOE and the conservative Partido Popular. As can be seen in table 2.1, there has been a substantial increase in the number of sessions since 1996, both of the Congress in plenary session and of its various committees. Written and oral questions introduced from the floor of the Congress have become dramatically more numerous, as have meetings of the *Mesa* (the presiding board) of the Congress and of the *Junta de Portavoces* (the committee of spokespersons). In general, both parties have availed themselves of parliamentary arenas and procedural devices in the increasingly two-party structure of partisan competition.

Table 2.1 Indicators of parliamentary activity in the Congress of Deputies, 1977–2008

Parliamentary activities (by legistature)	Constituent (1977–79)	1st 1979–82	2nd 1982–6	3rd 1986–9	4th 1989–93	5th 1993–6	6th 1996–00	7th 2000–4	8th 2004–8
Laws approved	–	352	187	108	109	112	172	173	240
Proposiciones de ley introduced[a]	68	193	132	148	173	157	328	338	295
Written questions	314	3,820	9,200	19,458	15,309	14,886	32,721	75,326	140,322
Oral questions	148	412	1,828	3,103	4,467	3,475	4,941	7,101	5,918
Interpellations	129	389	66	115	151	110	180	245	320
Plenary sessions	–	–	281	205	259	193	285	308	313
Committee sessions	–	–	564	645	866	874	1,082	1,123	1,197

[a] These are "private members' bills," introduced by the parliamentary groups of opposition parties. Between 5 and 12% of them became law.
Source: www.congreso.es

Table 2.2 Composition of the Spanish government (PSOE), 2008

President of the Government
First Vice-President and Minister of the Presidency
Second Vice-President and Minister of Economy and Finance
Minister of Education, Social and Family Affairs
Minister of Labor and Immigration
Minister of Industry, Tourism, and Trade
Minister of Justice
Minister of Defense
Minister of the Interior
Minister of Development
Minister of Culture
Minister of Agriculture and the Environment
Minister of Public Administrations
Minister of Health
Minister of Research and Development
Minister of Equality
Minister of Housing

The government

As in most West European parliamentary democracies, the government is the principal source of legislation and includes the heads of administrative departments that implement these policies. It is composed of a prime minister (officially titled President of the Government) and the individual members of the Council of Ministers. Each of the latter holds a specific ministerial portfolio, which gives them considerable authority over the drafting of new legislation pertaining to their respective areas of expertise. They also assume responsibility for carrying out policies within their respective jurisdictions. In addition, between one and three of these ministers are designated at the discretion of the prime minister as Vice-President of the Government, and are therefore in charge of coordinating policies within specified areas (e.g., economic affairs and "political affairs"). Also similar to other West European parliamentary systems, these individuals head ministerial departments and therefore preside over their respective segments of the state administration (bureaucracy). The government in office for the 2008 legislature, for example, consisted of 14 ministers and two vice-presidents (see table 2.2).

The Spanish system differs from several West European parliamentary systems insofar as it has clearly embraced the German-style "**Chancellor democracy**" model. As article 98.2 of the

Chancellor democracy This term is commonly used to denote parliamentary systems in which the prime minister is explicitly designated by the constitution as having the primary role in decision-making and policy implementation regarding the government's foreign and domestic policies. It was originally coined in the late 1950s to describe the dominant role of the prime minister ("chancellor," in the German system) Konrad Adenauer.

Box 2.3

Spanish prime ministers
During the course of over three decades of democratic government in Spain (see table 2.3), only five individuals have served as President of the Government. These are Adolfo Suárez (UCD, June 1977–February 1981), Leopoldo Calvo Sotelo (UCD, February 1981–December 1982), Felipe González (PSOE, December 1982–May 1996), José María Aznar (PP, May 1996–April 2004), and José Luis Rodríguez Zapatero (April 2004–).

constitution states, "The President [prime minister] shall direct the Government's actions and coordinate the functions of the other members thereof, without prejudicing the competence and direct responsibility of the latter in the discharge of their duties." In short, the President of the Government is much more than merely *primus inter pares* (the first among equals). Spanish prime ministers have greater powers and resources than their counterparts in most other Western European countries, and they (especially Felipe González and José María Aznar, who governed from 1982 until 2004) have used them to effectively dominate the processes of parliamentary government. Indeed, the fact that Spain had only two prime ministers over the course of nearly twenty-two years not only represents a remarkable record of stability among democratic systems, but also attests to their capacity to dominate politics at the national level. With regard to convening referendum elections, requesting a vote of confidence in the Congress, or proposing the dissolution of parliament, for example, the prime minister needs only to consult the other members of the government, whose approval is not required for such important initiatives.

The prime minister also has complete control over the appointment and dismissal of individual ministers, and can thus freely restructure the cabinet without parliamentary approval. Only the prime minister, and not the government as a collectivity, is subject to a parliamentary vote of investiture or no confidence (which will be discussed more extensively below). And debates over motions of no confidence focus fundamentally on the incumbent prime minister and the alternative proposed to replace him or her.

Collectively, these constitutional provisions and parliamentary procedures greatly reinforce the prime minister's control over government ministers, parties, and, in general, the policy direction of the country.

Executive–legislative relations

Majoritarianism in Spain's current democratic system is most clearly manifested in the formation of stable, single-party governments, and by the executive's domination of the legislative process. As we shall see in chapter 4, one of the principal determinants of the formation of stable single-party governments is the existence of an electoral system which helps to either manufacture absolute majorities for the largest party or magnify its share of parliamentary seats beyond the percentage of popular votes it received. A second institutional feature which has facilitated this development is the "constructive motion of no confidence." In addition, a variety of other institutional mechanisms have been adopted that strengthen the hand of government *vis-à-vis* backbench members of parliament.

Government stability and the degree of fragmentation of the parliamentary party system

The stability of Spanish governments since 1977 represents a dramatic departure from the pattern of unstable, multi-party governments, which helped to weaken the Second Republic (1931–6) and contributed to its collapse. As noted in chapter 1, that earlier unsuccessful experience with democracy was seriously weakened by an electoral system that greatly fragmented the parliamentary party system. In each of the three legislatures of the Second Republic, there were no fewer than 20 parties in parliament, and the largest party controlled no more than 24% of the seats. Accordingly, governments were formed by large, unstable multi-party coalitions and collapsed with disruptive frequency. Between April 1931 and July 1936 there were 19 different governments under 8 different prime ministers. This made the Second Republic the most unstable parliamentary regime in inter-war Europe, with an average "**cabinet durability**" of 101 days.

> **Cabinet durability** The length of time that a particular cabinet government remains in office is called "cabinet durability." It can be measured in different ways. One is based on the replacement of individual ministers. It is this measure that produces the 101-day lifespan of the average government during the Second Republic. If we were to use the replacement of the prime minister as the indicator of a change of government, the average cabinet durability between April 14, 1931, and the outbreak of the Civil War on July 19, 1936, would be just over 5 months. Whichever counting rule is used, the Second Republic emerges with a dramatically high level of cabinet instability.

In sharp contrast, the two largest parties in Spain's current democracy have always held at least 80 percent of the seats in the Congress of Deputies, and the largest party has always occupied at least 44% of the seats. Moreover, all of the governments formed since 1977 have been formed by only one party. Spain's parliamentary system has produced governments that are among the most stable in the democratic world. Between June 1977 and March 2004 there were only 9 governments under 4 different prime ministers. If we were to use Arend Lijphart's counting rules, the average cabinet durability of Spanish governments during this period would reach 107 months. This is second only to Australia (119 months, between 1945 and 1996) among all of the countries included in Lijphart's studies.

The constructive vote of no confidence

The stability of Spanish governments has been facilitated (in addition to the electoral system, which reduces the fragmentation of the parliamentary party system) by the inclusion of a "constructive vote of no confidence" (*moción de*

Box 2.4

Majority and minority governments
Of Spain's ten governments (see table 2.3), only the 1982 and 1986 PSOE governments of Felipe González and the 2000 PP government of José María Aznar were supported by an absolute majority of the Congress's 350 deputies. The PSOE occupied exactly half of the seats in the 1989 legislature, but a boycott of parliament by the Basque Herri Batasuna's four deputies made it possible to install a PSOE government by an absolute majority vote on the first ballot.

censura) in the constitution (article 113). Borrowed from the Federal Republic of Germany, this provision requires that a government can be removed from office only through the approval of a motion of no confidence supported by an absolute majority of all members of the Congress of Deputies, which must simultaneously designate a new prime minister who will automatically take office if the motion is approved. The investiture of a new President of the Government at the beginning of a newly elected Congress of Deputies, in contrast, requires only a plurality of votes in parliament on the second ballot. Thus, single-party governments can be easily formed, but can be dismissed only by surpassing a political hurdle that is virtually insurmountable.

By requiring the formation of a new government with the support of an absolute majority vote at the same time that the sitting government is dismissed, it is extremely unlikely that the opposition parties could ever reach agreement. In most legislatures, for example, this would have meant that a UCD, PSOE, or PP minority government could have been removed from office only if virtually all of the opposition parties (from the Communist Party or its broader coalition, Izquierda Unida, on the left, to the Alianza Popular or Partido Popular on the right, and including the major Basque and Catalan nationalist parties) were able to agree on the composition of a new government. Accordingly, over the course of three decades of parliamentary activity, only two *mociones de censura* have been introduced, and neither was successful. This provision has helped to strengthen the position of the government party to such a degree that 6 out of the 10 single-party governments between 1977 and 2007 were minority governments, i.e., formed by a party holding between 41 and 48% of the seats in parliament. And to date no multi-party coalition governments have been necessary.

The powers of the prime minister

The dominant position of the government *vis-à-vis* parliament is further reinforced by constitutional provisions that greatly strengthen the hand of the President of the Government.

- Only the candidate for President of the Government and his or her program are presented to parliament, debated over, and voted upon in the investiture process.
- In contrast with procedures in other parliamentary systems, the nominee for prime minister is not obliged to inform the parliament of the composition of the future government.
- In the investiture process, the vote of the Congress of Deputies is only in support of the candidate for President of the Government and not in favor of individual government ministers or the cabinet as a whole. Neither does the Congress have the ability to remove individual ministers from office.
- The prime minister is free to appoint or dismiss individual ministers as he or she chooses, without parliamentary approval.
- The President of the Government is also largely autonomous in deciding upon the dissolution of the parliament and, thereby, the holding of new parliamentary elections, as well as the holding of any type of referendum.

Even the rules governing the investiture of the prime minister have helped to reinforce the power of the executive *vis-à-vis* the opposition parties in parliament. An absolute majority of all of the members of the Congress is required on the first ballot, but if a candidate for prime minister fails to muster a majority, he or she can be elected with the support of a mere plurality on the second round. In actual practice, most candidates for prime minister will make great efforts to secure the support of other parties (usually by offering policy-relevant "side payments" during negotiations preceding the vote) in an effort to come to office with majority support on the first ballot. Thus, the institutional framework decisively stacks the deck in favor of government stability and executive dominance over parliament, and it strengthens governmental control over public administration and the establishment of policy priorities.

Box 2.5

Side payments

Side payments are made as part of "package deals," in which one individual or group will give something of value to another in exchange for the latter's support regarding a different matter. The side payments offered to other parties in exchange for support in voting to invest a new prime minister with governmental authority may be openly stated (as when the Catalan CiU supported the investiture of Felipe González in 1993 in exchange for a pledge that the CiU leader would be consulted on important policy matters) or "under the table" (such as when the small Socialist Party of Andalucía voted for the investiture of UCD prime minister Adolfo Suárez in exchange for various forms of assistance in the 1979 elections – which the UCD thought might undermine support for the PSOE in its regional stronghold).

> ## Box 2.6
>
> *Bargaining over legislation*
>
> Adolfo Suárez's first UCD government (1977–9) lacked a parliamentary majority and therefore had to bargain with other parties for their support in order to enact its legislative proposals. This bargaining was particularly extensive during the crucial period prior to approval of the constitution, since the "politics of consensus" (the consensual norms temporarily adopted during the transition to democracy, as described in chapter 1) meant that no important constitutional proposal or major piece of legislation should be completely unacceptable to any significant party. The "Pacts of the Moncloa" (October 1977), for example, involved negotiations among representatives of the UCD, the socialist PSOE, and the communist PCE, and dealt with a large number of policy matters relating to the social security and taxation systems, government price controls, reform of the education system, limitations on trade unions' wage demands, and the government's monetary policies. Under Suárez's second government (1979–81), the breakdown of discipline within his own party sometimes necessitated negotiations with representatives of factions within his own parliamentary delegation. As he described it in an interview, "Whenever they felt that they weren't getting what they wanted, 'mysterious illnesses' would break out among the deputies which could only be cured by granting them policy concessions."

Parliamentary groups

Executive–legislative relations in Spain, as noted earlier, are also characterized by the dominant position of the "parliamentary groups" in all phases of decision-making, as well as by the general inability of individual members of parliament to play important roles in the policy process. This dominance varies, however, according to the characteristics of specific governments and the level of discipline within their respective parliamentary groups (see table 2.3).

Center-right minority governments

From June 1977 through November 1982, governments of the center-right Unión de Centro Democrático (UCD) were weakened by the lack of a parliamentary majority, low party discipline, and the special requirements of the "politics of consensus" – the net effect of which was to give **backbenchers** considerable influence over the course of legislation. As we shall see in chapter 6, the enactment of every piece of legislation required considerable bargaining with opposition parties and even UCD backbenchers.

Backbenchers are members of parliament who hold no ministerial or sub-ministerial appointments and are not heads of committees or officially designated legislative leaders. This term was coined in Britain, where government ministers and members of the "shadow cabinet" occupy the front benches in the House of Commons.

Table 2.3 Spanish governments, 1977–2008

Prime minister	Time in office	Duration in office (months)	Government party	Parliamentary seats (%)	External support	Majority/ Minority
Suárez I	7/77–4/79	22	UCD	47	No	Min.
Suárez II	4/79–1/81	22	UCD	48	No	Min
Calvo Sotelo	2/81–10/82	21	UCD	48	No	Min.
González I	12/82–6/86	43	PSOE	58	No	MAJ.
González II	7/86–10/89	40	PSOE	53	No	MAJ.
González III	12/89–6/93	43	PSOE	50	No	MAJ.
González IV	7/93–3/96	33	PSOE	45	Yes (CiU)	Min.
Aznar I	5/96–1/00	45	PP	45	Yes (CiU, PNV, CC)	Min.
Aznar II	4/00–2/04	47	PP	52	No	MAJ.
Zapatero I	4/04–2/08	47	PSOE	47	Yes (IU, ERC)	Min.
Zapatero II	4/08–	–	PSOE	48	Yes	Min.

Majoritarian socialist governments

At the other end of the continuum were the Socialist (PSOE [Partido Socialista Obrero Español]) governments of the 1980s and the Partido Popular (PP) government that took office in 2000, when the executive was supported by absolute majorities in the Congress of Deputies and party discipline was much stronger. All parties had been so alarmed by the collapse and complete disappearance of the UCD in the early 1980s that the imposition of party discipline became paramount. Thus, by the time the PSOE came to power in 1982, the party's leadership had succeeded in establishing strict discipline among its deputies. Moreover, after the regime had been consolidated, and the norms and procedures of the "politics of consensus" were no longer regarded as necessary, PSOE elites decided that the economic crisis and the need for long-term restructuring required bold policy initiatives by a strong government. Following its near loss of an absolute parliamentary majority in 1989, the PSOE sought support from other parties in order to secure parliamentary support for its legislation, but its bargaining strategies were much closer to the majoritarian than the consensual model as it put together a series of *ad hoc* minimum-winning coalitions. The PSOE's principal partner in these efforts was the Catalan leader Jordi Pujol, who, in exchange, demanded considerable influence over government policy. A further drop in the PSOE's parliamentary representation in the 1993 elections substantially reinforced its dependency on the Catalan parliamentary group. While the Basque nationalist PNV was sometimes approached in efforts to secure its parliamentary support, the exclusion of all other parties from these kinds of deliberations clearly conformed to the majoritarian model of policy-making.

Center-right minority government

The Partido Popular, which formed a single-party minority government in May 1996, also followed the majoritarian model, but with some modifications. Since his party held only 45% of the seats in the Congress, prime minister José María Aznar negotiated a formal pact signed by the Catalan CiU (Convergència i Unió, a center-right coalition), the PNV, and the Coalición Canaria (the Canary Islands parliamentary group) that included a generic government program and commitments of support from the regional parties. This agreement enabled Aznar to receive an absolute majority of parliamentary support on his first vote of investiture, following which there were extensive discussions between the PP government and its parliamentary allies over their support for specific pieces of legislation (including the budget). The bargaining leverage possessed by the Basques and Catalans enabled them to extract a number of important policy concessions from the PP government with regard to such important issues as the financing of regional government activities and, implicitly, the balance of power and authority between central and regional levels of government.

PP majoritarianism

Following its attainment of a parliamentary majority in the 2000 elections, however, the PP no longer depended on the Basque and Catalan parties to enact its legislation, so Aznar was free to adopt a strongly majoritarian decision-making style. Particularly noteworthy was the extent to which the prime minister and his closest collaborators at the top of the PP hierarchy concentrated decision-making authority in their own hands.

Socialist minority government

With the election of a minority PSOE government in 2004, however, there was a return to the pattern of shifting, *ad hoc* legislative agreements similar to those of the UCD era. One difference from that earlier period (where legislative alliances changed almost from one piece of legislation to the next) is that the PSOE tended to rely at the outset on support from the leftist Izquierda Unida (IU) and Esquerra Republicana de Catalunya (ERC), and then moved to the center right in search of support from Converència i Unió and the Partido Nacionalista Vasco over a period of several months. Following the 2006 elections in Catalonia, however, the regional coalition forged among the Catalan branch of the PSOE, the ERC, and the Catalan branch of IU (Iniciativa per Catalunya) was reflected in a more or less durable legislative agreement among those parties in the national parliament as well. This clearly reflects the interactions between the regional and national levels of politics characteristic of the "multi-level governance" processes that we will analyze in the following chapter. In particular, it reveals how regional parties can use their delegations in the Congress of Deputies to exert pressure in support of additional transfers of government authority and resources from the central government to the autonomous communities.

■ Non-majoritarian and counter-majoritarian institutions

While government formation and executive–legislative relations at the national level have been characterized by majoritarianism, Spain's democratic system includes a number of institutions that are non-majoritarian or explicitly counter-majoritarian in nature. These include a number of "arbiter" institutions whose principal function is to oversee the fairness of the democratic competitive game, or to prevent partisanship from influencing the performance of important quasi-governmental institutions. This makes Spain's democracy different from the intensely majoritarian practices in the United States, for example, where even judicial appointments and oversight of the electoral process are highly partisan.

Consensual arbiter institutions

In Spain's democracy, consensualism applies to the staffing of certain government bodies that are intended to be non-partisan because of their fundamental roles as guarantors of the supremacy of the constitution, respect for basic civil or political rights, and/or the universalism of key state institutions. These include:

- the Constitutional Court;
- the Junta Electoral Central (which oversees the electoral process);
- the Tribunal de Cuentas (Court of Accounts);
- the Consejo General del Poder Judicial (the General Council of the Judiciary, which oversees the court system and plays a key role in the appointment and promotion of judges);
- the ombudsman (Defensor del Pueblo [defender of the people]); and
- the oversight board of the public broadcasting system (the Consejo de Administración de Radio Televisión Española).

The importance of maintaining non-partisanship or at least some minimal level of partisan balance in these institutions is reflected in the legal frameworks regulating them – either the constitution itself or various **organic laws** – which require that appointments be ratified by qualified parliamentary majorities (i.e., by at least 60% of all members of parliament). Since no parliamentary party has ever controlled that number of seats, inter-party agreements must be reached concerning all such appointments.

It is interesting to note, however, that the scope of inter-party consensus has sometimes gone well beyond minimal compliance with these oversized-majority requirements. In 1994, for instance, the PSOE could have met the three-fifths minimum requirement for the Congress's four

> **Organic laws** are those which establish or modify core governmental institutions or fundamental individual rights. They must be ratified by an absolute majority of all members of parliament, rather than by a "simple majority" of those voting on the measure. As noted in article 81 of the constitution, legislation pertaining to the statutes of regional autonomy, the electoral law, and basic civil rights are examples of subjects that must be dealt with as organic laws requiring absolute majority support.

Constitutional Court appointments by reaching agreement with just one party, the Partido Popular (as it had done in 1989, and as the UCD and PSOE had done in the 1970s). Instead, it also included a number of nominations by Basque and Catalan nationalist parties, as well as by Izquierda Unida (United Left, a coalition that includes the Communist PCE). Consensual norms even applied to some consultative bodies, such as the Council of State, where appointments do not have to be ratified by oversized parliamentary majorities. Similarly, the presidencies of the various committees in the Congress of Deputies and the Senate are parceled out proportionately among the various parliamentary parties.

The importance of guaranteeing non-partisanship in the performance of some of these institutions is obvious. Maintaining the fairness and integrity of the electoral process is important for the performance and legitimacy of democratic systems. Accordingly, the Junta Electoral Central includes 8 randomly selected members of the Supreme Court (Tribunal Supremo) and 5 professors of law or social sciences appointed by all significant political parties with parliamentary representation. This body has the ultimate responsibility for overseeing the conduct of elections nationwide and resolving disputes arising out of the electoral process, and these selection criteria make it impossible for any single party to dominate its deliberations or interfere with its performance of those duties. Similarly, it is essential that an ombudsman will intervene to protect the civil and political liberties of individuals in an absolutely impartial manner. Appointed by qualified majorities (60%) in the Congress and the Senate, the Defensor del Pueblo has effectively performed this function as originally intended.

The Constitutional Court

By far the most important of these counter-majoritarian institutions is the Constitutional Court. The Tribunal Constitucional has been used frequently both by the parliamentary opposition to restrain the central government's majoritarian impulses and by regional governments in the *comunidades autónomas*

Box 2.7

Diffuse and concentrated judicial review

In contrast with countries like the United States, where "diffuse" judicial review enables courts at all levels to rule on the constitutionality of the law (as long as that relates to a specific case brought before them), Spain and several other countries with civil-law traditions (e.g., Austria, Germany, France, and Italy) have a more "concentrated" process of review. A separate Constitutional Court rules on the constitutionality of the law, while the Supreme Court (Tribunal Supremo) deals with legal appeals that do not involve questions of constitutionality. This differs substantially from the United States, where a single Supreme Court both serves as the court of final appeal and rules on issues of constitutionality.

Cases received

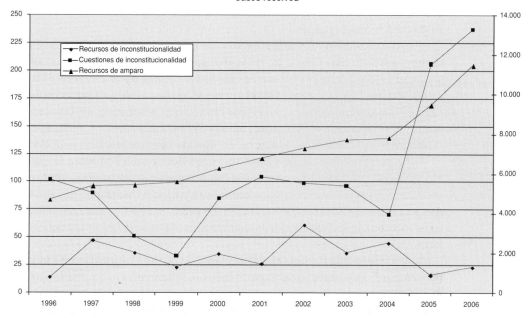

Figure 2.4 Cases accepted by the Constitutional Court, 1996–2006
Source: www.tribunalconstitucional.es/memorias/2006

(autonomous communities, or CCAA) to block what they regarded as uncon-stitutional infringements by the Spanish state on the rights and powers of the regions recognized in their respective autonomy statutes. The Constitutional Court, consisting of twelve members serving nine-year, non-renewable terms, was modeled after its German counterpart. Its members are selected through generally consensual procedures involving the Congress, the Senate, the government and the Consejo General del Poder Judicial. Its most impor-tant function involves the **abstract and concrete review** of legislation passed by the Spanish Cortes (Congress and Senate) and by the parliaments of the autonomous communities. Appeals may be filed by the prime minister, the ombudsman, any 50 deputies or senators, or by the regional governments or parliaments.

Abstract and concrete review Some judicial systems (such as that in the United States) limit rulings on the constitutionality of the law to specific cases which are appealed to the courts. In Spain, the Constitutional Court engages in both concrete review and abstract review, where a ruling can be issued even when no specific case is appealed to the courts.

The Constitutional Court also has responsibility for resolving conflicts between central and regional governments, or among regional governments, for redress of citizens' appeals against state actions allegedly violating funda-mental rights (*recursos de amparo*), and for determining the constitutionality of issues passed on to it by lower-court judges. As can be seen in the data in figure 2.4, the court has had to deal with an expanding number of cases, reflective of its increasing importance over the past decades. Particularly numerous are *recursos de amparo*, followed in terms of frequency by questions of constitutionality raised by other judges.

With the enactment of the *Ley Orgánica del Tribunal Constitucional* (Organic Law of the Constitutional Court) in 1979, the powers of the Constitutional Court were expanded to include *a priori* **review of legislation** approved by the parliament but before that law comes into effect. Since such appeals had the effect of suspending these new laws pending a verdict by an already overburdened Constitutional Court, this procedure enabled opposition parties in parliament to paralyze the implementation of legislation with which it disagreed. The abuse of this procedure by the Alianza Popular in the early 1980s led to the enactment of legislation by the Socialist majority that terminated this *a priori* review process in 1986.

> *A priori* **judicial review** allows a group of legislators to appeal the constitutionality of a new law to the Constitutional Court even prior to its coming into effect. Much more common is *a posteriori* review, in which the court makes a "corrective" decision regarding cases brought to it involving disputes over the constitutionality of a law only after it has been enacted.

The counter-majoritarian function of appeals to the Constitutional Court by the principal opposition party in parliament is closely reflected in the frequency of appeals of unconstitutionality between 1980 and 2002. In those legislatures in which the governing party lacked a parliamentary majority (1979–82, 1993–6, and 1996–2000), and which therefore required inter-party agreements for the enactment of legislation, only 2% of laws were subjected to *a posteriori* appeal by the principal opposition party. In contrast, in those legislative sessions in which the government was supported by an absolute majority in the Congress, nearly 7% of laws were appealed to the Constitutional Court by the parliamentary opposition. Thus, during the 1982–93 period of PSOE majoritarianism, the court provided the parliamentary opposition with an important veto point in the legislative process. Seen from a different perspective, variation in the frequency of such appeals in accord with political circumstances provides further evidence of the flexibility of Spanish political institutions.

Overall, the frequency of Constitutional Court involvement in the legislative process is not excessive: just 4.3% of laws passed between 1980 and 1999 have been subjected to appeal, a level roughly comparable to that of Germany. With regard to court involvement in center–periphery relations, however, this judicial role has been of extraordinary importance, in terms of both the frequency of appeals and the magnitude of the political issues at stake.

While high levels of judicial involvement are to be expected in all decentralized political systems (which frequently require resolution of disputes regarding the jurisdictions of the different levels of government), it is remarkable to note that the governments of Catalonia, the Basque Country, and Galicia filed 418 appeals between 1980 and 1999 – a figure vastly higher than the 26 such cases filed by *Länder* in Germany between 1951 and 1994. In part, this difference reflects the increasing relevance of the regional cleavage in Spain, as compared with its total absence in Germany, and the complete failure of the Spanish Senate to serve effectively as a chamber of territorial representation and dispute resolution, as compared with the exceptionally powerful Bundesrat of Germany. It also reflects the functioning of the court as a counter-majoritarian institution: under Spanish governments supported by an absolute parliamentary majority, 18% of bills enacted were appealed to the Constitutional Court by regional governments – a level which is more than twice that of periods under single-party minority governments (8%).

It is noteworthy that the frequency of regional government litigation before the Constitutional Court has declined dramatically since 1990. This reflects the fact that in earlier periods the specific jurisdictions and powers of newly created regional governments were not entirely clear, while broader consensual understanding of the proper roles of the central and regional governments has emerged as a product of cumulative experience.

Aside from the frequency of court involvement in reviewing legislation, the importance of the issues with which it has grappled provides clear evidence of the key political role played by the court in Spain. Judicial review has even led to the overturning of extremely important legislation that had been passed with the support of over 80% of the members of parliament in a crucial stage in the development of the *Estado de las autonomías*. In 1981, the two largest parties in parliament, the UCD and PSOE, both supported the passage of an "organic law for the harmonization of the autonomy process" (LOAPA, *Ley Orgánica de Armonización del Proceso Autonómico*, which will be discussed more extensively in the following chapter). If the most important clauses of that law had not been struck down by the Constitutional Court, they would have had a substantial effect on the nature and degree of decentralization of the Spanish state. And this, in turn, would probably have led the principal Basque and Catalan nationalist parties to challenge not only the legitimacy of that law, but also perhaps the legitimacy of the regime. Overturning many clauses of this law required much political courage (in the face of a huge parliamentary majority), as well as considerable political wisdom, which helped to preserve the consolidation of the new democratic regime. In general, since federal forms of government almost invariably generate conflict between the central and regional government bodies, the involvement of the court in resolving these disputes has been of the greatest importance.

Other government institutions

Some of the institutions intended by the authors of the constitution to be strictly non-partisan have not always lived up to those expectations in the performance of their duties. There are two main examples.

(1) **The Consejo General del Poder Judicial** (CGPJ). Designated by the constitution as the "governing body" of the judiciary, the CGPJ has responsibility for the appointment of judges and supervision of the administration of justice. The Congress and Senate each appoint 10 of its 21 members by qualified majority votes (60%). Among these 10 nominees, 4 are required to be experts

in legal affairs, and the other 6 are selected from among the pool of sitting judges and magistrates. The president of the Tribunal Supremo serves as president of the CGPJ. This institutional design (especially the super-majority requirement for appointment) was intended to create a council that would reflect Spanish society's political and ideological pluralism in a non-partisan manner. Nonetheless, the most conservative judicial professional associations have strongly and incessantly complained that the appointment functions performed by the two houses of parliament should be limited to ratifying nominations set forth by the judges' professional associations themselves. This confrontation has two consequences which run counter to the ostensibly non-partisan nature of the Consejo. The first is that the members of the Consejo are selected by parties on the basis of their respective shares of parliamentary representation, and, in turn, those members take stands in accord with the political objectives of their respective parties. The second is that parties can have an extraordinary veto power when they decide to block appointments to the Consejo or use threats of such opposition to bargain for government concessions on a variety of policy matters.

(2) The **Consejo de Administración de Radio Televisión Española**. Similar partisan rancor has occasionally interfered with the oversight role performed by the Consejo de Administración de Radio Televisión Española, which is charged with guaranteeing the objectivity, truth, and impartiality of information disseminated through public broadcasting media. Its 12 members are elected by the Congress and the Senate (6 members each) at the beginning of each legislative session by two-thirds majorities in each chamber. As with the CGPJ, its members are elected by partisan quota, based on the representation of the major parties in each house of parliament. Not surprisingly, once in office they tend to take stands consistent with the interests and viewpoints of their respective parties. However, in 2006 the Socialist government enacted a new Law for State Television and Radio (*Ley de la Radio y la Televisión de Titularidad Pública Estatal*) that should reduce the government's ability to influence news coverage. It provided for the election of the director of the national broadcasting networks by the Congress, rather than allowing the government to make such appointments without parliamentary accountability.

The authors of the Spanish constitution intended that all such counter-majoritarian institutions would remain immune from partisan interference. For the most part, some of these institutions – like the Constitutional Court and the Defensor del Pueblo – have fulfilled those objectives, and have countered the strong majoritarianism characteristic of executive–legislative relations in this parliamentary democracy. But the most important of the consensual elements in this model of democracy is the decentralization of the state, and the construction of the so-called *Estado de las autonomías*. In the following chapter we turn our attention to this unusual form of federalism.

■ Summary

In this chapter, we have examined the core governmental institutions that were created through enactment of the constitution in December 1978. As we have seen:

- Despite the fact that King Juan Carlos had been selected by the dictator Francisco Franco, he has behaved in a fully democratic manner (and has played key roles in establishing and protecting democracy in Spain) within a fully democratic constitutional monarchy.
- Despite the fact that the Spanish transition to democracy (described in chapter 1) closely conformed to the core tenets of *consensual* democracy, executive–legislative relations since the approval of the constitution have been strongly **majoritarian**.
- Legislative dominance by the lower house (the Congress of Deputies) also conforms to the majoritarian model, as do the regulations and internal structures of that body.
- However, the highly decentralized structure of the state since the early 1980s, the explicit protection of civil and political liberties by the very inflexible constitution (amended only once over the course of three decades) and a strong and active judiciary, and several counter-majoritarian "arbiter institutions," place Spain closer to the **consensual** end of the continuum with regard to the federal-unitary dimension.

■ Further reading

Bruneau, Thomas C., *et al.*, "Democracy, Southern European Style," in P. Nikiforos Diamandouros and Richard Gunther, eds., *Parties, Politics, and Democracy in the New Southern Europe* (Baltimore: Johns Hopkins University Press, 2001)

Capo Giol, Jordi, "The Spanish Parliament in a Triangular Relationship, 1982–2000," *Journal of Legislative Studies*, 9 (2003), 107–29

Colomer, Josep M., "Spain and Portugal: Rule by Party Leadership," in Colomer, ed., *Political Institutions in Europe*, 3rd edn. (London: Routledge, 2008)

Field, Bonnie, and Kerstin Hamann, eds., *Democracy and Institutional Development: Spain in Comparative Theoretical Perspective 1977–2007* (Basingstoke and New York: Palgrave Macmillan, 2008)

Guerrero, Enrique, *El Parlamento: qué es, cómo funciona, qué hace* (Madrid: Editorial Síntesis, 2004)

Magalhães, Pedro C., *The Limits to Judicialization: Legislative Politics and Constitutional Review in the Iberian Democracies* (PhD dissertation, Ohio State University, 2003), part of which has been published as Pedro C. Magalhães, Carlo Guarnieri, and Yorgos Kaminis, "Democratic Consolidation, Judicial Reform, and the Judicialization of Politics in Southern Europe," in Richard Gunther, P. Nikiforos Diamandouros, and Dimitri A. Sotiropoulos, eds., *Democracy and the State in the New Southern Europe* (Oxford: Oxford University Press, 2006)

Maurer, Lynn M., *El poder del Congreso: Parlamento y políticas públicas en España, 1979–2000* (Madrid: Centro de Estudios Políticos y Constitucionales, 2008)

Newton, Michael T., and Peter J. Donaghy, *Institutions of Modern Spain: A Political and Economic Guide* (Cambridge: Cambridge University Press, 1997)

Pasquino, Gianfranco, "Executive-Legislative Relations in Southern Europe," in Richard Gunther, P. Nikiforos Diamandouros, and Hans-Jürgen Puhle, *The Politics of Democratic Consolidation* (Baltimore: Johns Hopkins University Press, 1995)

Powell, Charles T., *Juan Carlos of Spain: Self-made Monarch* (New York: St. Martin's Press, 1996)

■ Websites

www.casareal.es	The official website of the Crown
http://www.la-moncloa.es	The prime minister's website
www.congreso.es	The Congress of Deputies
www.senado.es	The website of the Senate
http://www.map.es/enlaces/ administracion_general_del_estado.html	Information about the public administration and the Cabinet
www.tribunalconstitucional.es	The Constitutional Court
www.poderjudicial.es	Other judicial institutions
www.defensordelpueblo.es	The Spanish Ombudsman

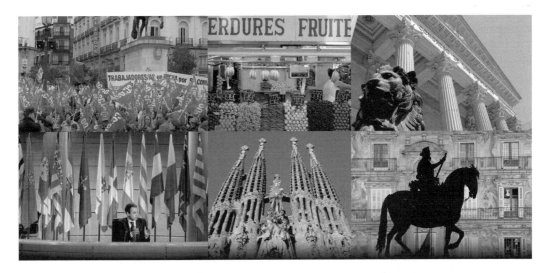

3 Multi-level governance: the *Estado de las autonomías* and the European Union

Under the Franco regime, Spain was one of the most centralized unitary states in Europe. And throughout the first two decades under Generalísimo Franco, Spain was largely isolated from the rest of the democratic world. With democratization, both of these aspects of government would be altered. Beginning in 1979, the state was substantially decentralized. And by the late 1980s, not only would Spain be an integral part of the European Union, but its former Foreign Minister, Javier Solana, would become Secretary General of NATO (the North Atlantic Treaty Organization), and, subsequently, the European Union's spokesperson on foreign affairs.

The ***Estado de las autonomías.*** Spain's quasi-federal system, called the *Estado de las autonomías* (state of the autonomies), was established in a piecemeal fashion through the granting of autonomy statutes to each of seventeen Spanish regions, called *comunidades autónomas* (autonomous communities). These give somewhat differing levels of autonomy to each region, representing a departure from the more uniform devolution of political authority to states in most federal systems.

In this chapter, we will examine the emergence of the quasi-federal ***Estado de las autonomías*** and Spain's integration within the European Union, as well as their implications for the processes of government. We will explore in detail:

- the processes through which the Spanish state was decentralized;
- the institutions and policy jurisdictions of the regional governments (the *comunidades autónomas*, or CCAA), as well as those of provinces and municipalities;
- the complex political relationships between the central and regional levels of government;
- Spain's increased involvement with international institutions, especially its integration within the European Union; and
- the varying ways in which the sub-national, national, and supra-national levels of government (i.e., involving the CCAA, the Spanish central government, and the European Union) interact with one another.

We will see that Spanish government and politics, both domestically and internationally, have been dramatically transformed since the days of international isolation and unitary government that characterized most of the Franco era.

◼ The decentralization process

Francisco Franco was a Spanish nationalist whose rebellion against the Second Republic (which had granted autonomy to Catalonia and promised self-government rights to the Basques) was in part a reaction against what he regarded as the disintegration of the Spanish nation. Accordingly, one of the most far-reaching steps taken by his authoritarian regime was the rigid re-centralization of the state, coupled with the suppression of Basque and Catalan regional nationalism. Indeed, even as late as 1980, fully 83% of all government expenditures were those of the central government, with the remainder representing the activities of municipal governments. While Spain was divided into fifty provinces, those provincial governments had almost no political authority or financial resources. It was clear to all observers that this state structure would have to be altered in order for the new democratic regime founded following the dictator's death to acquire **legitimacy**. Both Basques and Catalans demanded a restoration of their self-government rights that they had enjoyed throughout most of Spain's history.

Legitimacy of a state or political regime entails acceptance of and respect for its norms and institutions by the people. In Spain, continuation of a centralized state that denied self-government rights to historic regions (especially the Basque Country and Catalonia) would have been regarded as unacceptable, and its government authority would have been challenged by significant sectors of the population.

Accordingly, the post-Franco transition would have to involve political decentralization in addition to democratization.

The *Estado de las autonomías* that emerged from this decentralization process is an asymmetric form of federalism, in which the seventeen regions acquired different levels of autonomy and resources through different legal procedures at different times (see map 1.2). It has also been a relatively open-ended process, particularly insofar as the Basque and Catalan regional governments have frequently demanded and received increases in the level of their self-government authority, revenues, and staff resources. It has also been an expansive process, in which many regions that lacked historical traditions of self-government or even well-defined regional identities joined in the process of establishing their own autonomous government institutions. While this has often been a "messy" process, it was also largely inevitable, given the political demands and pressures of the transition to democracy.

The Spanish constitution did not, by itself, decentralize the Spanish state. Instead, it "recognizes and guarantees the right of autonomy for all nationalities and regions" (article 2), and establishes two different processes through which regions could apply for and secure self-government rights. Article 151 provides for the so-called "fast route" to autonomy, and article 143 establishes procedures commonly referred to as the "slow route" to acquiring self-government rights.

The three "historic regions" that had approved autonomy referendums under the Second Republic – Catalonia, the Basque Country, and Galicia – secured their respective autonomy statutes under the terms of article 151. The specific content of these autonomy statutes was determined through separate bilateral negotiations between, on the one hand, leaders of the Spanish government and, on the other hand, representatives of each region. Accordingly, the first steps towards decentralizing the Spanish state were *ad hoc* and sequential, with the Basques completing negotiations over their autonomy statute first, followed by the Catalans, and then by the Galicians. Their charters of autonomy were ratified through referendums held in 1979 (Basque Country and Catalonia) and 1980 (Galicia). The need to address Basque and Catalan demands for autonomy promptly in the transition to democracy was widely acknowledged. In particular, prime minister Adolfo Suárez was convinced that the legitimacy of the new democratic regime required Basque and Catalan acceptance of the new governmental framework, and this, in turn, required a restoration of their self-government rights. Accordingly, the "fast route" to autonomy was followed. Except for Galicia and Andalucía, all of the other regions secured their self-government rights via the "slow route," as provided for in article 143 of the constitution.

The Basque settlement

The urgency of addressing Basque autonomy demands was reinforced by the political environment of that period, characterized by pressure exerted in the Basque region through street demonstrations and terrorist violence by ETA. Indeed, this violence accelerated throughout the process of negotiating the Basque autonomy statute. Between 1968 and 1975 ETA assassinated 43 persons; but in 1978 the level of political violence increased to 65 assassinations, in 1979 to 78, and in 1980 to 96. This polarizing climate helped to strengthen the negotiating position of the PNV, which could claim that only the restoration of a high level of autonomy from the Spanish state would pacify the Basque country.

The actual process through which these autonomy statutes were written and approved was quite similar to that which was adopted in writing the

Box 3.1

ETA

Euskadi ta Askatasuna ("Basque Homeland and Liberty" in the Basque language) was founded in 1959 as a clandestine terrorist organization seeking to bring about the secession of four Spanish provinces (the three Basque provinces of Álava, Guipúzcoa, and Vizcaya, as well as Navarra) and three French *départments* (Basse Navarre, Labourd, and Soule) in order to create an independent Basque nation-state. Beginning in the late 1960s, in support of those demands, ETA launched a campaign of terrorist violence that, over the following four decades, claimed the lives of over 800 persons. In the 1970s, two souls coexisted within ETA. One faction (ETA-militar) sought to give preeminence to terrorist activities over political involvement, while the other (ETA-politico-militar) favored a strategy combining terrorism with mass-protest movements and participation in politics. After maintaining contacts with the two branches, in 1982 the UCD government was able to persuade ETA-político-militar to abandon terrorist violence and join forces with Euskadiko Ezkerra, which was simultaneously in the process of transforming itself into a loyal political party (which subsequently merged with the Basque branch of the PSOE). ETA-militar has managed to survive over the following two decades with the invaluable assistance of a network of allied social movements. It has continued to rely primarily on terrorist attacks, temporarily interrupted by two truces, in 1998 and 2005.

constitution of 1978. Formally, all authority for making these decisions rested with the Spanish parliament, which was to respond to a draft of an autonomy statute prepared by an assembly of the members of parliament elected from the Basque region. In actual practice, however, little progress was made in the formal public sessions of parliament, and the most decisive phase of negotiations took place behind closed doors between prime minister Suárez and the interim president of the Basque region, Carlos Garaicoetxa, with the occasional participation of their immediate collaborators as needed. Those talks went on for 15 days, with the final session lasting 30 hours. Suárez and Garaicoetxa reached final agreement over the Estatuto de Guernica at 12:20 a.m. on July 18, 1978 – which coincidentally happened to be the anniversary of Francisco Franco's 1936 uprising against the Second Republic. The text was enthusiastically supported by all Basque nationalist leaders except those in Herri Batasuna, the political party linked to ETA-militar. Even Euskadiko Ezkerra (a small party linked with ETA-político-militar, another branch of the Basque terrorist movement) fully supported the statute, initiating that party's shift towards full loyalty to the Spanish constitutional regime and its ultimate merger with the PSOE.

Continued terrorist attacks by ETA-militar, however, provided ample evidence that the text was regarded as insufficient by the most extreme of Basque nationalists. Moreover, it was challenged from time to time over the following decades by

> ## Box 3.2
>
> *The Estatuto de Guernica*
> This statute is the charter of autonomy for the Basque Autonomous Community, comprising the three provinces of Álava, Guipúzcoa, and Vizcaya. Navarra was established as a separate region through the enactment of the *Ley de Amejoramiento del Fuero* ("Law for the Improvement of the Charter" of autonomy). Guernica is the name of a Basque town of historic importance which gained international notoriety as a result of the massive bombing by German aircraft during the Civil War, depicted in Pablo Picasso's masterpiece cubist painting of the same name.

> ## Box 3.3
>
> *Terra Lliure*
> Terra Lliure was a Catalan terrorist organization with an extreme-left ideological orientation. Created in 1981, it had a much less developed organizational structure than ETA. In the course of its two decades of terrorist activities, it was involved in 200 attacks, with one person killed. Between 1991 and 1996 Terra Lliure was dissolved after the Spanish police dismantled most of its clandestine cells. Several of its members and leaders subsequently joined Esquerra Republicana de Catalunya, and by 1996 all of its convicts had been released from Spanish prisons.

leaders of even the mainstream Basque Nationalist Party (PNV), who demanded an increase in the level of autonomy granted to the region, including recognition of the right to self-determination.

The Catalan settlement

A similar procedure characterized deliberations over the Catalan autonomy statute, but this was not accompanied by mobilization in the streets or by terrorist violence of any kind – although a small and short-lived Catalan pro-independence organization, Terra Lliure (Free Land) killed one person in an act of terrorism. In this different political environment, progress toward resolution of disputes was maintained at a steady pace, and the actual negotiations were undertaken by government ministers and high-ranking officials of the governing party of Spain, the Unión de Centro Democrático (UCD), on the one hand, and the largest Catalan nationalist party, Convergència i Unió (CiU), on the other. Adolfo Suárez, the Spanish prime minister, did not have to intervene directly in these talks, although he maintained close contact with his representatives. Satisfaction with the statute was almost universal, and it was regarded as an adequate framework for Catalan self-government over the following two and a half decades.

However, shortly after the turn of the twenty-first century, and especially in the course of the 2003 Catalan regional election campaign, the statute was subjected to increasing challenges and renewed demands for higher levels of autonomy on the part of Catalan nationalists. This eventually led to renewed negotiations over extensive revisions in the Catalan statute, which were approved by a referendum in June 2006.

The Galician and Andalusian settlements

The third of the so-called historic regions, Galicia, was the next to secure its own charter of autonomy. It, too, negotiated this agreement in accord with the provisions of the constitution's article 151, and ratified that charter through a regional referendum in December 1980. However, by this time there were growing concerns that the autonomy process was getting out of hand and might lead to a "disintegration" of Spain. Accordingly, some proposed that this region should be granted autonomy via the "slow route," as provided for in article 143 of the constitution. This gave rise to considerable tension between the two major Spanish parties, the UCD and the opposition PSOE, which was resolved over the short term by a slight reduction in the extent of autonomy granted to that region.

A similar dispute broke out over the charter of autonomy for Andalucía, a region which had never previously demanded self-government rights. Nonetheless, politicians from the region (including a prominent UCD government minister) demanded that it, too, secure its autonomy via the fast route. Again, this demand was acceded to, and the crisis was resolved.

There were long-term negative consequences of these struggles: by taking a public stand in opposition to the use of article 151 for these regions, the UCD opened itself up to unfair accusations that it was committed to the preservation of a centralized Spanish state. This contributed to the eventual break-up of the party and its defeat in the 1982 election.

The slow route to autonomy

None of the other regions of Spain had previously demanded autonomy; neither did they have populations with strongly developed regional identities. However, having seen the concessions to the aforementioned three historic regions, they insisted upon rapid progress towards self-government authority of their own. This gave rise to great concern over a decentralization process that might spin out of control, leading to numerous expressions of concern over the "disintegration of Spain." Indeed, this was the reason stated by rebellious military officers in justifying their attempted coup in February 1981 (see chapter 2, pp. 47–48). The governing UCD and the principal party of opposition, the PSOE, responded by reaching an agreement that would force the other regions to secure autonomy via the "slow route" – article 143. By the end of this process (in 1983), the other regions had secured approval of autonomy statutes that provided for somewhat lower levels of self-government authority than had been secured by the three historic regions. These imbalances gave rise to more than a decade of debate over efforts to standardize relations between the central government and the seventeen autonomous communities that today make up the Spanish state. More recently, the passage of a new Catalan statute has given rise to numerous demands by other regions for the granting of similar expansions of their political authority and policy jurisdictions, even to the extent of copying language from the 2006 revisions in the Catalan statute. This has initiated a new phase in the decentralization process and the further weakening of the Spanish central government.

Spanish decentralization and federalism

Thus, in several ways, the *Estado de las autonomías* that emerged from this decentralization process is different from classic federalism.

- First, most federal systems transfer political authority and resources to regions through one single deliberative process in which representatives of all regions simultaneously discuss the extent of powers that they should receive. As we saw, in the case of Spain, the decentralization process has unfolded through several protracted series of bilateral negotiations between each individual region and the central government.
- Second, unlike most federal systems, there is no uniform distribution of legislative powers and fiscal authority to the various regions. Instead, particularly at the outset, there were significant differences among regions with regard to the level of autonomy that they received. This is a reflection of the fact that the constitution does not specify which powers would be devolved to the regional level, but instead, merely presents a menu of potential powers that *may* be transferred to the various regions. Accordingly, this could be regarded as an unbalanced federal system, or federalism *à la carte*.
- Finally, and most importantly, in many federal systems the allocation of power between central and state governments is stable if not entirely fixed. In contrast, the Spanish decentralization process is open-ended. In some cases, the statutes themselves may be revised (as occurred with regard to Catalonia in 2006), thereby formally redefining the powers to be granted to the regional government. But even lacking formal constitutional revisions, annual budgetary negotiations between the central and regional governments effectively redistribute powers and resources between the central and regional levels of government.

■ Autonomous communities, provinces, and municipalities

Regional government institutions closely resemble those of the central state, even though the constitution allows them considerable leeway for experimentation. All of the *comunidades autónomas* have established parliamentary systems in which governments are politically responsible to regional parliaments. They have all adopted proportional representation electoral systems (using the **D'Hondt formula** of seat allocation, to be described in chapter 4), as well as the constructive motion of no confidence (described in the previous chapter). In contrast with the Cortes Generales (the national-level Congress of Deputies and Senate), most regions initially fixed the terms of their regional parliaments at four years, although recent changes in autonomy statutes now enable all regional governments to dissolve their parliaments early and convene new elections.

> **Comunidades autónomas (CCAA)** Spain has been divided into seventeen "autonomous communities" (*comunidades autónomas*, or CCAA), each with its own regional parliament and some self-government rights (see map 1.2). For the most part, the boundaries of these regions correspond with those of the historic regions of Spain that we discussed in chapter 1, although in some cases (e.g., Cantabria), smaller CCAA were carved out of much larger and heterogeneous historic regions.

> **The d'Hondt formula** is a procedure for allocating seats among parties within each electoral district. It is a "highest averages" method that divides the number of votes by a series of divisors reflecting the number of seats awarded to each party on the previous round of seat allocation (in contrast with "largest remainder" methods that award seats in accord with numerical quotas surpassed by each party, and then allocates the remaining seats in accord with votes "left over" after the quotas have been taken into consideration). Compared with "largest remainder" systems, the d'Hondt formula has a slight majoritarian bias in its representation of parties in parliament.

Self-government authority of the autonomous communities

With regard to the actual governmental functions that have been taken on by the various CCAA, the picture is so complex as to defy detailed comparative description. Initially, the greatest differences among regions could be seen in the fields of education and health policy. From the beginning, the more autonomous "historic" regions (Catalonia, the Basque Country, and Galicia) assumed greater responsibility for education and the provision of health care, while those that took on fewer policy jurisdictions did not. Subsequently, however, agreements between the central government and the regions decentralized the education system, even to the extent of transferring state-run universities to the CCAA. By the end of the 1990s, the range of variation among regional governments had been narrowed considerably, with only differences concerning the provision of health services separating the more autonomous from the less autonomous regional communities. Finally, national health system institutions and services were transferred to regional governments in 2002, although the funding provisions of the transfer were contested by some regions.

All regional governments have responsibility for environmental policy, public works that do not spill over into other regions, social welfare policy (with

Box 3.4

Linguistic co-officiality

In an effort to reverse the harsh monolingual policies of the Spanish Nationalist Franco regime, the constitution recognizes the "co-official" status of regional languages within their respective regions. Accordingly, Basque and Spanish are co-official within the Basque region, Catalan and Spanish are co-official in Catalonia, etc. While this ostensibly coequal status was virtually unavoidable as a response to demands articulated during crucial stages of transition to a new democratic regime, it is inherently conducive to continuing tensions within the region. This contrasts with language policies in countries like Belgium (except Brussels) and Switzerland, where the single majority language in each political jurisdiction is official. In those systems, there is no doubt about which language should be used in specific areas. Within multilingual regions of Spain, however, individuals whose first languages differ from one another must select one language or the other, and this is inherently prone to tension and occasional conflict. In some regions (especially Catalonia, and to a lesser extent the Basque Country), moreover, regional-nationalist governments have pushed for "linguistic normalization" policies, which tend towards *de facto* monolingualism and the predominance of the regional language. This can be detrimental to the sizable immigrant communities within those regions, whose primary language is Spanish.

the exception of unemployment insurance), regional economic development, culture, language policy (if relevant), agriculture, herding and forestry, and the creation of regional television networks. The upper limit of this decentralization process is set by article 149 of the constitution, which defines as exclusive functions of the central government the conduct of foreign policy, defense, the basic framework for health and education policy, penal legislation, services and infrastructures that cross over regional boundaries, and the civil rights and liberties of Spanish citizens.

The magnitude of this political change can best be appreciated by examining language policy as it has evolved over the past decades.

Language policy

Despite its tradition of linguistic and cultural diversity, under the authoritarian regime of General Franco's Spain was forcibly castilianized. The public speaking of Basque and Catalan was illegal for several decades, and even names of individuals and towns were transformed into Spanish. In contrast, the constitution of 1978 establishes regional languages as "co-official" within the relevant autonomous communities. Virtually all citizens know Spanish, but special provisions have been enacted in several regional communities to encourage the use of the regional languages. The typical provision requires those in the regional

Table 3.1 Knowledge of regional languages in selected autonomous communities, 1996 (in %)

Autonomous community	Understands, speaks, and reads regional language	Understands and speaks regional language	Understands regional language	Does not understand regional language	(N)
Galicia	68	89	99	1	(679)
Catalonia	71	79	97	3	(1,006)
Baleares	56	72	93	7	(473)
Comunidad Valenciana	38	55	89	11	(771)
Basque Country	20	28	43	57	(613)
Navarra	7	16	23	77	(449)

Source: Miguel Siguán Soler, *Conocimiento y uso de las lenguas,* Opiniones y Actitudes 22 (Madrid: Centro de Investigaciones Sociológicas, 1999), 14.

bureaucracy and political institutions to respect the rights of those who wish to express themselves in either of the two languages.

Another set of policies establishes the predominance of regional languages in educational institutions. The governments of Catalonia and Galicia have opted for the model of "linguistic immersion," in which all elementary-school children are taught in the regional language but are also required to study Spanish. In the Basque Country, there are two main models: one of them involves linguistic immersion in Euskera, while the other requires the study of Euskera as a second language in Castilian-language schools. In upper levels of the education system, there is a tendency to allow each teacher to select one of the two languages, and at the university level, this is clearly established as a policy and is respected in practice.

The implications of these "linguistic co-officiality" policies vary considerably from one region to another concerning their impact on the daily lives of citizens, especially with regard to educational and employment opportunities. This is reflected in very substantial differences among multilingual regions with regard to the extent of knowledge and use of the regional language (see table 3.1). In Galicia, where the population is quite stable, there are few such difficulties, since about 9 out of every 10 inhabitants are reasonably fluent in both the regional language and Spanish, and can easily switch back and forth between the two languages. In contrast, in the Basque Country and Catalonia, where up to a third of the population was born in other parts of Spain, these policies pose significant problems for certain sectors of society. This is particularly true for Spanish-speakers when competitive examinations for public employment or advancement through the educational system are conducted in the regional language only. This has the effect of institutionalizing discrimination against those who are not native speakers of the regional language, and is particularly true of Catalonia, where the Catalan language is increasingly becoming the only language used in most spheres of public life.

Spanish decentralization in comparative perspective

Seen in comparative perspective, this decentralization process must be regarded as the most extensive institutional change in regional government to have taken place in Western Europe since the 1960s. In contrast with Britain, which granted limited autonomy to only a few regions (Wales, Scotland, and Northern Ireland), power and resources have been devolved from the center to sub-national government units throughout all of the territory of Spain. In contrast with the very limited powers devolved from center to periphery in France and Italy in the 1970s and 1980s, the scope of governmental authority and resources reallocated to the regional level in Spain is very extensive. And in contrast with the extremely protracted process that unfolded in Belgium, establishing a federal system over the course of several decades, the once unitary Spanish state was profoundly decentralized within a few short years.

The *comunidades autónomas* can establish laws that have the same force as those of the Spanish state, and their respective administrations are not subordinate to central control. The existence in many CCAA of regional police forces and television networks, and full jurisdiction in all regions over important policy areas such as education or health, make the autonomous communities of Spain more powerful than almost any other sub-national government structure in Europe. Accordingly, most observers regard Spain as having undergone not one transition following the death of Franco (from authoritarianism to democracy), but a second transition as well, from a rigidly centralized state to one that grants very extensive government powers and resources to sub-national units.

Provincial and municipal governments

Finally, while the most dramatic change in the governmental structure of Spain has involved the creation of new regional levels of government, it must be noted that the provincial and municipal government institutions that had existed since the nineteenth century continue to exist today within the various regions. To be sure, the powers of *Diputaciones Provinciales* (or provincial governments, which were strictly limited under the Franco regime) are even more constrained today, since many of their functions have been transferred upward to the regional government level, but these institutions continue to perform some government functions, particularly in provinces with less populated city capitals (see map 2.1). These include coordination among municipalities in the province, as well as maintenance of extensive rural road networks, some health services, rural development programs, and other public services like trash collection.

More significant is the municipal level of government. There are over 8,000 municipalities in Spain, governed by their own *ayuntamientos*, or municipal councils. Eighty-five percent of those municipalities have fewer than 5,000 inhabitants, and only 132 (1.6%) have more than 50,000 residents. As in most countries, municipal governments are "closest to the people" at the bottom of the hierarchy of government institutions. Their jurisdictional responsibilities include land-use planning and development, housing, public utilities, local roads, local environmental protection, and recreational activities.

■ The complexity of multi-level governance: center–periphery relations

From the standpoint of contributing to the consolidation of Spain's new democratic regime, the adoption of this flexible but somewhat uneven form of federalism has been quite positive. It has allowed for the restructuring of the state in a manner that adequately responded to the pressing demands of regional nationalist groups whose support was required for the legitimation and stability of the new political system. Moreover, over the long term, the existence of regional governments providing services for citizens throughout the country has generated substantial popular acceptance and support for this decentralized form of governance. However, the *ad hoc* nature of the decision-making process that brought this system into existence, the open-ended devolution of resources and jurisdictions, and the territorially uneven distribution of self-government rights have made this an extremely complex system that is difficult to coordinate and not as efficient as a more uniform federal system might have been.

The multi-level government structure that has emerged has important implications for:

(1) the administrative structure of the state;
(2) the raising and distribution of tax revenues;
(3) coordination among various levels of government; and
(4) the role of the Constitutional Court in resolving disputes.

Administrative structure

In order to carry out their respective functions, each level of government has developed its own sizable administrative structure. The magnitude of these municipal, regional, and central government bureaucracies (as well as the similar statistics for three other federal systems) can be seen in table 3.2. It should be noted that this is only a "snapshot" of an evolutionary process, in which the devolution of governmental functions to the regions has been matched by an expansion in regional administrative staffs. By the end of the twentieth century, regional governments accounted for more than one third of all public employees. The stated long-term goal of the Spanish government is that, in the end, 60% of public functionaries should be employed by the regional governments, with 20% employed by the central government and the remaining 20% by municipalities.

Table 3.2 Distribution of public employees by level of government (in %)

Level of government	Germany (1991)	Austria (1991)	United States (1990)	Spain (1992)	Spain (1998)	Spain (2006)
Central government	15	32	17	57	41	22
Regional/state	50	25	24	27	36	50
Local	35	23	59	16	23	24
Other						4

Sources: Braulio Medel Cámara and José M. Domínguez Martínez, "Descentralización fiscal y crecimiento del sector público: teoría, comparación internacional y evidencia empírica," *Hacienda Pública Española*, 2 (1994), 225; and Ministerio de Administraciones Públicas, *Boletín estadístico del Registro Central de Personal*, 2000 and 2006.

In a uniformly federal system, each of these levels of government would have its own clearly defined jurisdictions, all territorial units at each level would perform the same sets of functions, and each of them would have its own sources of revenues. As we saw earlier, this is not true of the *Estado de las autonomías*, within which different regions perform somewhat different functions, and none of them has its own sources of revenues separate from those of the state. In some regions, the central government's role in important policy areas was limited to establishing basic legislation, leaving in the hands of the CCAA the enactment of complementary legislation and the implementation of those policies. In other regions, however, complete control over important governmental functions remained within the jurisdiction of the Spanish state administration. This uneven distribution of functions has impeded efficiency in the delivery of services, particularly insofar as the central government's administrative organs must remain in place in order to guarantee continuity in the provision of services, even though the level of those services may be reduced. The inevitable consequence has been the duplication of bureaucratic structures and government programs, resulting in higher costs.

Sources and allocation of resources

In contrast with most federal governments, where the central government and the states have their own independent sources of revenue, tax revenues to support regional government activities in all regions – except in the Basque Country and Navarra – are collected by the Spanish central government. The specific amounts disbursed to the various regions are determined through negotiations between the central and regional governments over how much is needed by the CCAA to perform their government functions. For the Basque regional government, the process is reversed: it is the regional government which collects taxes and negotiates the amount that should be turned over to the central government in Madrid for the performance of national-level government functions. These negotiations take place typically

Table 3.3 Distribution of public expenditures by level of government, 1981–2005[a] (as percentage of total government expenditures)

Level of government	1978	1985	1990	1995	1997	2000	2005
Central government	89	73	66	65	61	59	53
Regional	–	14	20	23	26	27	33
Local	11	13	14	12	13	14	14

[a] Figures exclude interest payments and other financial charges.

Sources: Intervención General de la Administración del Estado, *Actuación económica y financiera de las Administraciones públicas* (Madrid: Ministerio de Administraciones Públicas, 1993); Eliseo Aja, *El Estado autonómico: federalismo y hechos diferenciales* (Madrid: Alianza Editorial, 1999), 236; and Ministerio de Administraciones Públicas, *Informe económico-financiero de las Administraciones territoriales, 2005* (Madrid: Secretaría de Estado de Cooperación Territorial, 2005).

once every five years. Implicit in the outcome of these negotiations is a redefinition of the balance of decision-making authority between these two levels of government.

Since these budgetary discussions are held in conjunction with the installation of the new government, an additional level of complexity is added to the process of allocating resources to sub-national units of government. In essence, representatives of the central government to be and of the regional parties are engaged in a two-level game, one level involving financial support for regional government, and the other parliamentary support for the formation of a new government. This is because most parliaments have lacked an overall majority for one party, and have also avoided coalition government. As a result, the largest party at the national level must secure parliamentary support from one or more of the regional parties in order to form a minority government and to enact its legislation. The negotiating power this gives the regionalist and nationalist parties makes it possible for them to extract concessions regarding not only their roles in the policy-making process at the national level but also the transfer of resources and powers from the central government to the respective autonomous communities. Throughout the 1990s, the Catalan CiU was remarkably influential, given its crucial role in sustaining minority PSOE and PP governments in power. It used this bargaining leverage to progressively expand the authority and resources at the disposal of the Catalan regional government. Consequently, as can be seen in table 3.3, the share of total government expenditures by the Spanish central administration has declined steadily since the creation of the *Estado de las autonomías*.

Transfers to poorer regions

In recognition of regional differences in levels of economic development and affluence, and in accord with the constitutional mandate regarding solidarity

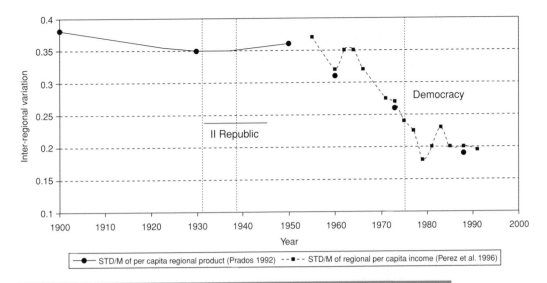

Figure 3.1 Evolution of inter-regional inequality in Spain, 1900–1996
Source: Carles Boix, "Spain: Development, Democracy, and Equity," prepared for the
World Development Report Background Papers (2006), 52

among the various regions of Spain (article 2), an Interterritorial Compensation
Fund (Fondo de Compensación Interterritorial) was established. This channels
investment capital from the wealthier regions to support the construction of
transportation and communications infrastructures in poorer regions. As can
be seen in figure 3.1, the distribution of these funds has reinforced the declining
trend in income inequality scores since the 1970s. The Interterritorial Fund also
supports professional training and other programs to benefit the less affluent
CCAA. These funds are distributed in accord with a formula involving per capita
income, unemployment, and emigration rates. After Spain's integration into
the European Union, these policy objectives were reinforced by the EU's own
regional development programs.

Coordination

The overlap between the activities of the Spanish state and those of the
autonomous communities requires a great deal of coordination. Constitution-
ally, this was supposed to have been one of the responsibilities of the Senate,
defined by article 69.1 as the "house of territorial representation." As explained
in the preceding chapter, however, it has never functioned effectively as such.
Instead, coordination is provided primarily by "sectoral committees," made up
of representatives of central government ministries and their regional counterparts. In a manner similar to the European Union's Council of Ministers,
the composition of the sectoral committees changes in accord with the policy area under consideration (agriculture, social policy, culture, etc.). The most

important of the sectoral committees is the Consejo de Política Fiscal y Financiera (Council for Financial and Fiscal Policy), which is largely responsible for allocating funds to the regions. For the most part, these sectoral committees function effectively and by consensus. However, their performance is somewhat uneven, and on occasion agreements cannot be reached.

The Constitutional Court

Under these circumstances, in particular, the Constitutional Court plays an important role in resolving disputes between regional governments and the Spanish state, as we discussed in the previous chapter. In the aggregate, roughly 10% of the laws passed by regional parliaments generate disputes that are appealed to the Constitutional Court for resolution. Most of these appeals are the result of jurisdictional ambiguity between the two levels of government. The fact that 60% of these conflicts have involved laws passed by the Basque, Catalan, and Gallego parliaments might suggest that they are a continuation of the historical conflict between the center and the regions. Most of these cases, however, were filed during the 1980s, when the newly decentralized system was being established. Thus, the most persuasive interpretation of these conflicts is that they were the predictable product of confusion and uncertainty over new institutions. During the 1990s, the frequency of these disputes was minimal (with only 12 filed in 1993, for example).

Following the election of a Partido Popular government backed by an absolute majority in parliament in 2000, however, the number of such appeals increased. To some extent, this was a product of a partial return to a Spanish-nationalist orientation by the PP, and reflected a polarization of center–periphery relations particularly concerning the Basques and Catalans. One product of that renewed polarization was a more militant stance taken by Catalan nationalists, especially in the Partit dels Socialistes de Catalunya (the Catalan branch of the PSOE), which began in 2003 to push vigorously for substantial revisions in the region's autonomy statute (which were enacted in 2006 and ratified in a referendum in that same year).

Center–periphery relations: an overview

Overall, the establishment of the *Estado de las autonomías* must be regarded as a political success, particularly insofar as it made possible the construction and consolidation of a new democracy that restored self-government rights to the historic regions, and devolved similar authority to all the other parts of Spain. Administratively, however, it has established institutions and procedures that are inevitably conducive to conflicts over the respective jurisdictions of the central and regional levels of government, as well as over the resources needed to fund those activities.

At the root of these potential conflicts is the tension inherent in two opposing concerns: first, the strategies of the nationalist parties in the historic regions to strengthen the regional cleavage and to expand their autonomy even further; and, countering this, the desire of central governments to "rationalize" the structure of the state for the purposes of efficiency and fairness to the less developed regions. The events which followed the revision of the Catalan statute in 2006 clearly illustrate these tensions, with various regions demanding greater autonomy and resources, on the one hand, and political leaders in the Partido Popular denouncing this rupture of the national unity of Spain. And the Basque government has continued to press its demands for even further autonomy, announcing (in violation of the terms of the Spanish constitution) a referendum on self-determination held in October 2008. In short, the process of political decentralization in Spain remains open-ended.

■ The international dimension

Similarly dramatic changes have characterized Spain's relations with the rest of the world, and with Western Europe in particular. In this respect, Spain's exceptional status substantially predated the authoritarian regime of General Franco. It had always maintained considerable distance and autonomy from the rest of Europe in both its formal foreign policy stands and its self-image. At no point in the nineteenth or twentieth century did Spain join the alliance structures that linked most other West European countries. Spain abstained from participation in both the first and second World Wars (with the exception of sending a "volunteer" division to assist the Nazi invasion of Russia). Indeed, until the 1960s most Franquist elites did not consider Spain as an integral part of Western Europe. Instead, the image of Spain that was disseminated for three decades, which served as the basis for most of its foreign policy orientations during that period, involved the metaphor of a bridge. But it was not one bridge leading in one direction, but several bridges leading in various directions.

- Spain saw itself as a bridge between Western Europe and Latin America – its former colonial empire and symbol of past greatness and world domination.
- Spain saw itself as a bridge between Western Europe and the Arab world – in part, as a consequence of its involvement in North African colonial territories, as well as of its geopolitical situation.
- Finally, Spain saw itself as a bridge between Western Europe and Africa. This was reciprocated by the dictum attributed to the father of French writer Alexandre Dumas (and which was widely disseminated) that Spain is best characterized by the phrase "Africa begins at the Pyrenees."

Spain's isolation from the rest of Western Europe was considerably deepened in the aftermath of the Spanish Civil War (1936–9) and especially World War II. General Franco's Nationalist forces received considerable assistance in the Civil War from Hitler and Mussolini. In the early stages of his authoritarian regime, he sought to establish a single party in the fascist mode to mobilize popular support in a badly divided, war-shattered country. Indeed, from 1939 until 1942, the regime took on all the superficial trappings of fascism, complete with blue-shirted militias and stiff-arm salutes. Germany's defeats at El Alemein and Stalingrad, both of which indicated that it would most likely lose World War II, led the authoritarian regime to quickly abandon its embrace of fascism, but its decade-long alliance with the fascist right led the victorious Allied powers to ostracize the country following the war. This ostracism took many forms, such as exclusion of Spain from the USA-funded Marshall Plan for the reconstruction of Western Europe after World War II, and from United Nations membership until the mid-1950s.

The isolation of Spain cut it off from foreign trade, and led to the adoption of corporatist autarky (a "go-it-alone" economic strategy), in which the state sought to guarantee the country's self-sufficiency by intervening heavily in the economy. To protect key industries and subsidize their production of strategically important goods, the state became the owner or co-owner of hundreds of "para-state" business firms. These were placed under the supervision of INI (the Instituto Nacional de Industria), which was modeled after Mussolini's IRI (Istituto per la Ricostruzione Industriale). Many of these heavily subsidized firms were inefficient and uncompetitive (which would prove to be a serious problem as Spain prepared for entry into the European Union (then, the European Community) in the 1980s).

The isolation of Spain from the rest of the world began to erode only in the 1950s.

- In 1953, a concordat was signed with the Vatican that regularized the role of the Church in Spanish society and provided Spanish Catholics with some international connections.
- In that same year, a visit by President Dwight D. Eisenhower to Madrid led to the establishment of American military bases on Spanish soil. While this enlisted Spain in an informal alliance against Soviet communism, Spain was not allowed to join NATO, as a result of continuing hostility from other West European countries, especially Great Britain.
- In 1956, with its admission to the United Nations, this diplomatic isolation began to soften.
- However, hostility towards the Franco regime on the part of other West European countries (some of whose political leaders had fought against Franco in the Spanish Civil War) led to repeated rejections of Spanish applications for membership in the newly emerging European Common Market. Other European leaders declared that no country governed by an authoritarian dictatorship could be allowed into the emerging European Community.

Nonetheless, even prior to the death of Franco, there was some real progress towards establishing economic and societal links with the rest of Western Europe. One factor that would dramatically contribute to the integration of Spain into Western Europe was the abandonment of autarky in 1959 and the rapid economic development that followed from 1960 until 1973. Increased contacts between Spanish government officials and businessmen, on the one hand, and their West European counterparts, on the other, began to establish linkages that would eventually facilitate Spanish membership of the European Community; in fact, Spain applied in the mid 1960s for membership in the European Community. At the same time, the massive expansion of international tourism led to the influx of up to 40 million foreign citizens into Spain each year – a considerable number, given that the population of Spain was less than 40 million.

However, as long as General Franco continued to serve as head of an authoritarian state, there could be no progress towards formal integration of Spain into the rest of Western Europe. Spain's isolation continued, despite the intense desire of Spain's business elites to gain access to West European markets, despite increasingly frequent contacts between the emerging "moderate opposition" and their Christian Democratic, social-democratic, and liberal counterparts in Western Europe, and despite the growing desire of many Spaniards to emulate the affluent West European tourists who increasingly clogged their beaches and restaurants.

The European Union

All of this changed following the death of Francisco Franco in November 1975. The new head of state, King Juan Carlos, undertook a series of international trips assuring American and West European governments that Spain would become democratic in the near future. The convening of the first democratic elections in June 1977 meant that other countries had no reason to continue the ostracism of Spain on the grounds that it was not democratic. Indeed, one of the very first acts of the first Suárez government, one month after Spain's first democratic election in over forty years, was to re-submit an application for admission to the European Community. While that long-standing goal would not be achieved until January 1, 1986, the delay in Spanish accession to the EC was not a product of its previous "exceptionalism," but rather resulted from complex and protracted negotiations over such matters as fishing rights and the strict conditions of the Common Agricultural Policy – the cornerstone of European Union (EU) budgetary negotiations. Spanish membership in the European Union was universally welcomed. Indeed, it is surprising that no opposition was expressed by any politically significant group – not even the Communist Party, which fully endorsed European Community membership.

Spain's involvement in the European Union even more fully reflects its integration into the mainstream of Western Europe. Massive increases in international trade, prompt abandonment of the last vestiges of autarky and subsidization of inefficient para-state industries, and achievement of important leadership positions within the European Union itself quickly followed its accession in 1986. Several prominent Spaniards have become members of the European

Commission, and the European Union's very first High Representative for Foreign Policy and Security was a Spaniard, once again distinguishing the international leadership role of Javier Solana. Moreover, Spain was extremely successful in launching in the mid 1990s the Euromediterranean Conference as a means of developing a common European foreign policy towards the countries of North Africa.

Mirroring the EU's embrace of its new Spanish members, Spanish public opinion has always been strongly supportive of the European Union. Public opinion polls taken at regular intervals since 1986 have consistently revealed that the proportion of the Spanish public who favorably evaluate EU membership has exceeded 50% of those interviewed, while the proportion of those regarding EU accession as a negative development has ranged between about 10% and 15% of the general public. And unlike voters in France and the Netherlands, the Spanish electorate voted overwhelmingly in support of the proposed European Constitution in the February 2005 referendum: 77% voted "yes" when asked to endorse that document.

NATO

Substantially more controversial was Spain's entry into the NATO alliance. A membership application was filed by the UCD government of Leopoldo Calvo Sotelo in 1981. This step was taken in the absence of prior consultation with other political parties, some of whom vehemently objected to the incorporation of Spain into an international military alliance for the first time since the early eighteenth century. The Communist Party (which had acquiesced to the continued presence of American military bases on Spanish soil on the explicit condition that Spain would not join NATO) strongly criticized this move and organized popular demonstrations against membership of the Atlantic alliance.

The position of the socialist party, the PSOE, was much more complex. In 1981 it strongly opposed entry into NATO, and attacked the UCD government for what it regarded as a betrayal of Spain's traditional foreign policy. The following year, however, the socialist party came to power, and was therefore faced with a serious dilemma. On the one hand, it had taken a strong stance against NATO membership, and made that a centerpiece of its 1982 election campaign manifesto. On the other hand, withdrawing from membership in the alliance would almost certainly have alienated the United States and other European countries, whose support was needed both in order to secure European Community membership and in the struggle to suppress ETA terrorism (much of which was conducted by individuals taking refuge on the French side of the border). The awkward position of the socialist party is best summarized by the tortured phrase that it used in its 1982 election campaign: "*OTAN* [NATO], *de entrada, no.*" This formulation was intended to justify the bizarre argument that it was wrong for Spain to have entered NATO ("*de entrada*"), but that it would be equally wrong for Spain to withdraw from NATO. The truth is that the party had clearly changed its mind about NATO membership, and was making a concerted effort to "cover its tracks." In any event, this problem was resolved by a referendum in March 1986, when 52.5% of Spaniards voted in favor of the government's resolution on continued NATO membership.

The full extent of the socialist party's conversion regarding this matter is reflected in the fact that, just one decade later, its former foreign-policy spokesman, Javier Solana, became Secretary General of NATO. There could be no greater symbol of the definitive abandonment of Spain's isolation from international military alliances. This change in its formal position was accompanied by active military involvement in many international peace-keeping, humanitarian, and/or antiterrorist operations, such as the first Gulf War, the military intervention to stop Serbian persecution in Kosovo, and in Afghanistan.

■ Multi-level governance and the European Union

Spain's entry into the European Union has profoundly altered the nature of political decision-making and policy implementation. This is manifested in many ways. From one perspective, the European Union requires that its member states comply with directives and meet a number of conditions that have important policy implications. However, looking at this relationship only from this top-down viewpoint substantially under-represents the extent to which the nature of governance in Spain has been irrevocably altered. It has not only reduced the autonomy of the Spanish state by requiring compliance with these Europe-wide policies, but it has also profoundly affected the nature of center–periphery relations within the newly decentralized Spanish state. No longer can we simply examine the interactions between representatives of the central government and the various regions; we also have to consider their complex interactions with European institutions. In addition to affecting the nature of decision-making and policy implementation, this has important implications for the national identities and nationalist aspirations of regional minorities.

Economic and industrial policy

We began this exploration of multi-level governance by examining the relatively simple one-way flow of directives from the European level to the national level. Even prior to European Community membership, the very anticipation of membership in a large common market led the Spanish government to adopt policies that would prepare Spanish businesses and the economy in general for the future rigors of competition. As noted earlier in this chapter, the autarkic policies pursued by the Franco regime included developing and subsidizing many inefficient para-state industries. Membership in the European common market is completely incompatible with this structure and these past practices.

At a minimum, the European Union requires the termination of subsidies in its overall efforts to encourage fairness in international trade. More broadly, the fact that Spanish business firms would be competing with much more efficient German, French, Dutch, etc., industrial giants made it necessary for the Spanish government to take bold steps to increase the efficiency of Spanish industry. During the transition to democracy, it was impossible to undertake these structural reforms, since they would almost certainly have increased strains on important sectors of Spanish society – in particular, on workers who would lose their jobs due to the closure of para-state industries. Accordingly, until Spanish democracy was consolidated (around 1982), subsidies continued, and in some instances the state actually increased its subsidies to industries that were faring poorly during this period of worldwide economic recession.

All of this changed following the electoral victory of the PSOE in 1982, which gave the party an absolute majority in parliament, and following the consolidation of Spanish democracy that same year. The first Socialist government of Felipe González undertook a series of bold steps that effectively closed down a large number of inefficient industries, particularly in the steel and shipbuilding sectors of the economy. While this created a great deal of dislocation over the short term, by the time Spain entered the European Community in 1986 it had been prepared to compete successfully, and it underwent a period of impressive economic growth.

Value-added tax

Upon entry into the European Community, Spain had to comply with a number of policies that are required of all of its members. The imposition of a

---

Box 3.5

The harmonization of tax systems

The European Union and all of its previous incarnations (the European Common Market, the European Community) has at its foundational core a common market, in which member states are forbidden to impose tariffs on one another's products, and which requires the imposition of a common tariff on imports from outside of the EU. A goal is the establishment and maintenance of free trade among member states, in which business firms can compete with one another on a "level playing field." In actual practice, this is often difficult to achieve, since there are often a number of "non-tariff barriers" to trade. One of these involves taxes (like sales taxes or excise taxes) that can effectively drive up the price of goods. In order to prevent one country from securing an "unfair" trading advantage by having lower indirect taxes on its goods, all EU member states are required to impose the same value-added tax (VAT) on goods for sale. (The VAT is like a sales tax, except that it is imposed on the item at each stage in the production process.) Making all of these kinds of taxes similar to one other among member countries is commonly referred to as the "harmonization" of the tax structure.

value-added tax and other steps towards the "harmonization" of its tax system are clear examples of this compliance with European policies.

The single currency

The next major impact of European Union membership on Spanish policies involved the EU's development of a single currency. Spain, which was one of the first participants in this process of monetary union, was required to meet a number of **"convergence criteria"** as the price of entry into this exclusive club. This imposed a number of constraints on budget balances, expansion of the money supply, and limits on inflation. Having succeeded in meeting these criteria, Spain abandoned its former national currency, the peseta, and embraced the euro on January 1, 2002.

These are but a few examples of where membership in the European Union requires the adoption of certain specific policies that are shared by all member states. It should be noted, however, that by its very nature, the European Union varies substantially from one sector of public policy to another in the extent to which it requires compliance. This loss of national autonomy is most extreme with regard to the tariff union, the Common Agricultural Policy, and certain other spheres of activity, but with regard to most social policies and some aspects of fiscal policy, member states continue to enjoy a great deal of autonomy.

> **Convergence criteria** Before they could abandon their separate national currencies and adopt the euro, EU member states had to meet a number of economic and fiscal-policy objectives. These were intended to maintain price stability following admission of new members to the euro zone. These "convergence criteria" included limits on the level of annual budget deficits, on rates of monetary inflation, on long-term interest rates, and on the size of the standing public debt.

The European Union and center–periphery relations within Spain

It would be a mistake to examine the implications of European Union membership only from the perspective of this top-down flow of directives to the member states. Much more intriguing is the manner in which European integration has profoundly altered the nature of center–periphery relations within Spain. In our previous discussion of the decentralization of the Spanish state, we focused only on two sets of actors – the central government and the autonomous communities. Their relations can be characterized in terms of a zero-sum power game – that is, there is a fixed amount of political power within the state, so that if the autonomous communities gained power, the central government would necessarily lose the same amount. This two-actor zero-sum game was profoundly altered by the imposition of an additional layer of government. The representatives of the Spanish state and of the regional communities are now no longer simply interacting with one another, but they are now also interacting with institutions and policies at the **supra-national** level. From the perspective of

> **Supra-national** institutions are those in which member states have transferred some real decision-making authority to a higher level of government that can make decisions that are binding on all member states by "qualified majority voting," rather than unanimity. The European Commission is an example of a supra-national institution.

the once entirely sovereign centralized state, this means that authority is being transferred both downward to the regional CCAA and upward to the EU level. From the standpoint of regional government leaders, European integration has created powerful supra-national institutions that have provided regional actors with new avenues for influencing decision-making.

Sub-national governments in Spain have taken advantage of these channels. Regional governments are directly represented in a number of European institutions – such as the Assembly of European Regions, Eurocities, the Conference of Peripheral Maritime Regions, the Association of Regions of Traditional Industry, the Union of Capital Regions, etc. – in which they can bargain directly on behalf of their own interests. One of the most intense debates regarding regional participation in the European institutions has been the right of the regional governments to participate in the agreements signed by the European Sectorial Councils – the intergovernmental–EU institutions that hold periodic summit meetings to establish specific regional policies. In 2004, the Socialist prime minister José Luis Rodríguez Zapatero granted this right to regional governments with regard to agriculture, fishing, the environment, social affairs, culture, education, and youth affairs. This also includes participation in the influential COREPER (Permanent Committee of Representatives) that has agenda-setting power and organizes the council's meetings. Zapatero also promised to allow regional governments to have a permanent representation in Brussels and to grant them access to the European Court of Justice in legal conflicts related to their regional government competencies. As a consequence, regional governments are no longer exclusively dependent upon representatives of the Spanish state functioning as intermediaries with the international arena. These new developments have not only increased their bargaining leverage with regard to access to European-level resources, but have also strengthened their hand in their relationships with the Spanish central government.

From one perspective, then, the European integration process can be seen to have undermined the sovereignty of the Spanish state. At the same time, however, it has created an incentive structure that undermines the rationale behind regional nationalists' demands for independence. As noted at the beginning of this discussion, prior to European Community entry the central government and the regions were linked in a zero-sum relationship in which further devolution of authority and resources from the center to the regions meant further loss of central power. The logical extension of this process could include complete independence from the Spanish state and the achievement of full sovereignty by a smaller but homogeneous nation-state.

With the imposition of a supra-national government (the EU) over both the Spanish state and its regions, however, the notion of independence and complete sovereignty in the international arena is no longer relevant. Instead, transfers of decision-making authority from the Spanish state to the regions imply only a relative increase in powers, as well as a shift of accountability to a different level of governance.

This, in turn, might have implications for the nature of national identities. Separatism implies a conception of national identity that is unique and exclusionary; European integration, in contrast, implies multiple, overlapping identities at different levels. In short, one could argue that this altered international arena should undermine the logic of separatism articulated by regional nationalists.

As we shall argue in the following chapter, however, it would be a mistake to regard national identities and demands for the restructuring of the state as merely a rational response to a material incentive structure. Instead, political elites play an important and independent role in articulating political demands concerning the territorial organization of the state.

■ Summary

In this chapter, we have explored profound changes in the structure of the Spanish state, as well in the relationships between Spain and the rest of the world.

- In contrast with the rigidly centralized state inherited from Franco, the establishment of the seventeen autonomous communities has been accompanied by a major devolution of decision-making authority and financial resources to the regional level.
- In contrast with ostracism by and isolation from the rest of Europe following World War II, Spain has become an integral member of the European Union, and several Spaniards have played important leadership roles within the EU.
- These two processes have interacted with each other, substantially affecting the nature of center–periphery relationships and even the nature of "national identities" within Spain.
- In contrast with the international non-alignment of Spain (dating back to the beginning of the nineteenth century), Spain has joined NATO and played an active role in international affairs.

■ Further reading

Aja, Eliseo, *El estado autonómica: federalismo y hechos diferenciales* (Madrid: Alianza Editorial, 1999)

Closa, Carlos, and Paul M. Heywood, *Spain and the European Union* (Basingstoke: Palgrave, 2004)

Field, Bonnie, and Kerstin Hamann, eds., *Democracy and Institutional Development: Spain in Comparative Theoretical Perspective 1977–2007* (Basingstoke and New York: Palgrave Macmillan, 2008)

Gibson, Heather D., ed., *Economic Transformation, Democratization and Integration into the European Union* (Basingstoke: Palgrave, 2001)

Linz, Juan J., Manuel Gómez-Reino, Francisco A. Orizo, and Darío Vila Carro, *Conflicto en Euskadi* (Madrid: Espasa-Calpe, 1986)

Llamazares, Iván, and Gary Marks, "Multilevel Governance and the Transformation of Regional Mobilization and Identity in Southern Europe, with Particular Attention to Catalonia and the Basque Country," in Richard Gunther, P. Nikiforos Diamandouros, and Dimitri A. Sotiropoulos, eds., *Democracy and the State in the New Southern Europe* (Oxford: Oxford University Press, 2006)

Mar-Molinero, Clare, and Angel Smith, *Nationalism and the Nation in the Iberian Peninsula* (Oxford: Berg, 1996)

Molina, Ignacio, "Spain," in Hussein Kassim, Guy Peters, and Vincent Wright, eds., *The National Co-ordination of EU Policy: The Domestic Level* (Oxford: Oxford University Press, 2000)

Muro, Diego, *Ethnicity and Violence: The Case of Radical Basque Nationalism* (New York: Routledge, 2008)

Newton, Michael T., and Peter J. Donaghy, *Institutions of Modern Spain: A Political and Economic Guide* (Cambridge: Cambridge University Press, 1997)

Subirats, Joan, and Raquel Gallego, eds., *Veinte años de autonomías en España: leyes, políticas públicas, instituciones y opinion pública* (Madrid: Centro de Investigaciones Sociológicas, 2002)

■ Websites

Regional governments

www.juntadeandalucia.es	Andalucía
www.aragob.es	Aragón
www.asturias.es	Asturias
www.caib.es	Balearic Islands
www.gobcan.es	Canary Islands
www.gobcantabria.es	Cantabria
www.jccm.es	Castilla-La Mancha
www.jcyl.es	Castilla-León
www.gencat.net	Catalonia
www.juntaex.es	Extremadura
www.xunta.es	Galicia
www.madrid.org	Madrid
www.camr.es	Murcia
www.cfnavarra.es	Navarra
www.euskadi.net	Basque Country
www.larioja.org	La Rioja
www.gva.es	Comunidad Valenciana
www.ceuta.es	Ceuta
www.melilla.es	Melilla
www.femp.es	Federation of Municipalities and Provinces
http://cor.europa.eu/en/presentation/contact_us_recruitment.htm	EU Committee of the Regions

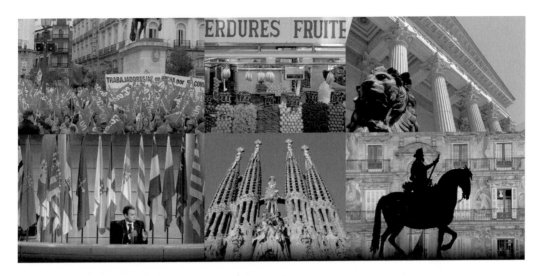

4   Parties and democratic stability

In the first chapter of this book we pointed out that Spain's only previous experience of fully democratic rule, the Second Republic, was one characterized by extreme instability, ideological polarization, and eventually the collapse of a democratic system. We also mentioned that the **party system** of the Second Republic was extremely fragmented, requiring the formation of multiparty coalition governments, and those lasted an average of only 101 days. It was also characterized by an exceptionally high level of "**electoral volatility**" – that is, there were huge shifts in the partisan composition of parliament from one election to the next. This further contributed to a high level of polarization among parties

Party systems are typically categorized in terms of the number of parties with significant representation in parliament, usually distinguishing among 2-party systems, moderately pluralistic systems (with between 3 and about 6 parties), and highly fragmented party systems (with 7 or more parties having significant parliamentary representation). Party systems involve the number of parties with significant parliamentary representation, their patterns of competition and cooperation, and their capacity to form durable governments.

Electoral volatility The magnitude of shifts in the popular vote from one election to the next is referred to as electoral volatility.

of left and right, and between parties favoring a strongly centralized state and those demanding the establishment or restoration of autonomy for the Basque and Catalan regions. Moreover, virtually all of the parties with significant representation in parliament were either anti-system or semi-loyal in their orientations towards the regime. Following the collapse of this system, the dictator, General Franco, asserted that Spain's inability to

Box 4.1

"Anti-system" and "semi-loyal" parties

An anti-system party, as we define it, is unequivocally opposed to the existing regime and refuses to make a binding commitment to respect the "democratic rules of the game." While they often participate in democratic elections, they deny the legitimacy of democracy and its requirement that governing parties must regularly submit themselves to free, democratic elections, and must leave office if they lose. While many anti-system parties participated in democratic elections (as did Hitler's Nazis and Mussolini's Fascist Party), they "participated in order to destroy" the democratic regime (as political scientist Hans Daalder put it). Semi-loyal parties and elites do not overtly reject the institutions or norms of a political regime, but instead they maintain an ambiguous stance towards that regime. They may operate within its institutional channels and follow its rules, but this behavior reflects a conditional or instrumental acceptance of the regime's rules and institutions, rather than an acknowledgment of their legitimacy. They also sometimes collaborate with anti-system groups and refuse to condemn their illegal behavior if that would help to advance their common cause. Their ambiguous stance towards the democratic regime often breeds reciprocal mistrust and polarization within the party system.

A ***caudillo*** is a charismatic figure who dramatically appears on the scene to restore order and provide leadership following a time of chaos. El Cid (who conquered and expelled the Moors from Valencia in the 11th century) was the very model of a *caudillo*. Francisco Franco claimed the title of *caudillo*, even though he was short and squat, spoke with a high-pitched voice, and looked somewhat silly when bedecked with the paraphernalia of a conquering military hero.

sustain a democratic system was rooted in fundamental aspects of the Spanish character. These "family demons" could be contained, he claimed, only by imposing over unruly Spanish society the strong leadership of a ***caudillo***. Given this tradition of conflict and instability, some observers feared that Spain might never be capable of governing itself within a democratic framework.

In sharp contrast with these dire expectations, we saw in chapter 2 that the parliamentary system set in place in 1977 is not only fully democratic but has made possible the formation of governments that are among the most stable in the Western world. In chapter 5, we will further argue that ideological moderation and mass-level acceptance of democratic institutions and rules of the game are widespread, if not universal.

In this chapter, we will explore some of those institutions that are most responsible for this Spanish success story. These are the political parties that have competed for power at the national, regional, and local levels. We will see that the party system is largely devoid of some of those undesirable characteristics that had undermined the stability of the Second Republic, and, instead, place Spain well within the mainstream of Western European democracies. Specifically, at the national level:

Box 4.2

Characteristics of the Spanish party system

The current party system is characterized by a moderate level of fragmentation, with the two largest parties holding over 80% of the seats in the Congress of Deputies, and with one of them typically holding an absolute majority or near majority. This facilitates the formation of stable, single-party governments. The two parties have been generally moderate in their ideological and programmatic commitments, and there has been a healthy alternation in power between parties of the center left and center right. In addition, with the exception of some small regional nationalist parties in the Basque Country and Catalonia, there are no electorally significant parties that are radical or extreme, and there are no anti-system parties. Finally, the electoral volatility of the party system has been generally low, except for the 1982 election, when a substantial realignment of the party system took place. The electoral dominance of the two largest parties, combined with the continuing existence of an electorally significant but much smaller Communist Party and a substantial number of regional parties leads many observers to refer to the Spanish system as a "two-plus" party system.

- fragmentation of the parliamentary party system is low;
- ideological polarization among nationwide parties is moderate;
- except in 1982, electoral volatility has been low, but at the same time has allowed for an alternation in government between parties of the center left and center right;
- there has been a very high level of cabinet durability;
- the two major parties (at least until 2000) have been "catch-all" parties of the center left and center right, and have competed with each other by gearing their electoral appeals towards moderate voters at the center of the political spectrum; and
- there are no anti-system parties at the national level.

We will also examine one institution, the electoral system, that has helped to craft and sustain this party system. It has reduced fragmentation and contributed to the formation of stable, moderate governments, while it has also allowed some smaller parties (especially those with regionally concentrated bases of support) an adequate level of parliamentary representation. Finally, we shall briefly analyze the dominant ideologies of Spain's political parties, as well as the behavioral style of most party leaders.

At the same time, regional party sub-systems exist that reflect a much higher level of pluralism if not (as in the case of the Basque Country) polarized pluralism. In some autonomous communities, the dynamics of electoral competition are totally distinct from those at the national level:

Box 4.3

Party system fragmentation and "polarized pluralism"

An important dimension of electoral competition in modern democracies is the extent of fragmentation of the party system. This refers to the number of parties that receive significant levels of electoral support or parliamentary representation. These two types of fragmentation are measured in two different ways. One of these involves the fragmentation of the popular vote, that is, the number of parties that receive significant shares of votes cast by the electorate. The other, which will be the focus of most of our discussion, refers to the fragmentation of the "parliamentary party system," that is, the number of parties that receive a significant number of seats in the legislature. As we will see, the two are not equivalent, since the electoral system can distort partisan preferences as a product of the way that it translates votes into seats. Political scientist Giovanni Sartori noted that highly fragmented party systems were often characterized by a dynamic process that he called "polarized pluralism." These party systems tended to polarize as a consequence of centrifugal drives growing out of parties "outbidding" each other for support and stressing their ideological distinctiveness from one another. And parties that are excluded from power for extended periods of time are free to engage in "irresponsible opposition," since they never have to deliver on the electoral promises they make. Bilateral contestation and irresponsible opposition lead parties to compete with one another for support from voters located on the extreme ends of the party system rather than the center, and electoral support for parties near the center of the political spectrum declines substantially. The Weimar Republic of Germany (1919–33) and the Spanish Second Republic are prototypical examples of polarized pluralism.

- Electoral conflict pits regional or regional-nationalist parties in Catalonia, Galicia, the Basque Country, and the Canary Islands against those with a nationwide basis of support, in addition to left–right competition among all parties, both regional and nationwide.
- While this higher level of party system fragmentation is most characteristic of elections to regional parliaments, national elections to the Spanish parliament are also affected by these different sets of competitive dynamics within those geographical areas.
- In the Basque Country, an ultra-nationalist secessionist movement exists that has given electoral support to a series of anti-system parties, and has sustained a campaign of political violence over several decades.

In short, our analysis of political parties must distinguish between characteristics of the Spanish party system at the national level and several regional party sub-systems.

■ The Spanish party system: fragmentation and the electoral system

One of the most common determinants of cabinet durability or instability in parliamentary systems is the degree of party system fragmentation. When parliament consists of large numbers of parties and no party comes close to having a majority of seats, it is difficult to form a government. Conversely, when the largest party commands a large number of seats, it may be able to form a single-party government or a coalition with just one additional party. Other things being equal, the larger the number of parties that must be included in a coalition government, the greater the probability that that coalition will break down.

As we saw in chapter 1, this was certainly characteristic of the party system of the Second Republic. The fact that the average government was able to maintain itself in office for just 101 days, and that there was a change of prime minister every 5 months, is to some extent the result of the fact that no party occupied more than 24% of the seats. Further complicating this picture was the fact that parliament included several large parties whose acceptability as reliable coalition partners was very much in doubt because of their semi-loyal or disloyal stances towards the democratic Republic. This certainly included the largest party of the right, the CEDA (Confederación Española de Derechas Autonómas), as well as the largest party of the left (the Partido Socialista Obrero Español [PSOE]).

Low party system fragmentation

In sharp contrast with the Second Republic, the average "effective number of parties" in the parliaments that have been seated since the first post-Franco election in 1977 is 2.8, and the two largest parties have occupied an average of 84.9% of the seats. Accordingly, it has never been necessary to form a coalition government. In five of the ten legislatures between 1977 and 2008, one party or the other (the PSOE, on the left of center, or Partido Popular, on the right) has held an absolute majority of seats. And even in those parliaments where no party held an absolute majority of seats, the largest party was close enough that, with the added support of the "constructive motion of no confidence" (which we discussed in chapter 2), it was able to form a single-party minority government.

This general pattern can be clearly seen in figure 4.1, which tracks the percentage of seats in parliament held by the larger nationwide parties. In the parliaments seated in the aftermath of the 1982, 1986, and 2000 elections, the largest party held an absolute majority of seats. In 1989, the PSOE won precisely half of the seats, but a boycott of parliament by the anti-system Herri Batasuna party gave it a functioning majority. In all of the other parliamentary sessions (six out of ten), the largest party was quite close to having a majority, and did not need to form a governing coalition with another party.

Box 4.4

Effective number of parliamentary parties

One measure of the degree of fragmentation of a parliamentary party system is a simple count of the number of parties with parliamentary seats. That way of estimating parliamentary fragmentation, however, does not accurately reflect the actual difficulty of forming a durable government. A parliament with a predominantly two-party (or "two-plus" party) system may often include one party with an absolute majority of seats (as has occurred in Great Britain following every election since World War II except one), but may also contain a large number of smaller parties (especially regional parties) whose support is not needed to sustain a government in office. Thus, by simply counting the total number of parties represented in parliament (usually six or more in the UK), one would have a hard time trying to understand why all British governments since World War II have been formed by one single party.

An accurate indication of the degree of difficulty of forming a government therefore requires a more complex means of estimating the degree of parliamentary party system fragmentation. The Laakso/Taagepera formula accomplishes this objective by mathematically weighting the parliamentary representation of the larger parties. In Spain's Congress of Deputies in 1977, for example, 12 different parties occupied seats. Among European parliaments, only the parliaments of Belgium and Italy have a larger number of parties. However, since 2 of Spain's parties controlled a combined total of 81% of the seats in 1977, the "effective number of parliamentary parties" was much lower – 2.9. It should be noted that the "effective number of parliamentary parties" (based on the number of seats allocated to each party) is different from the "effective number of electoral parties" (based upon the percentage of the popular vote received by each party), since the majoritarian biases of the electoral system will "manufacture" a larger share of seats than the two largest parties received as shares of the vote, while it will also under-represent, or deny parliamentary seats altogether, to the smallest parties. Accordingly, the nationwide effective number of electoral parties has averaged 3.8 since 1977, while the number of effective parliamentary parties is just 2.8.

Fair representation of regional parties

At the same time that the formation of governments at the national level has been facilitated by a low level of partisan fragmentation in parliament, small regional parties have been given fair levels of representation. As we argued in the opening chapter, this was an important element in the successful transition to and consolidation of the new democratic regime. If the small Basque and Catalan nationalist parties had been excluded from parliament, that would have greatly reduced the probability of their acceptance of the legitimacy of the new regime. Table 4.1 presents data summarizing the share of popular votes cast for each

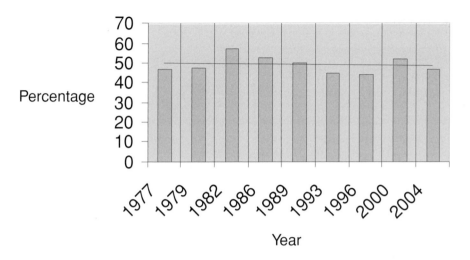

Figure 4.1 Percentage of seats in the Congress of Deputies held by the largest party

major party and the number of seats they were allocated in the Congress of Deputies.

As can be seen, the two largest nationwide parties have always received a larger share of the seats in the Congress than their percentage of the total popular vote, while smaller parties with geographically dispersed bases of support (e.g., the Spanish Communist Party [PCE] or the Izquierda Unida coalition) have been consistently under-represented in parliament. However, the major regional parties (the Basque nationalist PNV [Partido Nacionalista Vasco] and the Catalan Convergència i Unió [CiU]) have received a "fair share" of seats or have been somewhat over-represented in the Congress.

Accordingly, the structure of the party system in Spain can be regarded as optimal from several perspectives:

- its low level of fragmentation and the "magnification" of parliamentary representation for the largest parties facilitate the formation of stable governments;
- but this has not impeded the inclusion of regional-nationalist parties in the Congress of Deputies, which in turn has facilitated their integration into national politics and their acceptance of the democratic regime.

What explains these seemingly contradictory characteristics of the party system?

The electoral system

Spain's electoral system largely accounts for the relatively low level of party fragmentation and its high level of cabinet durability. It also has brought about a good balance between normally contradictory characteristics of

103

Table 4.1 Percentage of popular votes, number of parliamentary seats (and percentage of parliamentary seats) for major parties in national elections, 1977–2008

	Nationwide parties					Regional parties		
	LEFT		RIGHT					
	PCE/IU	PSOE/PSP	UCD/CDS	AP/PP	Other	PDC/CiU	PNV	Other
1977	9.2	28.9/4.4	34.0	8.0	7.8	2.8	1.7	3.2
	20	118/6	165	16	0	11	8	6
	(5.7)	(35.4)	(47.1)	(4.6)	0	(3.1)	(2.3)	(1.7)
1979	10.8	30.5	35.1	6.1	6.8	2.7	1.7	6.3
	23	121	168	9	1	8	7	13
	(6.6)	(34.6)	(48.0)	(2.6)	(.3)	(2.3)	(2.0)	(3.7)
1982	4.0	48.4	6.5/2.9	26.5	2.5	3.7	1.9	3.6
	4	202	12/2	106	0	12	8	4
	(1.1)	(57.7)	(3.4/.6)	(30.3)	(0)	(3.4)	(2.3)	(1.1)
1986	4.5	44.6	9.2	26.3	3.7	5.1	1.6	5.0
	7	184	19	105	0	18	6	11
	(2.0)	(52.6)	(5.4)	(30.0)	(0)	(5.1)	(1.7)	(3.1)
1989	9.1	39.9	7.9	25.9	5.5	5.1	1.2	5.4
	17	175	14	107	0	18	5	14
	(4.9)	(50.0)	(4.0)	(30.6)	(0)	(5.1)	(1.4)	(4.0)
1993	9.6	38.8	1.8	34.8	3.8	4.9	1.2	5.1
	18	159	0	141	0	17	5	10
	(5.1)	(45.4)	(0)	(40.3)	(0)	(4.9)	(1.4)	(2.9)
1996	10.6	37.5	–	38.8	1.8	4.6	1.3	5.4
	21	141	–	156	0	16	5	11
	(6.0)	(40.3)	–	(44.6)	(0)	(4.6)	(1.4)	(3.1)
2000	6.1	34.7	–	45.2	3.2	4.3	1.6	5.0
	9	125	–	183	0	15	7	11
	(2.6)	(35.7)	–	(52.3)	0	(4.3)	(2.0)	(3.1)
2004	5.0	43.3	–	38.3	2.5	3.3	1.7	5.9
	5	164	–	148	0	10	7	16
	(1.4)	(46.9)	–	(42.3)	(0)	(2.9)	(2.0)	(4.6)
2008	3.8	43.6	–	40.1	5.3	3.1	1.2	2.9
	2	169	–	154	1	10	6	8
	(0.6)	(48.3)	–	(44.0)	(0.3)	(2.9)	(1.7)	(2.3)

parliamentary representation. Usually, a reduction of party system fragmentation causes serious representative distortions, most often by eliminating or seriously under-representing all but the two largest parties, as is the case with many single-member plurality systems. In the Spanish case, however, **majoritarian**

biases in the representation of parties with a *nationwide* base of support have facilitated the formation of stable governments by over-representing the two largest parties, while, at the same time, small parties with *regionally concentrated* bases óf support are given a fair share of parliamentary representation. The Spanish electoral system allocates seats in accord with a proportional representation formula, but it also includes majoritarian "correctives" intended to reduce party system fragmentation. Meanwhile, the adoption of the province (of which there are 50, in addition to the North African enclaves of Ceuta and Melilla – see map 2.1) as the electoral district facilitates the fair representation of regional-nationalist parties, as we shall see below.

> **Majoritarian biases in electoral laws**
> Consistent with the definition of the concepts of "majoritarianism" and "consensualism" set forth in chapter 2, consensual electoral laws are those which allocate parliamentary seats to parties strictly in accord with the percentages of the popular vote they received in the preceding election. Majoritarian electoral laws, in contrast, are those which systematically over-represent the largest party (or, as in Spain, the two largest parties), while under-representing smaller parties or denying them parliamentary representation altogether. They "magnify" electoral pluralities, sometimes to the extent of "manufacturing" an absolute majority in parliament for a party that received less than half of the popular votes cast.

The electoral system adopted in 1977 reflected a compromise among the conflicting demands of the emerging parties whose leaders were consulted by prime minister Adolfo Suárez.

- The Socialist and Communist parties (the two largest parties of clandestine opposition to the Franco regime) demanded the adoption of proportional representation.

> ## Box 4.5
>
> *Main features of Spain's electoral system*
> There are several features of Spain's electoral law that result in significant majoritarian biases in parliamentary representation. The first is the small size of the parliament (350 seats) in combination with the large number of electoral districts (the 50 provinces, plus the North African territories of Ceuta and Melilla). The product is a relatively small number of deputies elected from each district (an average of 7), which leads to over-representation of large parties and under-representation of small parties in each district. The d'Hondt formula for translating popular votes into parliamentary seats for parties in each district (as compared with the "largest remainder" and other proportional representation seat allocation formulas) further reinforces these majoritarian biases. Conversely, the minimum-vote requirement, which is commonly used to reduce fragmentation in countries like Germany, Sweden, and Poland, has very little effect, since the 3% threshold is applied only within each province. Finally, voters cast ballots for "closed lists" of candidates whose position on the ballot is determined by each party's leaders, rather than a "preferential ballot" that enables voters to select individual candidates.

- Conversely, Alianza Popular, a party founded by some of the most prominent figures from the Franco regime, demanded a **first-past-the-post**, single-member constituency system as the best means of manufacturing stable governments.
- And regional-nationalists insisted upon an electoral system that would not impose a nationwide threshold or calculate parliamentary seats on the basis of nationwide percentages of the vote, since both of those features would have excluded them from parliament.

At the same time, prime minister Suárez and other members of his government (who were in the process of founding the UCD [Unión de Centro Democrático]) were carefully calculating how they could maximize their own representation in designing this new electoral system.

The meaningless minimum-vote threshold

One of the so-called "correctives" incorporated within this electoral law is minimal if not irrelevant in its role in reducing party system fragmentation: this is the inclusion of a 3% minimum-vote requirement. This commonly used technique is normally powerful in its denial of parliamentary representation to small political parties. In the case of Spain, however, the 3% minimum is applied at the *provincial* level (rather than on the basis of a party's share of the total nationwide vote), and could conceivably deny a party parliamentary representation only in the largest district, Madrid, where a party with just 2.9% of the vote might otherwise win seats. If the 3% minimum-vote requirement had been imposed at the national level rather than within each province (as some political elites have sometimes suggested), no regional party except the Catalan CiU (Convergència i Unió) would have been represented in the national parliament. As we argued in chapter 1, the exclusion of regional parties from the constituent parliament of 1977–9 would have undermined the process of democratic consolidation.

Small district magnitude

The principal means by which this electoral system over-represents the two largest parties and under-represents smaller parties with geographically dispersed bases of support derives from the large number of electoral districts sending only a few deputies to the national parliament. As can be seen in table 4.2, at present 9 provinces elect just 3 deputies to the lower house of parliament, 9 elect 4, and another 9 provinces elect 5 members. These 27 districts make up 52% of all constituencies electing deputies to the Congress. As classic studies of electoral systems demonstrated decades ago, proportional representation

Table 4.2 The number of deputies elected from each electoral
district: 1977 and 2004

District magnitude	Number of electoral districts of that size		Number of seats in that size district
	1977	2004	(2004)
1	2	2	2
3	7	9	27
4	8	9	36
5	13	9	45
6	3	5	30
7	6	5	35
8	5	3	24
9	2	4	36
10	2	1	10
11	–	1	11
12	1	1	12
15	1	–	–
16	–	1	16
31	–	1	31
32	1	–	–
33	1	–	–
35	–	1	35
TOTAL	52	52	350

systems can have strong majoritarian biases if multi-member constituencies elect a small number of deputies, and the fewer the number of deputies, the more powerful the majoritarian bias. Conversely, districts electing seven or more deputies tend to be more proportional in their allocation of seats, and the extent of disproportionality increases with reductions in district magnitude.

It is not accidental that the average number of deputies elected in Spain from each district is 7, and fully 140 deputies (out of a total of 350) are elected in small districts – i.e., those represented by fewer than 7 members of parliament. This serves to maximize parliamentary representation of the two largest parties, giving the largest party a near majority of the Congress (as we saw in figure 4.1), and, occasionally, to "manufacture" parliamentary majorities out of mere pluralities of the popular vote. Overall, the net effect of the predominance of small electoral districts (in addition to the use of the **d'Hondt formula** for seat allocation, which marginally

The d'Hondt formula is a procedure for allocating seats among parties within each electoral district. It is a "highest averages" method that divides the number of votes by a series of divisors reflecting the number of seats awarded to each party on the previous round of seat allocation (in contrast with "largest remainder" methods that award seats in accord with numerical quotas surpassed by each party, and then allocates the remaining seats in accord with votes "left over" after the quotas have been taken into consideration). Compared with "largest remainder" systems, the d'Hondt formula has a slight majoritarian bias in its representation of parties in parliament.

Box 4.6

Electoral disproportionality

Electoral systems are purely proportional if the percentage of parliamentary seats allocated to each party is equivalent to the percentage of votes they received. "Electoral disproportionality" measures the extent to which the share of seats deviates from pure proportionality. The higher the disproportionality score (representing the absolute value of the average departure from strict proportionality), the greater the "majoritarian bias" of the electoral system. Single-member-district systems tend to be more disporportional than PR (proportional representation) systems. Accordingly, the electoral disproportionality scores for several illustrative single-district electoral systems are as follows: France 11.8, Canada 11.7, New Zealand 11.1, the United Kingdom 10.3, and Australia 8.9. What is noteworthy is that the majoritarian bias of Spain's "PR" system (8.2) is stronger than that of the single-member-district system of the United States (5.3). Other PR systems' electoral disproportionality scores are: Norway 4.9, Portugal 4.0, Belgium 3.2, Germany 2.6, Austria and Switzerland 2.5, Sweden 2.1, Denmark 1.8, and the Netherlands 1.3. Among West European PR systems, only that of Greece (8.1) includes majoritarian "correctives" comparable to those of Spain.

strengthens these majoritarian biases) is that Spain's electoral system is the most disproportional among all proportional representation systems in Western Europe, and almost as disproportional as most single-member district systems.

Fair representation in some large districts

However, as noted above, this electoral law is a compromise that included elements designed to placate other parties in advance of the crucial "founding election" of 1977. Since the Socialist and Communist parties anticipated receiving higher shares of the vote in large urban and industrialized provinces, they were assured of a significant level of parliamentary representation in large districts like Madrid and Barcelona (which in 1977 elected 32 and 33 deputies, respectively). More importantly, the use of the province as the principal electoral district allowed for the fair (indeed, almost perfectly proportional) representation of small regional-nationalist parties. In several provinces within which regional or nationalist parties receive substantial electoral support, moreover, district magnitudes are relatively high (e.g., in the provinces of Barcelona, Vizcaya, La Coruña, etc.). Within those provinces where support for regional parties is concentrated, the largest parties may be regional or nationalist, and therefore would benefit from the majoritarian biases of this electoral system, despite the fact that their shares of the nationwide vote total may be quite small.

Box 4.7

"Majoritarian" and "conservative" biases in representation

The "majoritarian" bias in parliamentary representation that results from the presence of a large number of electoral districts that elect 3, 4 or 5 deputies reduces the level of fragmentation of the party system by over-representing the two larger parties and under-representing smaller parties with regionally dispersed bases of electoral support. While that form of bias affects the number of parties that will be given significant representation in the Congress of Deputies, the "conservative" bias affects *which* parties will be over- or under-represented. It is the product of malapportionment of districts, in which rural provinces (whose voters tend to be conservative in their political preferences) are allocated more seats than can be justified on the basis of their small populations, while large and predominantly urban districts receive fewer deputies per voter. This violation of the principle of "one person, one vote" means that rural votes count for more than an equivalent number of urban votes in terms of their representation in parliament. In the 1977 election, for example, the province of Soria elected one deputy for every 34,636 persons, while the province of Barcelona was allocated only one seat for every 136,554 inhabitants. Over the past three decades, this has systematically benefited the center-right UCD and the more conservative Partido Popular.

The conservative bias

Finally, the biases of the electoral system include over-representation of sparsely populated rural provinces. These kinds of electoral districts include relatively conservative voters who could be expected to favor the moderately conservative UCD (whose founders wrote the electoral law) and, since 1982, the much more conservative Partido Popular (PP). This is referred to as a "conservative bias" of the electoral law, as distinct from the "majoritarian bias" discussed above. Accordingly, in both the 1977 and 1979 elections, the UCD received nearly 13 percentage points more as a share of seats in parliament than it had earned as a share of popular votes cast. And in 2004, the *second-placed* PP received in seats 4% more than it would have been allocated strictly in terms of its share of the vote, while the victorious PSOE received only 3.6% more than its "fair share" of seats.

The net impact of these two kinds of bias (majoritarian and conservative) can be seen in table 4.3, which presents the "advantage ratio" for each major nationwide party. This figure is calculated by dividing the percentage of seats won by the share of the votes received by each party. Thus, scores of "1.0" indicate perfect proportionality in the allocation of seats, numbers lower than that represent under-representation, and larger numbers indicate over-representation.

"Psychological effects" and "wasted votes"

It is often noted that electoral systems influence the structure of party systems both through their short-term or "mechanical" effects (i.e., in the process

Table 4.3 Advantage ratios for parliamentary representation of Spanish parties, 1977–2008

Year	PCE/IU	PSOE	CDS	UCD	PP	PNV	CiU
1977	0.61	1.15	–	1.36	0.58	1.25	1.11
1979	0.61	1.13	–	1.37	0.43	1.31	0.85
1982	0.28	1.20	0.20	0.46	1.15	1.21	0.93
1986	0.43	1.19	0.58	–	1.15	1.11	1.02
1989	0.53	1.26	0.50	–	1.16	1.14	1.01
1993	0.56	1.17	–	–	1.16	1.15	0.98
1996	0.57	1.07	–	–	1.15	1.12	0.99
2000	0.42	1.02	–	–	1.15	1.25	0.93
2004	0.28	1.08	–	–	1.10	1.17	0.87
2008	0.15	1.20	–	–	1.08	1.42	1.02

Source: For 1977–96, Alberto Penadés, "El sistema electoral español," in José Luis Paniagua and Juan Carlos Monedero, eds., *En torno a la democracia en España* (Madrid: Taurus, 1999), 310; updated for 2000, 2004, and 2008 by the authors.

of translating popular votes into parliamentary seats) and over the long term, when voters and party leaders adjust their behavior in accord with the anticipated effects of the system. These so-called "psychological" influences have had a significant impact on the structure of the Spanish party system. Voters who do not want to waste their votes on a party with no realistic prospect of electing a deputy in a particular district shift their support to a somewhat less preferred (but acceptable) party with a greater probability of securing parliamentary representation. This leads them to vote "strategically" by casting a "useful vote" (*voto útil*), rather than wasting their ballots on their most preferred but smaller and electorally unviable party. This has the effect of further penalizing smaller parties above and beyond the mechanical effect of under-representation.

Over the long term, this psychological effect has a particularly strong impact on the behavior of leaders of smaller parties. Accordingly, parties that anticipate being seriously under-represented may choose to **merge** with ideologically compatible but rival parties. This was the case, in particular, with regard to the absorption in 1978 of the Partido Socialista Popular by the much larger PSOE, as well as the merger between the Catalan socialist PSC (Partit dels Socialistes de Catalunya) and the regional branch of the PSOE in that same year. They also may choose to **form a durable coalition**, while retaining their separate organizational structures. One prominent example is the Catalan CiU [Convergència i Unió], which has served as the electoral vehicle for candidates of the Convèrgencia Democràtica de Catalunya and Unió Democrática de Catalunya. Another is the Izquierda Unida coalition formed in 1986 by the Communist Party in the aftermath of its devastating electoral defeat in 1982. Alternatively, small parties with no realistic chance of electoral victory may simply choose to **go out of business** altogether, as was the case with the Equipo de la Democracia Cristiana in 1977, the Centro Democrático y Social in 1993, or, most dramatically, the UCD following its disastrous electoral performance in 1982. This further contributes to the consolidation of the party system and, in turn, facilitates the formation of stable governments.

Closed lists

One final noteworthy characteristic of the electoral law is that its provincial-level lists of candidates for the Congress of Deputies are "closed" – that is, voters cast ballots only for lists of candidates whose rank-ordering is established by the party. Voters are not allowed to express their preferences for individual candidates or otherwise determine the order in which candidates will take their seats in parliament. Insofar as the top-ranking leaders of a party control the candidate nomination process, this enhances their ability to enforce party discipline: members of parliament who do not respect party discipline can be punished by being given places on the provincial list that are so low that they could never be elected. A noteworthy exception to this general pattern is that of the UCD, whose leader, Adolfo Suárez, did not actively participate in the candidate selection process. Accordingly, elite-level disputes erupted over the year and a half preceding the 1982 election, culminating in the party's disastrous defeat

Box 4.8

Elections to the Senate

Some people have complained that closed lists are "undemocratic"– that leaving the selection of individual candidates in the hands of party leaders deprives voters of the ability to choose "the best man/woman for the job," and thereby undermines the quality of democracy. Spain provides us with an excellent test case to see if voters really do know enough about most legislative candidates to cast an informed ballot, and to "vote for the man/woman, not the party." While elections to the Congress of Deputies present voters with "closed lists" of candidates whose rank-ordering on the party's list is determined by party leaders, elections to the Senate allow voters to split their three votes among parties, and vote for individual candidates irrespective of their position on the ballot. Senate elections are conducted according to a "limited-vote" variant of the plurality system, with multimember districts within which each voter can cast up to 3 votes for candidates on "open lists" to fill the 4 seats representing each province. Rather than splitting their votes among candidates for different parties (as the critics suggest voters would do in selecting the best individual for the job), the overwhelming majority of voters cast all 3 votes for candidates for the same party for which they had voted in the election to the Congress of Deputies. And rather than picking and choosing the best 3 from among the 4 candidates nominated by each party, the overwhelming majority of voters support candidates in accord with the *alphabetical ordering* in which their names appear on the ballot!

(a traumatic event that, as we shall see, convinced leaders of all other parties of the need to maintain party discipline).

Moderation

In contrast with the ideological radicalization and electoral polarization of the Second Republic, the party system established in the 1970s was noteworthy for its moderation. Relatively moderate and fully democratic parties have always garnered the overwhelming majority of votes, and the government has always been headed by either a party of the center right (the UCD from 1977 to 1982 and the Partido Popular from 1996 to 2004) or of the center left (the PSOE from 1982 through 1996, and since 2004). In addition, this democratic system has been characterized by a healthy **alternation** between left and right at the national level of government, in contrast with the "immobilism" of governments in the French Fourth Republic (1946–58) or the permanent Christian Democratic domination of governments in the Italian "first republic" (1946–94).

Another manifestation of moderate political pluralism is that control of the national-level parliament by a single party has not been paralleled by similar domination of regional governments throughout the country. This has been particularly important for the Basque and Catalan nationalist parties (PNV and CiU), as well as for the PSOE (in Andalucía, Extremadura, and Castilla-La Mancha) and the PP (in La Rioja, Castilla-León, or Galicia), which have controlled their respective autonomous communities for most of the current democratic era.

This is not to say that inter-party competition has been devoid of conflict. Indeed, at times opposition parties have intensified their attacks on the government as part of a strategy for dislodging the incumbents from power. But these episodes of intense inter-party conflict, with some exceptions that will be discussed later, have not become permanent features of Spanish party politics and they were never translated into extra-parliamentary conflicts among citizens at the mass level. In addition, the tactical objective of these attacks was to separate the governing party from its moderate base of electoral support in a **centripetal** (or center-seeking) competition over the moderate majority of Spanish voters. Attacks were never oriented towards "outbidding" for support from the extreme poles of the political spectrum, which might have contributed to ideological polarization to a degree that might have posed a threat to the stability of democracy.

The overall moderation of electoral competition in Spain is, as we shall see in the following chapter, partly a product of the fact that Spanish voters following the death of Franco have consistently maintained moderate attitudinal

Centrifugal vs. centripetal drives in party systems Party systems characterized by polarized pluralism have, as the name implies, "centrifugal" tendencies, resulting from each party's pursuit of voters from the more extreme ends of the political spectrum. When most parties appeal primarily to voters near the center of the left–right continuum, the drives inherent in partisan competition are "centripetal," the aggregate result of which is that they adopt more moderate stands that would appeal to centrist voters.

Box 4.9

Catch-all parties

The term "catch-all" was first coined by the political scientist Otto Kirchheimer to describe changes in many parties that were becoming apparent by the second half of the 20th century. Mass-based "cleavage parties" (including both social-ist and Christian democratic parties) were tending to downplay their ideologies and programmatic commitments, weaken their defense of the interests of their respective electoral clienteles, shift control of the party from congresses of dues-paying members and their elected executive committees to the highest-ranking party leaders, focus their election campaigns on the personal qualities of party leaders, and broaden their electoral appeals beyond their traditional clienteles (e.g., the working class). Kirchheimer concluded that these parties were evolving into "catch-all parties."

orientations regarding politics. A second important explanatory factor involves the behavior of the leaders of Spain's principal political parties. In this regard, the contrast with the Second Republic could not be greater: while political leaders in that earlier era often engaged in dogmatic, radical, and occasionally sectarian and rancorous behavior, the party leaders of the new democratic regime have generally been characterized by the moderation of their interactions with their rivals (although verbal clashes between the PP and PSOE have become some-what more rancorous since 2000). These patterns of behavior can be traced to "catch-all" electoral strategies that they adopted since the very earliest elections, which not only helped to determine the configuration and dynamics of the party system but also contributed to the consolidation of democracy.

In the case of all but one of these national-level parties, this orientation could not be taken for granted at the time the new democracy came into existence. Only the governing UCD was founded as a moderate centrist party. In the cases of the PSOE, Alianza Popular (now the Partido Popular), and the communist PCE, considerable efforts were made to moderate initially radical stands on poten-tially divisive issues. In each of these cases, that conversion caused considerable internal party conflict and, in 1982, a massive party system realignment. In order to understand the dynamics of these parties' respective conversions to moderate democratic orientations, it is best to briefly recount these evolutionary processes party by party.

■ Spain's principal nationwide parties

Four political parties (in addition to regional parties, which will be discussed later) emerged from the first post-Franco democratic election with the largest

The left–right continuum Over more than a century of democratic politics in Western Europe, parties have often been referred to as of the "left," "right," or "center." The left–right continuum is a simplifying device that captures several aspects of political ideology or party program. While the meaning of left and right has evolved over time, and varies from country to country, in the early twenty-first century parties of the "right" have tended to be more religious, opposed to taxes and government spending, favorable towards the socioeconomic status quo, and strongly in favor of "law and order." Parties of the "left" have tended to favor individual freedoms and protection of civil liberties, and a more egalitarian distribution of income, and have been non-religious or sometimes anticlerical.

shares of the vote nationwide. Moving from **left to right on the political spectrum**, these were:

- the Partido Comunista de España (PCE);
- the socialist PSOE (Partido Socialista Obrero Español);
- the Unión de Centro Democrático (UCD), and
- Alianza Popular (AP).

Only one of these parties, the UCD, was from the time of its founding explicitly committed to presenting itself as a centrist party and to attracting voters from the modal center of the electorate, which contributed to its electoral victory in 1977. The other three, intentionally or through miscalculation, were seen as too extreme for most voters (in the cases of the PCE and AP) or inconsistent in ideological orientation (the PSOE). Over the following two years, they, too, sought to position themselves closer to the center of the left–right continuum. But this generated considerable intra-party tension and conflict.

Balanced two-party competition, 1977–1982

Over the short-term, the UCD enjoyed another electoral triumph in 1979, in large measure by capitalizing on the success of the process of democratization that had culminated in the endorsement of a new constitution in December of the preceding year. In the first two elections, Spain had what looked to be a balanced "two-plus" party system at the national level, with the PSOE and UCD emerging as the predominant parties competing with each other near the center of the political spectrum (see table 4.1 and map 4.1).

Paradoxically, the one party that was unable to survive into the mid 1980s was the UCD. By the mid 1980s, the PSOE and Alianza Popular were able to stabilize internally – enforcing strict party discipline in support of an unchallenged leadership team – and establish themselves as the principal competitors for the majority of voters near the center of the political spectrum. The Communist Party was incapable of resolving its internal contradictions, culminating in a serious electoral setback in 1982, followed by schisms and defections by several of its most prominent national figures. And the UCD was completely destroyed in that same election, following two years of unseemly leadership struggles and the departure of many of its leaders (including its founder, Adolfo Suárez!).

The predominance of the PSOE, 1982–1993

After the electoral earthquake of 1982, Spain had a highly unbalanced, predominant two-plus party system in which the overwhelmingly dominant PSOE

UCD (37)
PSOE (13)
PNV (2)

Map 4.1 General election results, 1979[a]
[a]Numbers in parentheses are districts in which the party received the largest number of votes.
Source: www.electionresources.org/es/index_es.html

governed in the absence of a credible threat from either its left (the PCE) or its right (Alianza Popular and the tiny Centro Democrático y Social [CDS], founded by Adolfo Suárez as a centrist successor to the by now defunct UCD) (see map 4.2). Eventually, the CDS was unable to survive the highly detrimental effects of the majoritarian electoral law on small nationwide parties, and became extinct following the 1993 election. The Communist Party was also largely unable to develop as a credible leftist alternative to the PSOE, although it has survived as the core member of the Izquierda Unida coalition. For over a decade, from 1982 to 1996, the PSOE dominated Spanish politics, fully commanding the center of the political spectrum, while AP struggled valiantly to convince voters that it was a party of the moderate center-right. It eventually succeeded, but only

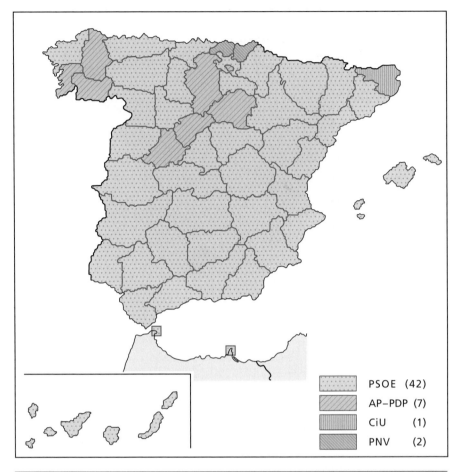

PSOE (42)
AP–PDP (7)
CiU   (1)
PNV   (2)

Map 4.2 General election results, 1982[a]
[a]Numbers in parentheses are districts in which the party received the largest number of votes.
Source: www.electionresources.org/es/index_es.html

after a major demographic turnover among its leaders and a change of name – becoming the Partido Popular in 1989.

The return of two-party balance, 1993–2008

By the mid 1990s, the Spanish party system once again resembled a balanced two-plus party system, with a moderate catch-all party of the center left, the PSOE, competing for power with a rising catch-all challenger of the center right, the PP (see map 4.3). In the 1996 election (see table 4.1 and map 4.4), the Partido Popular finally succeeded in defeating the PSOE, which was punished by voters for numerous corruption scandals and for an economic downturn. After struggling for fourteen years to reposition itself as a party of the center right,

	PSOE	(24)
	PP	(25)
	CiU	(2)
	EAJ–PNV	(1)

Map 4.3 General election results, 1993[a]
[a]Numbers in parentheses are districts in which the party received the largest number of votes.
Source: www.electionresources.org/es/index_es.html

the PP formed a single-party minority government of the center right. It thus appeared as if electoral politics in Spain had returned to the same pattern that had characterized the first two democratic elections, with a moderate center-right party in government facing a center-left PSOE opposition. After the smashing election victory of the PP in 2000, however, this picture began to change (see map 4.5). The PP government shifted markedly to the right, even to the extent of taking positions on certain policy matters that effectively revived the religious cleavage in Spanish politics. Ideological polarization was further reinforced by the PP government's decision to send troops to participate in the extremely unpopular war in Iraq. Accompanying this polarization of issue stands was a shift towards rancorous partisan conflict that had been scrupulously avoided

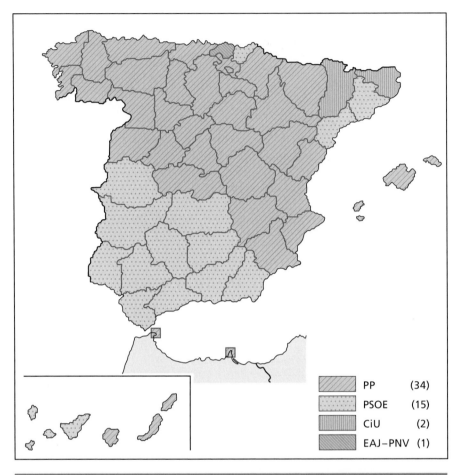

during the transition to democracy and its aftermath. Even after the defeat of the PP in the 2004 election (see map 4.6), it continued to maintain its newly extreme stands on many issues, and rancor continued to characterize politics among party leaders.

The strategy pursued by the Partido Popular as the principal opposition party in the 2004–8 parliament was to undermine electoral support for the PSOE by taking a Spanish nationalist stance with regard to the regional cleavage, accusing the government of being weak on terror and allowing ETA to reorganize and re-arm by naively attempting to negotiate with it during the "truce" of 2006. The PP also allied itself with the Catholic Church in organizing mass protests against some of the government's social policies, and it encouraged a xenophobic public

PP (42)

PSOE (6)

CiU (2)

EAJ–PNV (2)

Map 4.5 General election results, 2000[a]
[a]Numbers in parentheses are districts in which the party received the largest number of votes.
Source: www.electionresources.org/es/index_es.html

response to the growing wave of immigration. Coupled with its continuing, completely unwarranted assertions that the PSOE had somehow colluded with ETA in bringing about the terrorist bombings that immediately preceded the 2004 elections, and the rancorous tone it adopted in articulating its attacks on the PSOE, relations between the governing and principal opposition parties deteriorated to unprecedented levels.

In the end, this strategy was unsuccessful. While the PP increased its share of parliamentary seats from 148 to 154 in the 2008 election, the PSOE was returned to power with its parliamentary delegation increasing from 164 in the 2004 legislature to 169. Indeed, one by-product of the polarization between the two principal nationwide parties was an increase in their joint share of votes cast

PSOE (21)
PP (29)
EAJ–PNV (2)

Map 4.6 General election results, 2004[a]
[a]Numbers in parentheses are districts in which the party received the largest number of votes.
Source: www.electionresources.org/es/index_es.html

and seats allocated – largely at the expense of regional parties (particularly the Catalan ERC, as will be discussed below). The combined share of votes that went to the PSOE and PP increased from 81.6% in 2004 to 83.7% in 2008, while their seats in the Congress of Deputies rose from 89% to 92%. For the first time, either the PSOE or the PP won pluralities in each of Spain's 52 electoral districts, including those in Catalonia and the Basque Country, where regional nationalist parties previously held sway (see map 4.7).

In short, while the first two decades of Spanish democracy were characterized by partisan moderation and competition for support from the center of the political spectrum, the dawn of the new millennium witnessed a reversal of the centripetal or "center-seeking" drives in the Spanish political system. In the

Map 4.7 General election results, 2008[a]
[a]Numbers in parentheses are districts in which the party received the largest number of votes.
Source: www.electionresources.org/es/index_es.html

following section of the chapter, we will examine the origins and evolution of these major nationwide parties over the course of the three decades following the death of Generalísimo Franco. And in the concluding section of the chapter, we will see how some of these same trends can be observed with regard to partisan conflicts involving the regional and regional-nationalist parties.

■ Moderation and centripetal competition: 1977–2000

The Socialist Party

The Partido Socialista Obrero Español was founded as a Marxist-socialist party in 1879. Indeed, portions of the ideological declarations in the party charter

> ## Box 4.10
>
> *Socialism and social democracy*
>
> The core ideological principles of the socialist parties of Western Europe can be traced back to Karl Marx's belief that private ownership of the means of production inevitably leads to inequality, exploitation, and social injustice. Socialist parties, however, have typically included some individuals who maintain a commitment to the maximalist objective of nationalizing the means of production in order to eliminate the source of inequality, and others who accept capitalism and private ownership of most business firms but who seek to use government policies (especially social welfare policies and public education) to reduce economic inequality and provide an equal opportunity for all citizens within a competitive market economy. While there has always been disagreement about the use of these terms, in Southern Europe the latter group – the more moderate reformists – have typically been referred to as "social democrats," even though both social democrats and more maximalist socialists are normally committed to democratic forms of government.

were written by Karl Marx himself. However, like nearly all socialist parties in Western Europe, the PSOE included both radicals and moderates. In the Second Republic, the parliamentary leadership of the party tended to be more moderate in its programmatic orientation, while the head of the party's allied trade union, the Unión General de Trabajadores (UGT, the General Workers Union) – the self-described "Spanish Lenin," Francisco Largo Caballero – adopted a much more militant stance, including a prominent role in leading in the 1934 revolt in Asturias, which was viciously suppressed by Spanish troops under the command of General Francisco Franco. The party was banned throughout the Franco regime, and completely disappeared from most parts of Spain until about 1973, when new branches of the party spontaneously formed in clandestinity. Throughout most of the four decades of *franquismo*, the official leaders of the party remained in exile.

Ideological inconsistency and electoral frustration

In 1974, 32-year-old Felipe González was elected head of the party at its congress in Suresnes, France. This marked the definitive end of leadership of the party by those of the Civil War generation, and it set in motion two contrary trends with regard to this chapter's central theme of ideological moderation. On the one hand, González presented himself as the PSOE's candidate for prime minister as a moderate, pragmatic social democrat. And throughout his fourteen years as Spain's prime minister (1982–96) he governed from the center. At almost the same time as he was elected party leader, however, the formal ideological and programmatic stands of the party lurched to the left. At the 27th Congress of the PSOE in December 1976, the term "Marxist" was *added* to the party's

Figure 4.2 Felipe González at an election rally in Barcelona, 1989

Declaration of Principles for the first time in its history, and some radical stands were incorporated within the party's program, such as calls for "socialization of the means of production, distribution and exchange by the working class," and for elimination of the religious sector of education.

This radicalization of the party's formal ideological and programmatic declarations did not fit with the moderate image the party sought to project in the first two democratic elections, particularly that of 1979, by which time the PSOE had clearly established itself as the principal rival of the governing UCD. Felipe González adopted a catch-all electoral strategy and attempted to attract votes from the center by adopting moderate campaign stands and emphasizing its responsible and constructive behavior throughout the transition to democracy. These messages, however, were undermined by the maximalist rhetoric in the party's official declarations of principles (which were seized upon by many UCD politicians during the 1979 campaign in an effort to portray the PSOE as an irresponsible and radical party), by the undisciplined and sometimes unruly style of its internal deliberations, and by public confrontations between moderates and more traditional socialists over a variety of issues.

González therefore sought to formally alter the party's ideology by, among other things, removing the self-designation "Marxist" at its party congress in May 1979. Instead, rejection of his proposals by the congress provoked him to resign as party leader. Over the following several months he worked to convince party members and middle-level party officials of the wisdom of ideological moderation, and to make sure that his supporters would be selected as delegates to attend the Extraordinary Congress of the party that was held in September of that year. At that crucial meeting, the leadership position of Felipe González and his close collaborator Alfonso Guerra was clearly established, the term "Marxist" was eliminated from the party's self-definition, and a typically social-democratic reformist program was adopted. Having resolved its internal crisis, the PSOE was able to focus its efforts on the tasks of opposition to the UCD government, as well as present itself as a stable and credible alternative for voters from a wide variety of social, ideological, and political backgrounds.

The predominant status of the moderate PSOE

This change in the party's image helped it to capitalize on the decomposition of the governing UCD and achieve a sweeping election victory in 1982. For the following fourteen years, Spain was governed by prime minister Felipe González and a series of PSOE single-party governments. Thousands of party members occupied official and elective posts in the Cortes, regional parliaments, and municipal governments, as well as in the state administration. And throughout this period (as we will see in the concluding chapter of this book), the public policies enacted by the Socialist majority and its *ad hoc* legislative allies in the Cortes were generally centrist. In accord with the party's social-democratic principles, programs associated with the social welfare state and public education were expanded. However, the González governments also adopted "neoliberal" monetary and industrial policies, at least in part in an effort to increase the competitiveness of the economy in advance of Spain's entry into the European

---

Box 4.11

Neoliberal economic policies

In the early 1980s, some governments in advanced industrialized countries (especially the Thatcher government in Great Britain) adopted a variety of economic and social policies that sought to reverse important aspects of Keynesianism (in which the government used its taxation and spending policies in an effort to regulate the aggregate level of "supply" and "demand" in the economy) and the social-welfare state. These policies took a wide variety of forms, but all shared a belief that government intervention in society and economy should be minimized in order to allow "free-market" incentives to drive economic growth, that barriers to free trade should be eliminated, that budgets should be balanced, and that monetary policies should be stable and non-inflationary. In countries with corporatist traditions and large para-state industrial sectors, these policies also included privatization of state and para-state enterprises. (See chapter 6 for further discussion.)

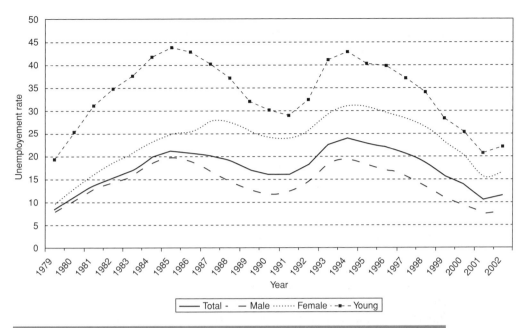

Figure 4.3 Unemployment in Spain, 1979–2002
Source: Carles Boix, "Spain: Development, Democracy, and Equity," prepared for the
World Development Report Background Papers (2006), 41.

Community (now European Union) in 1986. This generated intense intra-party conflict.

In the early 1980s, of particular concern to the party's traditional trade-union ally, the UGT (Unión General de Trabajadores), was the closure of hundreds of inefficient industrial firms owned or controlled by the state, especially in the steel, shipbuilding and other heavy-industrial sectors. Thousands of workers were laid off, and the overall unemployment rate was allowed to exceed 20% of the labor force. In addition, "tight-money" policies restricted credit and further reduced the economy's capacity to create or maintain high levels of employment over the short term. In the end, the UGT definitively separated from the Socialist Party, terminating a collaborative relationship that dated back to the late 1880s. In 1988, the UGT collaborated with the other major union, the once predominantly Communist Comisiones Obreras (CCOO), in organizing a nationwide general strike against the Socialist government after announcing a far-reaching labor market reform. The González governments' economic reforms eventually paid off, however, and by the late 1980s Spain had one of the most rapidly expanding economies in Europe. Unemployment levels declined accordingly (see figure 4.3). But great intra-party and party-union tensions were an unintended by-product, as workers and party members favoring more traditionally socialist programs opposed what they regarded as the PSOE's "neoliberal" policies.

Throughout this period, the PSOE behaved as a "catch-all party," seeking votes from the great bulk of Spanish voters near the center of the political spectrum. The moderate image of its leadership under Felipe González and the centrist social-democratic policies it pursued in government enabled it to compete most successfully for electoral support from those voters from 1982 until 1996.

The defeat of the PSOE in the 1996 election (in part, a natural response by an electorate to the "exhaustion" that comes with governance by a single party after a period of fourteen years, and in part a reaction against a series of corruption scandals that had involved a number of PSOE leaders over the previous decade) threw the party into confusion and chaos. These problems were exacerbated by certain features of the processes adopted for selecting a new party leader and candidate for President of the Government in the next elections, following the resignation of Felipe González, which contributed to a protracted leadership struggle. The impact of this internal chaos on the party's performance in the 2000 election was disastrous: the PSOE was disoriented, its supporters divided, its leadership weakend, and an electoral alliance with the left-wing Izquierda Unida further alienated many moderate voters. The new Secretary General, Joaquín Almunia, resigned in the aftermath of this electoral debacle, plunging the party into yet another vortex of conflict and uncertainty.

Box 4.12

The PSOE's leadership struggles
In June 1997, the PSOE held its first party congress as an opposition party after 14 years in government. This brought to a climax the long-simmering conflict within the party among *"felipistas"* (loyal supporters of Felipe González), *"guerristas"* (allies of his once close collaborator, Alfonso Guerra), and *"renovadores"* ("renewers" or reformists who demanded significant change in the party's leadership). Felipe González unexpectedly resigned and designated as his successor secretary general Joaquín Almunia, a *renovador* who had previously served in several important government posts. In response to criticism that his designation as party leader lacked legitimacy, Almunia convened a "primary election" the following year, in which all PSOE members could choose their party's candidate for prime minister in the next general election. Against all expectations, Almunia was defeated by an outsider, José Borrell, by a margin of 55 to 44%. This gave rise to considerable confusion and conflict within the party between supporters of Borrell and of Almunia, who retained his position as secretary general of the party. Internal struggles precluded the programmatic and organizational renovation that the party so badly needed after a decade and a half in government. The situation further deteriorated when Borrell was forced to step down as his party's candidate in the aftermath of financial scandals involving some of his close collaborators. Thus, on the eve of the 2000 election, Almunia became the party's candidate for prime minister, although his own credibility had been seriously damaged by losing the primary election.

At a new party congress, held in July 2000, a previously unknown backbencher, José Luis Rodríguez Zapatero, won a narrow victory (42%, to 41% for his next-closest rival) to become the new party leader. Surprisingly, Zapatero succeeded in pacifying the party, consolidating its organization and leadership, and initiating a successful opposition in parliament to the PP government of José María Aznar. His election as prime minister in the 2004 election was equally surprising, and was made possible by a dramatic series of events on the eve of balloting, as we will see. Noteworthy successes under his first government included high rates of economic growth, a significant reduction in unemployment, and enactment of a number of innovative social policies. Despite some other shortcomings – most importantly, the failure of efforts to end ETA's violence, as well as a somewhat erratic regional policy – his party was victorious in the March 2008 election. Indeed, the number of votes received by his party (nearly 11.1 million) was the highest ever received by a Spanish party, and the level of voter turnout in this election (75.3%) was extraordinarily high.

The Unión de Centro Democrático

The UCD was the principal rival of the PSOE in the first two democratic elections (1977 and 1979 – see table 4.1). The UCD emerged victorious from both of those elections and, under the leadership of Adolfo Suárez, formed single-party minority governments. From the very beginning, it was the quintessential catch-all party. Its founders included both reformists with origins in the Franco regime (including Suárez, who had served as secretary general of the Franco regime's single "party," the National Movement, and director of RTVE, the state broadcasting corporation) and members of the moderate opposition to that authoritarian system. In terms of their ideological orientation, it included Christian democrats, social democrats, and liberals. This heterogeneity and moderation helped it to attract electoral support from a broad array of voters near the middle of the political spectrum.

Internal dissension

However, several prominent leaders of the factions that made up the elite of the party rebelled against what they regarded as the party's ideological vagueness and incoherence, demanded a stronger defense of the interests of their respective clienteles, and were offended by some of the compromises made by Suárez and his collaborators in the course of "the politics of consensus" (see chapter 1), even though this "consensual" behavior contributed to widespread acceptance of the new constitution, as well as the party's victory in the 1979 election.

- Christian democrats favored a much more resolute defense of the interests of the Church, particularly with regard to the education system. They also demanded institutional linkages between the party and religious organizations, along the lines of those established by the Christian Democratic Party

Figure 4.4 From right to left, Adolfo Suárez, Leopoldo Calvo Sotelo (who succeeded Suárez as prime minister in February 1981), and Catalan leader Jordi Pujol in the Congress of Deputies during its opening session following the first democratic election in 1977

in Italy. They were also outraged by the UCD government's enactment of a law that legalized divorce for the first time since the Second Republic.

- Liberals close to big business and the banks favored more conservative monetary and fiscal policies, and some were outraged by a decision by Suárez to allow foreign banking institutions to open branches in Spain.
- And social democrats became alienated from the party beginning in early 1981, as the UCD government under its new leader, prime minister Leopoldo Calvo Sotelo, shifted more towards the center right.

In short, the same programmatic and ideological heterogeneity that was so appealing to a wide array of voters contributed to the eruption of unseemly factional squabbles during the two years preceding the 1982 election.

The party was unable to cope with these elite-level disputes, in large measure because it was not adequately institutionalized. That is, it was deficient in the kind of institutional loyalty and commitment that had helped the century-old PSOE to weather its ideological storms. In part, this was the result of a lack of agreement among the party's leaders concerning what kind of party it

on the support of three center to center-right regional parties for the passage of its legislation further reinforced its propensity towards moderation in both the content of its policies and its rhetorical style.

Following its securing of an absolute parliamentary majority in 2000, however, the Aznar government lurched sharply to the right, deeply cutting taxes and government spending (especially on infrastructure and social welfare programs), and sending troops to Iraq as part of George Bush's "coalition of the willing" – a foreign policy stand that was strongly opposed by the overwhelming majority of Spaniards.

From the standpoint of polarization along the lines of traditional social cleavages, the most important change in partisan behavior involved religion. While the leaders of all major parties had scrupulously avoided taking polarizing positions on religious issues ever since the first post-Franco democratic elections, the Aznar government took highly visible stands on potentially polarizing religious issues. It substantially increased financial support for privately owned but publicly funded schools (mostly religious), and reintroduced religious instruction into the public school curriculum. In general, the PP adopted positions that followed very closely the dictates of the Church concerning a wide variety of issues (such as its rejection of the PSOE's 2005 legislation legalizing gay marriage, as well as of stem-cell research). The consequence of this close public embrace of the Catholic Church was to reactivate the religious cleavage in Spanish politics, at least to the extent that religiosity would once again become a powerful determinant of the vote. This was not reflected in the link between partisan preferences and religiosity *per se*, which remained at the same moderate level as in 1993. But there was sharp polarization along partisan lines regarding attitudes towards religion and abortion. This trend towards greater polarization has continued since the 2004 election.

Polarization was not restricted to religious issues, however. The Partido Popular abandoned the traditionally united stance of Spain's nationwide parties against Basque terrorism and ETA, and sought to use the PSOE's unsuccessful efforts to negotiate an end to this decades-old conflict as evidence of its "weakness" in the face of terrorism in order to undermine electoral support for the socialist government of Rodríguez Zapatero.

The basic behavioral styles of party leaders and their mobilization strategies also reflected an increased polarization of partisan politics. The harshness of the rhetorical clashes between the leaders of the two parties stands in sharp contrast with the restraint and mutual respect that characterized the first several years of Spain's post-Franco democratic era. In short, "*la política del consenso*" (the politics of consensus) was replaced by "*la política de la crispación*" (the politics of rancor). And the PP's frequent recourse to massive protest demonstrations against the PSOE government harks back to the mass-mobilization strategies employed by parties of the left during the first six months following the death of Franco.

Why did the PP adopt this rancorous opposition strategy? Some analysts have interpreted its behavior as a long-term strategy to achieve three partisan

Figure 4.6 José Luis Rodríguez Zapatero in the Moncloa Palace, 2004

objectives: first, to mobilize the electoral base of the PP, while at the same time to discourage and alienate those who had supported the PSOE in the 2004 election; second, to distract public attention from the policy accomplishments of the Zapatero government (especially the impressive performance of Spain's economy or the popularity of its social policies); and third, to recast the political debate in terms of emotional "valence issues," such as terrorism and the "unity of Spain," by accusing the PSOE government of weakening the nation and coddling terrorists.

Certain characteristics of the 2004 election also had some impact in transforming the elite-level political culture. Indeed, the 2004 election was remarkable in several ways. The surprising victory of the PSOE (receiving 43% of the vote and 47% of parliamentary seats, vs. the PP's 38% of the vote and 42% share of seats in the Congress of Deputies) shocked the PP and its electoral supporters. For the first time in Spanish electoral history, a governing party that had held an absolute majority in the previous parliament was ousted from office. In the days before the election, public opinion polls had indicated that voters were evenly divided between the two major parties. The dramatic terrorist attacks that took place on March 11, however, mobilized and traumatized the electorate.

But the electoral backlash against the PP was primarily motivated by the government's partisan and misleading manipulation of information about the attack, rather than the terrorist act itself. Despite clear evidence that the murder of nearly 200 persons in or near the Atocha railway station, in downtown Madrid, was the result of bombs planted by Islamist terrorists linked to Al Qaeda (confirmed by the conviction in December 2007 of a group of Al Qaeda terrorists and their accomplices in the first ever trial against the organizers of a terrorist attack), the Aznar government persisted in attributing this attack to ETA, not only during the three days prior to the election, but for three years following the election in a protracted effort to challenge the legitimacy of the PSOE's electoral victory. PP spokespersons and their allies in the media claimed that the PSOE had somehow colluded with ETA and Al Qaeda in an effort to prevent the PP's certain electoral victory.

This strategy can be understood only within the particular configuration of partisan forces surrounding this election. Following the 2003 Catalan regional elections, the Catalan branch of the PSOE (the Partit dels Socialistes de Catalunya) formed a government in coalition with two left-wing Catalan parties, Iniciativa per Catalunya and the Catalan nationalist Esquerra Republicana de Catalunya. One of the most prominent ERC leaders in this regional government subsequently engaged in secret negotiations with ETA, and then publicly announced that he had negotiated a "truce" with ETA, which agreed to terminate all terrorist attacks *in Catalonia* only. The ERC leader's collusion with ETA was denounced throughout the rest of Spain as a self-serving sellout to terrorists. PP strategists during the 2004 electoral campaign sought to capitalize on the PSOE's presence as a coalition partner within the Catalan regional government to discredit the Socialist Party on the eve of the 2004 elections.

Over the following three years, the PP has added to its accusations against the PSOE its alleged weakness in approving revisions in the Catalan autonomy statute that increased that region's autonomy, and in allowing the ERC to return to the Catalan regional government following the 2006 regional elections. The PP's continuing effort to seize upon center–periphery relations and terrorism (which previous Spanish government and opposition parties had dealt with through bipartisan consensus) for partisan purposes, and to challenge the legitimacy of the government, represents a style of opposition politics without precedent in the post-Franco era.

Finally, the polarization that followed the 2004 election is to some degree the result of a shift to the left by the PSOE under Zapatero. In part, this is a product of the configuration of partisan forces present within the parliament that was seated in the aftermath of the 2004 election. Instead of negotiating an agreement with regional parties located near the center of the political spectrum (as had sustained the PSOE government of 1993–6), the Zapatero government depended on parliamentary support from parties of the left – Izquierda Unida (the coalition that includes the PCE), and two left-wing Catalan parties, Esquerra Republicana de Catalunya (ERC) and Iniciativa per Catalunya (which includes the Catalan Communist Party). The inclusion of IU and the Communist Party within this parliamentary alliance (under its new leader, Gaspar Llamazares) is particularly noteworthy, since IU's previous leader, Julio Anguita, had rejected virtually all forms of collaboration with the PSOE in parliament. This pushed the "center of gravity" of the policy process decidedly to the left, in sharp contrast with the moderating influences of parliamentary alliances between 1993 and 2000. The collapse of electoral support for both IU (which lost 3 of its 5 seats in the Congress of Deputies) and the ERC (which lost 5 of its previous 8 seats) in the 2008 election meant that his former partliamentary coalition could not have produced a majority in support of his investiture. The major regional parties (CiU, PNV, and CC) would have been logical alternatives. However, Zapatero was not willing to give in to what he regarded as excessive demands by those regional parties, so he chose to form a minority government in the absence of a standing commitment from other parliamentary parties. His investiture on the second ballot, which requires only a plurality vote, was only the second such occasion when this constitutional provision was utilized (the other being the investiture of Leopoldo Calvo Sotelo in 1981). Accordingly, the second Zapatero government returned to the legislative practices of the UCD governments of 1977–1982, in which parliamentary support for individual bills is secured through shifting *ad hoc* coalitions. It is likely that this will move the PSOE back towards the center in the legislative session that began in April 2008.

In short, strategic and tactical decisions made by political elites have had a marked impact on the degree of polarization of the Spanish party system. In contrast with the first twenty-three years of Spanish democracy, when leaders of all parties sought to position themselves towards the center of the political spectrum (both in order to maximize their share of votes and to help consolidate Spanish democracy), there has been a significant increase in polarization between the two major nationwide parties. In part, this is the result of a change in coalition-building strategies, in which the previous practice of seeking support from moderate regional parties was temporarily replaced by a reliance upon left-wing allies. It was also a direct product of the electoral strategy pursued by the Partido Popular. The mass-level manifestation of this re-polarization will be examined in the following chapter. It remains to be seen if a restoration of the previous coalition-building strategy and a change in the behavioral style and opposition tactics of the PP will reverse this process of polarization.

Parties and party systems in the *Estado de las autonomías*

In the first chapter of this book, we examined the origins of the Spanish state and the multilingual, multicultural, and plurinational character of its population. In chapter 3, we saw how this complex pattern of regional diversity culminated in the creation of a highly decentralized state, the so-called *Estado de las autonomías*. In chapter 1, we explored the nature and origins of social and cultural cleavages in Spain – especially regarding class, religion, and region – that have had an impact on politics and political development in Spain over the past two centuries. We now turn our attention to the extent to which this has affected the parties and regional party systems that have emerged in various parts of Spain since the reestablishment of democracy and decentralization of the political system in the 1970s and 1980s. Although our central concern is with the Basque and Catalan cases, there are relevant non-nationwide parties in most of the other fifteen communities.

In terms of their programs and electoral appeals, some of them are nationalist (like the CiU and ERC in Catalonia, PNV in the Basque Country, and the Bloque Nacionalista Galego [BNG] in Galicia); others are strongly autonomist (like the Unión del Pueblo Navarro [UPN] or the Partido Andaluz [PA] in Andalucía); and others are just regionalist (like the Partido Regionalista de Cantabria [PRC] or the Partido Riojano Progresista [PRP] in La Rioja).

In terms of their organizational strategies and tactics, some of them have established a durable federal structure (such as the Catalan CiU) or permanent pacts with a nationwide party similar to the one between the Bavarian Christian Social Union and Christian Democratic Union (as in the case of UPN and Partido Popular in Navarra); others have reached more *ad hoc* arrangements for specific elections (like the Partido Aragonés and PP in Aragón). These parties play extremely important roles in both national and regional political arenas, particularly insofar as they have participated in coalition governments within their respective CCAA and have provided key parliamentary support for the formation of minority governments in Madrid. Others may lack significant representation in the Spanish parliament, but nonetheless play important roles in the political and institutional arenas of their respective communities.

These differing regional developments defy simple explanations, particularly those which would hypothesize a political trajectory on the basis of social-structural or cultural factors alone. Valencia and the Balearic Islands are noteworthy for the weakness of nationalist and regionalist parties despite the fact that they both followed particular historical trajectories and have distinctive regional languages that are widely spoken by their respective populations. Similarly, the fortunes of regionalist or nationalist parties in Galicia have fluctuated wildly (until the apparent consolidation of the BNG), despite the fact that use of a regional language is more widespread than in any other part of Spain. The Canary Islands are characterized by the existence of both island-specific parties and the archipelago-wide Coalición Canaria, but they do not question the structure of the Spanish state and have given crucial parliamentary support to center-right governments in Madrid. Finally, Navarra is a particularly complex community because of the coexistence of three identities (Navarrese, Spanish, and Basque) and their particular reflection in electoral alignments.

Regional party systems and sub-systems

Spain is a multicultural, multinational, and multilingual society that in some respects is even more complex than other linguistically or nationally heterogeneous countries like Switzerland or Belgium. This complexity – which, as explained in chapter 1, became more evident in the nineteenth century with the irruption of nationalist parties – contributed to the crises of the Second Republic in the 1930s, and resurfaced during the transition. In the new democracy, the regional cleavage has been manifested in several aspects of electoral behavior and party systems.

- First, in the emergence of *regional voting* – that is, significant variations in the distribution of the vote across most communities.
- Second, in the presence of strong nationalist parties in a few communities and a wide variety of regionalist parties in nearly all the rest.
- And third, in the asymmetric presence of the regional cleavage that has given rise to the multi-layered character of the Spanish party systems, including a nationwide party system and several regional party systems and sub-systems.

The resulting mosaic has been labeled the *electoral Spains*, in reference to the great diversity of patterns of party competition in the different communities.

Regional differences in electoral preference

Figure 4.7 presents two types of data that illustrate the extent of regional variations in electoral behavior. The simpler of the two presents the average of the vote within each autonomous community for regionalist and nationalist parties in the nine general elections held between 1977 and 2004. A more complex indicator measures the electoral distinctiveness of each autonomous community: the Index of Regional Voting measures the extent to which electoral support

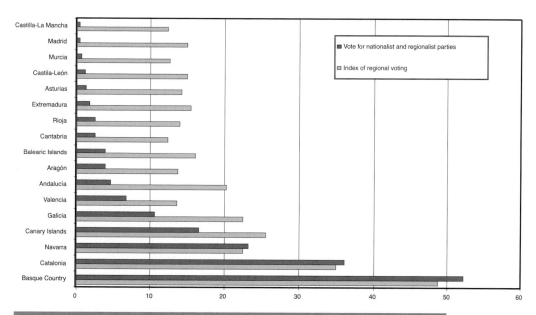

Figure 4.7 Index of regional voting and vote for nationalist and regionalist parties (in percentages)

for each party deviates from its nationwide average level of support. It is calculated by subtracting the percentage of the vote received by each party within each region from the percentage of the vote that it received nationwide, then by adding together the absolute values of those differences and dividing by two. A high score can result from levels of electoral support for nationwide parties that depart markedly from the nationwide average level of support for each party (e.g., if a region were much more conservative or much farther to the left than the country as a whole). But it would also result from purely regional parties receiving a large percentage of the vote in a particular region. In either case, this figure provides a general indication of the distinctiveness of partisan preferences within each region. Nearly all the communities have high indices, which, moreover, have remained remarkably stable (in 1977, for example, the mean of regional voting was 21.7, while in 1996 it was 17.1). In comparative terms, the Spanish levels of regional voting are among the highest in Europe: nearly all the autonomous communities score higher than the overall mean of 13.6 for 118 regions of eleven European countries between 1979 and 1993.

The distinctiveness of regional voting is particularly high in those communities with nationalist or regionalist parties. No other European region (except for the exceptional case of Northern Ireland) surpasses the percentages found in the Basque Country or Catalonia, and no European country has as many regions in which the non-nationwide parties are as significant as Spain. Moreover, the nationwide share of the vote for nationalist and regionalist parties has increased somewhat over time (from 9.7 in the 1977 elections, to 12.7 in 1993, and to 10.9 in

1996), and has always been higher in elections for the autonomous communities' regional parliaments.

Regional party systems and sub-systems

The regional cleavage is particularly deep in the Basque Country, Catalonia, and Navarra, where a number of nationalist parties ranging from the extreme left to the center right compete with one another and with nationwide parties. Indeed, these autonomous communities have distinct regional party systems rooted in historical, cultural, and political features that have generated conflictive perceptions of national identities. In other communities lacking such deep historical traditions, regionalist parties have benefited from the opportunities offered by the decentralization process and the institutional consolidation of the *Estado de las autonomías*. Political decentralization has given nationalist parties and regionalist entrepreneurs the possibility to compete successfully with the nationwide parties, to use the political resources generated by the new regional government bureaucracies, and to foster national and regional identities. In some instances, this has provided incentives for the demagogic articulation of claims of relative deprivation with respect to other communities and the central government.

The dynamics of partisan competition varies substantially from one region to another. Table 4.4 illustrates three dimensions of these competitive dynamics in 1996, relating to the number of parties within each party system or sub-system, their respective placements on the left-right scale, and the extent to which their supporters regard themselves as nationalist or regionalist. In the Basque Country, Catalonia and, to a lesser extent, Navarra, both the number of parties and their patterns of interaction clearly diverge from the general pattern of the nationwide party system. In these regional party systems, electoral support for nationwide parties is relatively weak, and several regional parties, with both distinctive ideological and nationalistic profiles, receive considerable electoral support. In the Basque Country and Catalonia, moreover, regional and nationwide elections are conducted at different times from all the other CCAA (which hold regional and municipal elections on the same day), and nationalist parties have dominated or held important roles in regional governments that control substantial resources.

Several other regions of Spain can be regarded as having nationwide party *sub*-systems. These differ from the more distinctive regional party systems of Catalonia, Navarra, and the Basque Country insofar as the degree of party system fragmentation is lower and the dynamics of inter-party competition are simplified by the absence of a strong nationalist cleavage. Accordingly, these sub-systems tend to reproduce the general patterns of the state-wide party system, albeit with some minor modifications.

These different patterns of partisan competition have a significant institutional impact with regard to the governments and parliaments of the autonomous communities, as can be seen in table 4.5. Some nationalist parties may play minor roles in the Spanish Congress of Deputies, but within their

Table 4.4 Party systems and party sub-systems in Spain, 1996[a]

	Nationwide parties				Nationalist parties				Regionalist parties			
	Party	Vote	Ideology	Nationalism/ regionalism	Party	Vote	Ideology	Nationalism/ regionalism	Party	Vote	Ideology	Nationalism/ regionalism
Party systems												
Spain	IU	10.6	2.9	5.5								
	PSOE	37.5	3.7	6.1								
	PP	38.8	6.5	7.2								
Basque Country	IU	9.2	2.7	4.1	HB	12.3	2.5	8.4				
	PSOE	23.6	4.0	5.7	EA	8.2	4.5	7.6				
	PP	18.3	6.2	4.5	PNV	25.0	5.1	7.2				
Catalonia	PSOE	39.3	3.8	5.6	ERC	4.2	2.9	9.0				
	PP	18.0	6.5	5	IC-EV[b]	7.7	3.1	7.1				
					CiU	29.6	5.2	8.1				
Navarra	IU	12.5	3.2	7.6	HB	8.2	2.3	7.1	CDN	5.3	5.9	6.7
	PSOE	30.2	3.5	6.8	EA	3.8	4.7	9.4				
	PP-UPN	36.8	7.4	7.8								
Party sub-systems												
Galicia	IU	3.7	2.5	5.8	BNG	10.1	2.9	7.0				
	PSOE	33.0	3.7	5.8								
	PP	48.5	6.6	5.9								
Andalucía	IU	13.5	2.7	7.0					PA	3.1	4.5	7.4
	PSOE	46.5	3.6	7.1								
	PP	35.5	6.2	6.4								

(cont.)

Table 4.4 (*cont.*)

	Nationwide parties				Nationalist parties				Regionalist parties			
	Party	Vote	Ideology	Nationalism/regionalism	Party	Vote	Ideology	Nationalism/regionalism	Party	Vote	Ideology	Nationalism/regionalism
Canary Islands IU		5.5	2.5	7.4					CC	25.2	5.0	7.4
PSOE		29.8	3.9	7.8								
PP		37.7	7.1	7.5								
Valencian Community IU		11.1	2.9	5.7					UV^c	3.5	5.2	6.1
PSOE		38.2	3.7	5.4								
PP		43.8	6.2	5.7								
Madrid IU		16.5	2.9	4.0								
PSOE		31.3	3.7	4.9								
PP		49.3	6.8	5.6								

[a] *Vote* refers to the percentage of valid votes in the general election of 1996; *ideology* refers to the means for voters of each party on ten-point left–right scales; and *nationalism/regionalism* refers also to the means for voters of each party on eleven-point scales in which 0 is minimum and 10 is maximum nationalism (for voters of nationalist parties) or regionalism (for voters of nationwide and regionalist parties). For *Spain* only the nationwide parties have been included despite the representation enjoyed by both nationalist (i.e., HB, BNG, ERC, EA, PNV and CiU) and regionalist (i.e., CC and UV) parties. For the latter parties, percentage of the vote and ideological and nationalism/regionalism means have been calculated at the level of their respective autonomous communities.

[b] Iniciativa per Catalunya-Els Verds (the Greens).

[c] Unió Valenciana, a center-right regionalist party in the Comunidad Valenciana.

Source: Banco de Datos, Centro de Investigaciones Sociológicas.

Table 4.5 Regional parliaments: distribution of seats, number of parties, and type of government, 2005–2008[a]

Community	Parties IU	PSOE	PP	Nationalist or regionalist	Total of seats	Number of parties[b]	Type of government[c]
Basque Country	3	18	15	39[d]	75	7	PNV + EA
Catalonia	12	37	14	69[e]	135	6	PSOE + IU + ERC
Navarra	2	12	22	12[f]	50	6	UPN
Canary Islands		26	15	19[g]	60	3	**CC + PP**
Balearic Islands		20	28	11[h]	59	6	**Unió Mallorquina, Bloc per Mallorca, y Eivissa pel Canvi**
Galicia		25	37	13[i]	75	3	**PSOE + BNG**
Aragón	1	27	22	17[j]	67	5	PSOE + Par
Cantabria		10	17	12[k]	39	3	**PSOE + PRC**
Asturias	4	21	20	0	45	3	**PSOE**
Rioja		14	17	2[l]	33	3	**PP**
Castilla-León		33	48	2[m]	83	3	**PP**
Andalucía	6	56	47	0	109	3	**PSOE**
Valencia		38	54	7[o]	89	3	**PP**
Extremadura		38	27	–	65	2	**PSOE**
Castilla-La Mancha		26	21	–	47	4	**PSOE**
Madrid	11	42	67	–	120	3	**PP**
Murcia	1	15	29	–	45	3	**PP**

[a] Communities are ranked by the percentage of seats obtained by nationalist and regionalist parties. Regional elections were held in 2006 in Catalonia, in 2008 in Andalucía, in 2005 in Galicia, in 2005 in the Basque Country, and in 2007 in the other 13 communities.

[b] Index of effective number of parliamentary parties according to the criteria of Rein Taagepera and Matthew S. Shugart, *Seats and Votes: The Effects and Determinants of Electoral Systems* (New Haven: Yale University Press, 1989).

[c] Bold type denotes majority governments; otherwise they are minority governments.

[d] Euskal Herrietako Alderdi Komunista (formerly Herri Batasunna) (9 seats), Eusko Alkartasuna (7), Partido Nacionalista Vasco (22), and Aralar (1).

[e] Esquerra Republicana de Catalunya (21 seats) and Convergència i Unió (48).

[f] Unión del Pueblo Navarro (in coalition with PP, 22 seats), Centro Democrático de Navarra (2), and Nafarroa Bai (12).

[g] Coalición Canaria (17 seats) and Coalición Canaria Agrupación Herreña Independiente (2).

[h] Partido Socialista de los Socialistas de las Islas Baleares (20 seats), Unió Mallorquina (3), Eivissa pel Camvi (2), and AIPF (1).

[i] Bloque Nacionalista Galego (13).

[j] Partido Aragonés (8 seats) and Chunta Aragonesista (9).

[k] Partido Regionalista de Cantabria (12 seats).

[l] Partido Riojano Progresista.

[m] Unión del Pueblo Leonés.

[n] Partido Andalucista (5).

[o] Compromís pel País Valencià (7).

respective regions they function as governing parties that, in some instances (as in the Basque Country and in Catalonia until 2003), dominated regional politics over two decades or more. Other regional parties may have no significant role to play in Madrid (or not even have representation in the Congress of Deputies), and have a relatively minor impact on governance within their respective regions.

These differing regional patterns of partisan competition have also affected the nature of these parties' participation in politics at the nationwide level. In contrast to the German Free Democratic Party or the Greens (which are held electorally accountable by voters throughout Germany), the nationalist parties of Catalonia and the Basque Country are responsive only to their own electorates. They have little or no interest in entering the Spanish government; indeed, to do so would contradict some of their nationalist positions and allow their nationalist competitors to accuse them of blatant opportunism. They are rewarded by voters, not necessarily for their role in the nationwide politics of Spain, but rather for their representation of the particular interests of their nationalist voters and the political interests of the regional governments they control. Indeed, by remaining outside of the Spanish governments of 1993–6 and 1996–2000, regional parties were able to avoid having to take stands on potentially divisive policy issues that might have alienated segments of their respective electorates, helping them to maintain their claims of representing "all of the people" within their respective nationalist constituencies.

In exchange for casting votes for the formation of the new nationwide government, they were rewarded primarily through transfers of resources and additional government authority from the central to the regional levels of government, in contrast with the more typical pattern of receiving ministerial posts in majority coalition governments. This is not to say that they have not had an impact on policy and politics of the central Spanish government. Since the major regional-nationalist parties are generally centrist with regard to their left–right ideological orientations, they have served to moderate policies adopted and implemented by the governing parties in Madrid – moving the Socialist government of 1993 more towards the center left or center, and similarly restraining the more conservative impulses of the PP government of 1996–2000. In this respect, they have contributed to the centripetal (center-seeking or moderating) drives of Spanish politics at the nationwide level. Their demands for ever greater levels of autonomy, however, in combination with the semi-loyal manner in which they have realized the "blackmail potential" (as described by Giovanni Sartori) inherent in the governing Spanish party's dependence upon their parliamentary support, has exerted a decidedly centrifugal force on the dynamics of center–periphery relations in Spain.

Regional party system fragmentation

In most autonomous communities since 1982, competition has essentially been between the two major nationwide parties, the PSOE and the PP, with some regionalist parties that enjoy representation only at the regional level occasionally playing an important role in the formation of the autonomous governments. Accordingly, most regional party sub-systems can be classified as *imperfect* two-party systems: the "effective number of parties" is very low, electoral preferences are concentrated in support of the PP and the PSOE, and third parties are either marginal or increasingly irrelevant.

Again, the Basque Country and Catalonia stand in sharp contrast. The Basque party system is characterized by "polarized pluralism" (see Box 4.3), while the Catalan case approached that of **a predominant-party system** until 2003, with CiU as the dominant party; since then the party system belongs to the category of moderate pluralist. Moreover, in both cases, nationalist parties enjoy a greater and more influential presence than the nationwide parties in institutional arenas other than the parliament in their respective communities. In table 4.6 the Basque Country and Catalonia are compared with Galicia and Andalucía, the other two communities which share the possibility of holding separate elections and are entitled to the greatest powers and resources in the new *Estado de las autonomías*.

> **A predominant-party system** (as described by political scientist Giovanni Sartori) is one in which one party "outdistances all the others," that is, it obtains a share of seats that is sufficient to form a government supported by an absolute majority or a large plurality in parliament over at least three successive elections, and in which the second largest party receives at least 10 percentage points fewer votes. This is a system within which there is democratic competition, but without electoral competitiveness.

In the Basque case, the profound fragmentation among nationalist and nationwide parties in both the Spanish and the Basque parliaments disappears at the local level: due to the small size of many of the municipalities in the region and the strong nationalist sentiments found in rural areas and many small towns, the nationalist parties enjoy overwhelming superiority. This reflects the very different level of support for the nationwide parties in the large, urban, highly industrialized cities with large Spanish immigrant populations, and in the periphery, where nationalism, even extreme nationalism, holds sway.

The Catalan case differs at the parliamentary level because of the duality between the PSOE's strong presence in the central parliament and the CiU's dominance of the regional parliament. But at the local level the CiU also enjoys a disproportionate presence: once again, the strength of nationalist parties lies in the enormous number of small towns, whereas the PSOE is particularly well established in the industrial zones surrounding Barcelona, which has a substantial immigrant population and where the majority of the population lives. The contrast with Galicia (another region with a distinctive language and some nationalist sentiments) and Andalucía could hardly be greater: in both cases nationwide parties dominate representation at every institutional level.

■ The main regional parties

Let us now explore some of the more important characteristics of the most important regional parties. Given their large number, we must limit our attention to those in the Basque Country, Catalonia, Navarra, and Galicia that have had the greatest impact on politics over the past three decades. These are the Basque

Table 4.6 Presence of nationwide, nationalist and regionalist parties in the autonomous communities of the Basque Country, Catalonia, Galicia, and Andalucía, 2004–2008 (In percentages of the total number of seats assigned to each chamber)

Party	MPs	Senators	Reg. MPs[a]	Mayors	Councilors	Euro MPs[b]
Basque Country						
IU		–	3	0.4	4	
PSOE	50	75	18	7.5	24	
PP	16.7	–	15	1.2	16	
EH (HB)		–	9	13.3	–	
EA		–	–	5.9	7	
PNV/EA	33.3	25	29	50.2	31	1
Aralar	–	–	1	–	–	
(N)	(18)	(12)	(75)	(255)	(2,159)	
Catalonia						
IC	2.1	–	12	1.5	9	
PSOE	53.2	75	37	21.2	32	
PP	15	–	14	1.1	10	
ERC	6.4	–	21	12.8	12	1
CiU	21.3	25	48	44.1	25	1
C-PC[c]	–	–	3	–	–	
(N)	(47)	(16)	(135)	(953)	(8,595)	
Galicia						
IU	–	–	–	–	1	
PSOE	47.8	25	29	33.0	29	
PP	43.5	75	37	50.9	40	
BNG	8.7	–	13	10.1	19	
(N)	(23)	(16)	(75)	(318)	(3,737)	
Andalucía						
IU	–	–	5	7.8	12	
PSOE	59	75	51	63.6	41	
PP	41	25	44	17.3	32	
PA	–	–	–	0.5	6	
(N)	(61)	(32)	(108)	(774)	(8,716)	
Rest of Spain						
IU	0.5	–	4	0.8	3	2
PSOE	25.1	89	41	35.3	35	25
PP	30.8	101	49	48.7	36	24
UPyD[d]	0.3	–	–	–	–	
(N)	(350)	(208)	(785)	(8.111)	(42,923)	(54)

[a] The regional elections in the Basque Country and Galicia were held in 2005, in Catalonia in 2006, and in Andalucía in 2008. For the rest of Spain, they were held only in the 13 communities not included in this table.

[b] Since the country constitutes a single district for European elections, the figures are the actual number of European MPs who belong to each party.

[c] Ciutadans-Partido de la Ciudadanía.

[d] Unión Progreso y Democracia.

Partido Nacionalista Vasco, Eusko Alkartasuna, and the various parties that have supported ETA and demanded independence from Spain (Herri Batasuna, Batasuna, Euskal Herritarrok, and, most recently, Euskal Herrietako Alderdi Komunista and Acción Nacionalista Vasca); the Catalan Convergència i Unió and Esquerra Republicana de Catalunya; the Unión del Pueblo Navarro; and the Bloque Nacionalista Galego.

The Basque Country

We begin this examination of regional parties in the Basque Country, whose party system is the most distinctive from the rest of Spain (as indicated by its score on the Index of Regional Voting) and whose voters give the lowest level of support to nationwide Spanish parties.

Partido Nacionalista Vasco

The Basque Nationalist Party is one of the oldest parties in Spain. It was founded in 1893 by Sabino Arana in reaction against immigration into the rapidly industrializing Basque region by poorer Spaniards from other regions. As we noted in chapter 1 and shall further discuss in the following chapter, this initially led to the formulation of a racial definition of the Basque national identity *vis-à-vis* these so-called *maketos*. Initially, it was a religious and conservative party, as reflected in its slogan, "God and the Old Laws."

The party's ideology and policy demands have evolved substantially since then, but have generally been characterized by chronic ambivalence, particularly with regard to the Basque nation's proper relationship with the Spanish state. In particular, party leaders have adopted stands vacillating between calls for increased autonomy within Spain and outright independence. During the Civil War, the lack of consistency in the party's ideology was worsened due to its support for the Republic (which had granted it self-government authority), and the resulting alliance of this bourgeois, conservative, religious party with socialists, anarchists, and anticlericals. Harsh repression of Basque nationalism, language, and culture under the Franco regime, coupled with another wave of massive immigration as the regional economy grew rapidly in the 1960s, further exacerbated ideological tensions, leading to the creation of the terrorist organization ETA, by young Basque nationalists who found the then clandestine PNV insufficiently aggressive in its pursuit of independence.

The core of the party's ideology and program is Basque nationalism, but continuing ambiguity in its ultimate intentions led to what political scientist Juan Linz has described as a "semi-loyal" stance (see Box 4.1). On the one hand, it collaborated with pro-democratic forces in the transition to democracy and in negotiations over its autonomy statute (the Estatuto de Guernica). On the other hand, it abstained from the parliamentary vote on the 1978 constitution, and encouraged its supporters to abstain from the December 1978 constitutional referendum. Since then, its ambiguity is reflected in its shifting demands regarding more autonomy or independence, as well as in its stance towards ETA's terrorism, which has caused the death of over 800 people since the end of the 1960s. In the late 1990s, for instance, the PNV and EA reached an agreement with political representatives of ETA to exclude non-nationalist Basque parties from the region's political institutions and to push the Spanish state to acknowledge the region's right to self-determination. Finally, under the leadership of Xabier Arzallus and the *lehendakari* (president) Juan José Ibarretxe, it announced its intention to hold a referendum on self-determination following procedures explicitly prohibited by the Spanish constitution and the Basque autonomy statute.

Aside from its Basque nationalism, the party's ideology and programs can generally be characterized as moderately conservative and residually Christian democratic. It is a member of the European Popular Party (Christian democratic) in the European Parliament. Electorally, the party has adopted a catch-all strategy, extending its appeals to all social classes, but within the Basque nationalist camp. It has an extensive organizational structure, with a sizable mass-membership base, a dense network of local party branches, and its own trade union. Prior to a schism in 1986 (which led to the creation of Eusko Alkartasuna [EA] – discussed below), it had a confederal organizational structure, with provincial branches of the party enjoying considerable autonomy, but it has reinforced the authority of its central office since then. Nonetheless, there remains a strong tradition of "sovereignty" on the part of local- and provincial-level organizations in Álava, Guipúzcoa, and Vizcaya.

Its long period of control of the regional government contributed to a *de facto* dual leadership of the party that sometimes gave rise to conflict and inconsistency. The formal head of the party (the president of the Euskadi Buru Batzar [EBB, or executive committee]) controls the party apparatus, while the *lehendakari* (president) of the *comunidad autonóma* presides over extensive regional government institutions and resources. This *de facto* dual leadership has given rise to confusion over questions of accountability to party members and voters. On occasion, it has generated tension and conflict between the two, especially when *lehendakari* Carlos Garaikoetxea clashed with EBB president Xabier Arzallus in the early 1980s; subsequently when Arzallus undermined the collaborative relationship in the late 1980s between *lehendakari* José Antonio Ardanza and the PSOE government in Madrid; and most recently, in 2007, when the new president of the EBB, Josu Jon Imaz – who favored autonomy within the Spanish state and the integration of non-nationalists into Basque political life – was obliged to resign following a confrontation with the *lehendakari* José Antonio Ibarretxe.

Electorally, the PNV has been most successful. It has won every regional election since the establishment of the Basque *comunidad autonóma* in 1980, and every *lehendakari* has been a representative of the party, sometimes as head of coalition governments (with the regional branch of the PSOE or with EA and IU). Its political dominance has allowed it to exert an extraordinary influence over the development of the regional government's institutions: indeed, the region's flag, its anthem, and its symbols are those of the PNV. Over time, regional elections have consolidated into competition between two blocs of parties, pitting *soberanistas* (those parties favoring independence from Spain) against *autonomistas* or

constitucionalistas (those favoring the current or somewhat greater levels of autonomy within the Spanish state). To date, the PNV has always emerged as the largest
party, but the balance of electoral support between the two camps has become
more equal. The PNV has always been the largest *soberanista* party, joined by a
shifting group of smaller parties, including the now defunct Euskadiko Ezkerra,
EA, Herri Batasuna and its successors (to be discussed below), and increasingly IU
(whose Basque regional branch has drifted ever closer to extreme Basque nationalism). The PSOE has always been the largest party in the autonomist camp,
followed by the center-right PP (and prior to 1982, the UCD). This high level of
party system fragmentation and polarization makes the politics in the region a
classic example of "polarized pluralism" (see Box 4.3).

Eusko Alkartasuna

"Basque Solidarity" was created in 1986 as the result of a schism within the
PNV. As noted above, the dual leadership structure gave rise to much tension
and conflict between party president Xabier Arzallus and *lehendakari* Carlos
Garaikoetxea. In addition to personal animosity between these two individuals, they clashed over several serious party and policy matters. Arzallus favored
continuation of the PNV's traditional conservatism and religious commitment,
while Garaikoetxea held more social-democratic sociopolitical values. Arzallus
defended the decentralization of the party and the structure of regional government, while Garaikoetxea preferred to strengthen the Basque autonomous community's authority at the expense of the provinces. Finally, this struggle pitted
the *soberanista* (more militantly nationalist and pro-sovereignty) Arzallus against
the more pragmatic autonomist Garaikoetxea, who had successfully negotiated
the terms of the Basque autonomy statute through face-to-face discussions with
Spanish prime minister Adolfo Suárez.

The schism in 1986 divided the PNV from the top down to its local branch
organizations. Initially, EA was enormously successful, attracting nearly 16% of
the vote in the 1986 regional elections (compared with 24% for the PNV). It has
subsequently declined in electoral support, losing about half of its electorate over
the following decade and a half. Given its electoral weakness and the retirement
from political life by both Arzallus and Garaikoetxea, the PNV and EA have
increasingly collaborated with each other in forming both pre- and post-electoral
coalitions. In the aftermath of the 2005 regional election, for example, they
formed a coalition minority government with Ezker Batua, the regional branch
of Izquierda Unida.

Eusko Alkartasuna is unequivocally a Basque nationalist party, although its
ideology and programmatic demands differ from those of the PNV. With even
greater intensity than the PNV, EA considers the Basque Country as a nation
divided between the Spanish and French states, and calls for the reunification
of these territories as an independent nation-state. And, like the PNV, it believes
that this can be achieved through peaceful negotiations, within the framework
of the European Union, and it rejects the violence of ETA. EA claims to represent

a "third way" between the (until recently) moderate nationalism of the PNV and the radically pro-independence, anti-system Herri Batasuna (HB) and its successor parties).

But unlike the PNV, the electorate of EA is decidedly to the left of center. The party describes itself as modern, progressive, and social-democratic. Accordingly, with regard to its placement on the left–right continuum, it is located (in accord with its self-description as representing a "third way") between the conservative PNV and the extreme left HB. Thus, EA has been able to differentiate itself from its Basque nationalist rivals and survive politically over at least two decades in the very crowded Basque regional party system. Paradoxically, this high level of fragmentation has contributed to the viability of a small party like EA, since the PNV and other parties have found it increasingly indispensable as a coalition partner in forming regional governments.

HB / Batasuna / EH / EHAK / ANV

The extreme-left, ultra-nationalist end of the Basque political continuum has been occupied by parties or electoral coalitions named Herri Batasuna (Unity of the People), Batasuna (Unity), Euskal Herritarrok (Basque Citizens), Euskal Herrietako Alderdi Komunista (Communist Party of the Basque Peoples), or more recently Acción Nacionalista Vasca (Basque Nationalist Action). These political organizations, and several other allied groups or social movements, belong to the so-called *abertzale* (patriot) camp. They all defend in more or less explicit terms the use of terrorist violence (including extortion, blackmail, and assassination) in pursuit of their political objectives. In addition to demanding the creation of an independent Basque nation-state, they share a radical leftist socioeconomic agenda, and they reject democratic forms of participation and conflict regulation. Given their connections with ETA and their repeated violations of the democratic "rules of the game," one after another has been recently declared illegal by Spanish courts and prohibited from running candidates for office. But like the elusive furry creature in the carnival game Whack-a-Mole, just as one organization is forced underground, another one with a different name pops up to take its place.

Herri Batasuna was born in April 1978 as the product of a schism within Euskadiko Ezkerra (Basque Left). The EE deputy in the Congress of Deputies, Francisco Letamendía, had consistently taken the most extreme stands in opposition to the Spanish constitution that was being negotiated at that time, alienating more moderate, pragmatic members of EE. HB emerged as a Marxist-Leninist party that advocated a "no" vote in the constitutional referendum, and actively worked for rejection of the constitution in the 1978 referendum. It also opposed the Basque autonomy statute of 1979 on the grounds that it did not acknowledge the right of Basque self-determination, and it did not include Navarra as an integral part of the Basque regional community. Even though HB regularly fielded candidates in both regional and nationwide elections (receiving about 15% of the vote in most of those contests), its elected representatives refused to take their seats in the Spanish parliament. The party's anti-system stance was further manifested in its explicit approval of political violence as a legitimate form of political participation and as the principal means of securing independence. While party representatives sometimes deny that they explicitly endorse terrorism, they do not deny that HB "does not" (as stated by Letamendía) "rule out any form of struggle which could bring about an advance for the people."

HB's anti-system stance and its continuing connections with ETA-militar, the most extreme and violent wing of the Basque terrorist organization, stand in contrast with what remained of Euskadiko Ezkerra following the schism. EE (which, itself, had been linked with ETA-político-militar) urged a "yes" vote in the 1979 autonomy referendum, its elected deputies played active roles in both the Basque and Spanish parliamentary bodies, after 1981 they explicitly denounced ETA's terrorist violence, and the party subsequently merged with the Basque branch of the PSOE. Herri Batasuna's relationship with ETA also contrasts with that between Sinn Fein and the IRA in Northern Ireland, in which the party controlled the strategy of the terrorist organization. In the Basque case, it is the reverse: the political front organization (whatever its name at the time) follows the lead of ETA. This has had a significant impact on Spanish politics, as in 2005, when ETA declared a ceasefire and attempted to initiate negotiations with the central government. The representatives of Batasuna were not authorized to make binding commitments that might have led to a permanent settlement of conflict within the region. Instead, ETA resumed its campaign of terrorist violence in December 2006 with the killing of two in Madrid.

Catalonia

The second most distinctive regional party system is that of Catalonia. It includes major nationalist parties or coalitions – Convergència i Unió (CiU, Convergence and Union) and the Esquerra Republicana de Catalunya (ERC, Republican Left of Catalonia) – but, in addition, the regional branches of two major nationwide parties have been substantially "catalanized." The region's communist party, the Partit Socialista Unificat de Catalunya [PSUC, Unified Socialist Party of Catalonia], has enjoyed a substantial level of autonomy from the PCE ever since the Second Republic. This regional identity has been maintained following the coalition between the communist party and various post-materialist groups that formed Izquierda Unida: in Catalonia, it is named Iniciativa per Catalunya (IC, Initiative for Catalonia). Even more significantly, the Partit dels Socialistes de Catalunya (PSC) was formed in 1978 through the merger of the regional branch of the PSOE (which received considerable support from the substantial immigrant population from other parts of Spain) and the two factions of a Catalan party, the PSC-Congrés and the PSC-Reagrupament. Catalan nationalists have increasingly dominated the leadership of the PSC, and at times (as in negotiations over an expansion of the Catalan autonomy statute in 2006) have more stridently articulated the demand for greater regional autonomy than has the more explicitly nationalistic CiU.

In contrast with the Basque Country, Catalan politics is not so highly fragmented or polarized. Its party system is moderately pluralistic, and extremism has been generally absent, despite the great importance of the regional cleavage and the widespread embrace of a Catalan nationalist identity. As we shall argue in the following chapter, this is in part a reflection of the multiple, overlapping nature of national identity in the region, in which the great majority of the population regard themselves as both Spanish and Catalan, and do not regard Catalan nationalism as incompatible with the region's continuation within the Spanish state.

Convergència i Unió

The CiU is structurally unique in Spain. Like the German CDU and its Bavarian ally, the CSU, it is a durable coalition between parties that maintain their own organizations. One of these, Convergència Democràtica de Catalunya [CDC, Democratic Convergence of Catalonia], was founded in 1974 in clandestine opposition to the Franco regime. The other, Unió Democràtica de Catalunya (UDC, Democratic Union of Catalonia), is a centrist Christian democratic party that dates from the Second Republic. These two parties formed the CiU coalition in 1978, and dominated the Catalan regional government – the Generalitat – from its founding in 1980 until 2003 under the leadership of Jordi Pujol, the founder of the CDC. The CiU coalition has presented a common slate of candidates (with 75% from the CDC and 25% from the UDC) for all elections, and orchestrates parliamentary collaboration between representatives of the two parties between elections. In the early 1990s, tension between the two parties arose over the CDC's preference for the creation of a unified party structure dominated by the CDC. This was resolved through a compromise that established a federal relationship between the two parties, but which continued the leadership of the party under a CDC representative (Artur Mas) when Pujol retired in 2003.

The CDC is a moderate nationalist party that derives most of its support from the middle class. It has some religious roots, but its primary ideological stance is centrist or center right, drawing eclectically from the liberalism and social democracy of the 1970s, as well as the Catalan conservatism of the 1930s. In short, it is a moderate, nationalist catch-all party. Despite its ideological heterodoxy (and unlike the now defunct UCD), there have been no significant intra-party conflicts. The more militantly Catalan-nationalist stance of some younger party activists has been effectively utilized by Generalitat president Pujol to enhance his bargaining leverage in his negotiations with the Spanish central government.

CiU has been extremely successful electorally, both in dominating the regional government for over two decades, but also in politics at the nationwide level. One of the unusual features of Catalan electoral behavior is the so-called "dual vote," through which the CiU has always won elections to the regional parliament, while the PSC-PSOE has received the largest share of the vote in general elections for the Congress of Deputies. Its over two decades of domination of the Generalitat came to an end in 2003 with the formation of a coalition government that included the PSC, ERC, and IC. CiU once again won the largest share of the vote in the early regional elections in 2006, receiving nearly 5% more votes than the PSC. Nonetheless, the coalition of left and center-left parties retained control of the regional government.

Given its moderation and pragmatism, the CiU has been a crucial partner with both the PSOE and the PP in supporting Spanish governments. Indeed, under the 1993–6 PSOE government of Felipe González, the influence of Generalitat President Pujol was so great that he was regarded in the press as the "vice-president of the government," even though he occupied no seat in the Congress of Deputies. And in the final stages of negotiations over revisions in the Catalan autonomy statute in 2006, the Socialist government of José Luis Rodríguez Zapatero preferred to negotiate with representatives of the CiU rather than with the Socialist president of the Generalitat.

Esquerra Republicana de Catalunya

The ERC was formed in 1931, and dominated Catalan politics during the Second Republic. Under the Franco regime, the Catalan government in exile was often headed by ERC leaders, such as Josep Tarradellas, who was elected as President of the Generalitat (in exile) in 1959. His return to Spain following the death of Francisco Franco and his appointment by Spanish prime minister Adolfo Suárez as interim head of the Catalan "preautonomy" government was of great symbolic importance, contributing to the legitimation of the transition to democracy within the region and, over the long term, to the moderation of Catalan nationalism.

Nonetheless, throughout the current democratic era, the ERC has been electorally weak (receiving less than 6% of the regional vote in Spanish elections from 1977 through 2000), and its ideology is relatively radical. The party declares itself to be of the non-Marxist left, embraces post-materialist and ecological issues, and favors establishing a republic (alone, in this respect, among all significant parties in Spain) and an independent Catalan nation-state, consisting of the so-called Països Catalans (Catalan Countries) including not only the current autonomous community of Catalonia, but also the communities of Valencia and the Balearic Islands, as well as parts of Aragón, the French region of Rousillon, Andorra, and the city of Algher in Sardinia, Italy. It pledges to pursue this nation-state-building via peaceful means, through democratic institutions, and within the framework of the European Union, and it rejects violence as a political instrument.

Following a protracted series of internal crises and changes of leadership, in the mid 1990s the party improved its electoral fortunes under the leadership of Josep Lluís Carod Rivera. It became the third party in the region (receiving over 16% of the vote in the 2003 regional elections and nearly 15% in 2006), but still well behind the CiU and PSC-PSOE. But the lack of parliamentary majorities for those parties made it possible for the ERC to serve as an essential coalition partner for both the CiU and the PSC-PSOE. Its acceptability to both of the major parties in the region as a coalition partner is enhanced by the nature of its ideology: its nationalism appeals to the radical wing of the CiU, and its leftist orientation is consistent with the traditional stance of the Socialist Party.

Its participation in Catalan regional governments and its support in the Spanish Congress of Deputies for the Socialist government of Rodríguez Zapatero have led to tensions within the party's leadership and with the radical sector of the party, which favors an organizational style including more direct democracy. This has led the party to adopt a series of puzzling stands, including its refusal to support the revised autonomy statute in the 2006 referendum. The most damaging of these stands (as described earlier in this chapter) was the negotiation by party leader Carod of a truce with ETA that was restricted exclusively to the Catalan region. This subjected the party (and its PSOE coalition ally) to attacks by the PP, during the 2004 election, alleging that it is a disloyal collaborator with Basque terrorism. Over the long term, the ERC's erratic and semi-loyal behavior alienated many of its supporters. Indeed, in the 2008 election, the ERC lost half of the votes it had received four years earlier (declining from 2.5% of the nationwide total to 1.2%), and its representation in the Congress of Deputies shrank from 8 to 3.

Galicia

One of the most striking aspects of politics in Galicia over the past century is the weakness of nationalistic sentiments and political parties or movements, despite the fact that nearly 90% of its population speaks Galego (which, as we saw in chapter 1, is a dialect of Portuguese). Even though there were some regionalist or nationalist groups within the region during the Second Republic, they received low levels of electoral support.

This does not mean that regionalist or nationalist sentiments are absent. An effort to grant Galicia autonomy via the "slow route" (under article 143 of the constitution) provoked a rebellion within the regional branch of the PSOE that forced the Spanish government to place the region's autonomy process on the fast track via article 151. What was most remarkable was the conversion to an aggressive regionalism on the part of its regional government (Xunta) president Manuel Fraga, who had been the founder of the Spanish nationalist Alianza Popular. Over time, regionalism has been embraced by leaders of both major parties, while a significant minority of the population (17% in 2005) regard themselves as belonging to a "nation." This has culminated in the emergence of an electorally significant nationalist party which, despite its radical origins, has become more moderate and has served in regional coalition governments.

Bloque Nacionalista Galego

The BNG began in the 1980s as a leftist, anti-system nationalist party, which received only 4% of the vote in the 1985 regional elections. It was supported primarily by young, well-educated male voters of the left to extreme left, who favored recognition of Galicia as a nation of the same kind as Catalonia and the Basque country. Over time, however, the BNG absorbed a number of smaller nationalist groups, and its bases of support have broadened considerably. The party has become a catch-all party of the nationalist left whose members have a wide variety of ideological orientations, from Maoism and Marxism to social democracy, environmentalism, pacifism, feminism, anti-militarism, and "Euroskepticism." Its electoral strategy has been successful in converting the party to the third largest in the region, receiving nearly 19% of the vote in the 2005 regional election.

This broadening of the nature and appeals of the party has been accompanied by a moderation that included the abandonment of its former anti-system stance. In 1990 it also abandoned its earlier support for independence, and its primary political objectives are expansion of the powers of the regional government and the advancement of the regional language. It now works entirely within the institutional rules of Spanish democracy, and, accordingly, has become a regional government coalition partner of the Partido Socialista de Galicia (the regional branch of the PSOE). In addition, it supported the investiture of the PSOE government of José Luis Rodríguez Zapatero in the Spanish Congress of Deputies in 2004.

Navarra

Perhaps the most complex and fragmented region of Spain is Navarra. This is largely due to deeply rooted conflicts over national identity within this region bordering on the Basque Country. Much of the population residing in the north speak Basque and identify themselves as Basque. Over three quarters of the population, however, do not speak Basque, firmly reject assertions that they belong to the Basque region either politically or culturally, and identify themselves as either *Navarros* or as both Spanish and *Navarros*. Indeed, historically there never was a link between the two. As noted in chapter 1, the Basque region was part of the Kingdom of Castilla-León, while Navarra was a separate kingdom until 1512, long after Ferdinand and Isabella had united Castilla-León with the confederal Kingdom of Aragón to create Spain. Subsequently, the Basque region and Navarra had their own separate *fueros* (charters of autonomy within the Spanish state). In the Civil War of 1936–9, moreover, most Basques fought on the side of the Republic, while the conservative Carlist Traditionalists who dominated politics in Navarra supported Franco's rebellion.

These conflicting traditions and national identities have had a substantial impact on politics under the current democratic regime. During negotiations over the constitution and the Basque regional autonomy statute, Basque nationalists demanded that Navarra be included within the Basque autonomous community (and aspire ultimately to have it incorporated within an independent Basque nation-state). Instead, Navarra received its own autonomy statute, awkwardly named the *Ley Orgánica de Reintegración y Amejoramiento del Régimen Foral* (Organic Law for the Reintegration and Improvement of the region's *Fuero*), which dates back to legislation approved in 1839 and 1841, at the end of the First Carlist War (1833–40). However, a transitional disposition of the Spanish constitution allows for the possible incorporation of Navarra within the Basque autonomous community. While this provision may have temporarily satisfied the PNV during a very difficult stage of the Spanish transition to democracy, it has fueled disputes over the status of the region ever since.

This historic conflict is reflected in the party system of the region today. Between 15 and 20% of the region's voters have regularly cast ballots for Basque nationalist parties (the PNV, Eusko Alkartasuna, Euskadiko Ezkerra, and Herri Batasuna and its successors). A measure of the extent of polarization over this cleavage is that the ultra-nationalist, anti-system HB has always far outdistanced the more moderate Basque nationalist parties in terms of electoral support. The PSOE is strong within the region (and has often participated in regional governments), and Izquierda Unida and some smaller Spanish parties also receive electoral support. The most noteworthy feature of the regional party system is that, following the collapse of the UCD in 1982, the center right was dominated by a regional party, the Unión del Pueblo Navarro (UPN, Union of the Navarrese People). Neither Alianza Popular nor its successor Partido Popular succeeded in establishing viable autonomous party branches within the region (receiving less than 7% of the vote in the 1977 election, and not fielding its own candidates since that time). Instead, the UPN has formed a durable alliance with the AP/PP, much as the Bavarian Christian Social Union collaborates with the German Christian Democratic Union, but with a distinction between regional and nationwide elections. Candidates in regional elections run under the UPN party label, but in national and European elections they are listed as representing the PP. The UPN politicians elected to the Spanish parliament through this procedure are fully integrated within the PP delegation.

Unión del Pueblo Navarro

The UPN was created in 1979 as a product of a schism within the regional branch of the UCD (which received 30–32% of the vote in the first two democratic elections). The schism was triggered by the concession made by prime minister Adolfo Suárez to the PNV in the form of a transitional disposition added to the 1978 constitution that allowed a potential merger between Navarra and the Basque Country. This is the only statement allowing such an institutional arrangement between regions. This infuriated many UCD leaders and voters within the region, who felt that they had been "sold out" by their party leaders in Madrid. The defense of the region's interests and its autonomous status, they concluded, could be maintained only by a regionalist party. With the demise of the UCD in 1982, a substantial political space near the center to center right of the political spectrum was opened up, and was quickly filled by the UPN. Fully two thirds of the rapidly collapsing UCD's regional leaders entered the UPN, and quickly established the new party as the region's second largest (receiving nearly 25% of the vote in 1982, compared with the UCD's 10%). While the PSOE won the largest share of the vote within the region in the 1982 and 1986 general elections, by 1989 the UPN had become the largest party in the region, and since the mid 1990s it has dominated the region's government.

The UPN is a conservative party that defines itself as "*navarrista.*" This regionalist party has consistently opposed demands for the incorporation of Navarra within the Basque region, and has called for repeal of the transitional disposition through a reform of the Spanish constitution. In defense of the language, culture, and identity of the region, it has opposed demands from the Basque-Navarrese minority for the strengthening of the Basque language in public life and, especially, in the region's education system.

■ Summary

In this chapter we have explored the basic characteristics of the Spanish party system, as well as of its major parties. We have seen that

- At the national level, there is a low level of fragmentation, facilitating the formation of stable, single-party governments. Spain's electoral system has contributed substantially to this low level of party system fragmentation.
- Some regional party systems, however, are characterized by higher levels of fragmentation.
- At the national level, electoral politics has been characterized by a low level of polarization, and competition over formation of new governments has always pitted a catch-all party of the center left against a catch-all party of the center right. Since 2000, however, there has been a significant polarization between those two parties as a result of changes in electoral and parliamentary strategies and tactics of political elites.
- Regional party systems vary considerably, with the Basque and Navarrese party systems highly polarized, the Catalan party system more moderately polarized (although support for higher levels of autonomy and even independence have increased in recent years), and the other regional party systems or sub-systems characterized by moderation.
- Electoral volatility was extremely high in 1982, but has been low in most other elections, particularly with regard to "inter-bloc" volatility (i.e., shifts across the barrier separating parties of the left from parties of the right).
- Some parties (particularly the PSOE and AP/PP, and the major regional parties) have adapted to evolving political circumstances and have successfully stabilized their electoral bases of support, while others (especially the UCD and PCE) failed to do so.

■ Further reading

Acha, Beatriz, and Santiago Pérez-Nievas, "Moderate Nationalist Parties in the Basque Country," in Lieven de Winter and Huri Türsan, eds., *Regionalist Parties in Western Europe* (London: Routledge, 1998)

Alcántara, Manuel, and Antonia Martínez, eds., *Las elecciones autonómicas en España: 1980–1997* (Madrid, Centro de Investigaciones Sociológicas [CIS], 1998)

Astudillo, Javier, and Elena García-Guereta, "If It Isn't Broken, Don't Fix It: The Spanish Popular Party in Power," in Anna Bosco and Leonardo

Morlino, eds., *Party Change in Southern Europe* (London and New York: Routledge, 2007)

de Winter, Lieven, Margarita Gómez-Reino, and Peter Lynch, eds., *Autonomist Parties in Europe: Identity Politics and the Revival of the Territorial Cleavage* (Barcelona: Institut de Ciències Polítiques i Socials, 2007)

Diamandouros, P. Nikiforos, and Richard Gunther, eds., *Parties, Politics, and Democracy in the New Southern Europe* (Baltimore: Johns Hopkins University Press, 2001)

Gunther, Richard, José Ramón Montero, and Joan Botella, "Elections and Parties," in Gunther, Montero, and Botella, *Democracy in Modern Spain* (New Haven: Yale University Press, 2004)

Gunther, Richard, Giacomo Sani, and Goldie Shabad, *Spain After Franco: The Making of a Competitive Party System* (Berkeley: University of California Press, 1986)

Linz, Juan J., and José R. Montero, eds., *Crisis y cambio: electores y partidos en la España de los años ochenta* (Madrid: Centro de Estudios Constitucionales, 1986)

"The Party Systems of Spain: Old Cleavages and New Challenges," in Lauri Karvonen and Stein Kuhnle, eds., *Party Systems and Voter Alignments Revisited* (London: Routledge, 2001)

Marcet, Joan, *Convergència Democràtica de Catalunya* (Madrid: CIS, 1987)

Marcet, Joan, and Jordi Argelaguet, "Nationalist Parties in Catalonia," in Lieven de Winter and Huri Türsan, eds., *Regionalist Parties in Western Europe* (London: Routledge, 1998)

Méndez, Mónica, "Turning the Page: Crisis and Transformation of the Spanish Socialist Party," in Anna Bosco and Leonardo Morlino, eds., *Party Change in Southern Europe* (London and New York: Routledge, 2007)

Montero, José Ramón, Ignacio Lago, and Mariano Torcal, eds., *Elecciones generales 2004* (Madrid: Centro de Investigaciones Sociológicas 2007)

Morlino, Leonardo, *Democracy Between Consolidation and Crisis. Parties, Groups, and Citizens in Southern Europe* (Oxford: Oxford University Press, 1998)

■ Websites

www.psoe.es	PSOE
www.pp.es	Partido Popular
www.izquierda-unida.es	Izquierda Unida
www.nodo50.org/pce/	Partido Comunista de España
www.ciu.cat	Convergència i Unió
www.esquerra.cat	Esquerra Republicana de Catalunya
www.iniciativa.cat	Iniciativa per Catalunya
www.eaj-pnv.eu	Partido Nacionalista Vasco
www.euskoalkartasuna.org	Eusko Alkartasuna
www.ehak-english.blogspot.com	EHAK
www.coalicioncanaria.org	Coalición Canaria
www.bng-galiza.org	Bloque Nacionalista Galego
www.upn.org	Unión del Pueblo Navarro

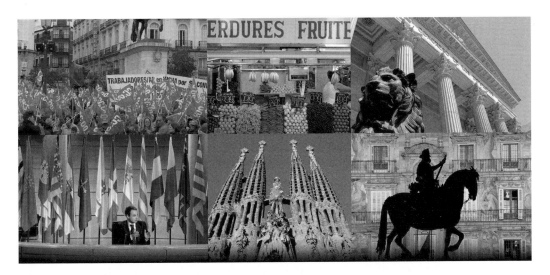

5   Citizens and politics in Spain

In previous chapters, we have seen that many factors contributed to the transition to democracy after Franco's death in 1975, and to the stability of the democratic system in the decades that followed. Crucial in this respect was the development of a moderate party system, the behavior of political elites (especially King Juan Carlos and the leaders of the major parties), and the adoption of an electoral system that encouraged both democratic representation of the electorate and the emergence of stable governments. Decentralization of the centralized and authoritarian state created by Franco was also important.

However, political leaders can be successful only if the institutions operate in a way that meets with the approval of citizens, and if parties and elites reflect the preferences of voters. In this chapter, therefore, we shall examine politics in Spain at the level of ordinary citizens – particularly with regard to their attitudes, organizational affiliations, and patterns of political behavior. What is the role of the general public in Spanish politics? Have the old ideas of the Franco regime been replaced by attitudes and behavior that support democracy? How strong is support for democracy today? What impact have civic organizations and secondary associations had on the transition to democracy? How has the existence of regional languages and identities been reconciled with national integration and the current structure of the state? What is the relationship between the social and economic structure of modern Spain and the political attitudes and behavior of its citizens?

In an effort to answer these and related questions, this chapter will explore the following issues:

- the long-term effects of the Franco regime's anti-democratic propaganda on current mass attitudes towards democracy;
- the strength of popular support for democracy;
- the role of civic organizations and secondary associations;
- the role of public opinion and behavior in the democratic system, especially with regard to ideological polarization and traditionally divisive social cleavages; and
- the varying relationships between regional identities and "Spanish" identity.

■ Political institutions, leaders, and citizens

As we saw in the preceding chapter, the party system of Spain today does not reflect any of the characteristics that doomed democratic politics under the Second Republic. At the national level, there are no anti-system parties to challenge the legitimacy of the democratic regime. The level of fragmentation of the parliamentary party system is moderate, facilitating the formation of single-party governments with the capacity to remain in office over extended periods of time. Polarization among parties is relatively moderate, certainly compared with the party system of the Second Republic. Perhaps most importantly in that regard, all nationwide parties behaved in an extremely restrained and constructive manner during the critical early stages of establishing a new democratic regime. That contributed greatly to the consolidation of a fully democratic and legitimate political system in Spain today. The only partial exceptions to this pattern can be seen, as we explained in chapter 4, in the Basque Country, where much higher levels of polarization and partisan fragmentation have emerged, as well as some anti-system parties and social movements.

Explaining successful democratization

In previous chapters, we argued that these developments were, in part, consequences of political institutions set in place following the transition to democracy, as well as the behavior of political elites.

- **Elite norms and behavior.** Key political elites played an extremely important role in establishing the stable democracy that has enabled Spain to join the mainstream of Western European countries. The constructive role of King Juan Carlos was crucial during the earliest stages of dismantling the former authoritarian regime and setting in motion the transition to democracy, as well as in defending democracy from the attempted coup in February 1981. The leaders of Spain's principal political parties also played constructive roles in overcoming the divisions and mutual hostilities of the past, setting Spain firmly on the path of peaceful democratic competition.

- **Burying past grievances**. Despite the bloodletting of the Civil War (1936–9) and the political repression of the Franco regime (1939–75), party elites behaved in accord with an informal and unspoken agreement to "forget the past" and avoid recriminations that could have revived potentially destabilizing, deep-seated animosities – as occurred for instance in the early 1990s in post-Tito Yugoslavia.
- **The electoral law** contributed substantially to these generally positive outcomes. It reduced the potential for fragmentation of the parliamentary party system, thereby facilitating the formation of stable governments, while at the same time it gave significant political forces that had opposed the Franco regime (most importantly the communists, socialists, and Basque and Catalan nationalists) a fair share of representation in parliament during the crafting of a new democratic constitution.
- **Moderate catch-all parties.** Party leaders also contributed to the moderation of partisan conflict in Spain by creating "catch-all" parties, focusing their electoral appeals on moderate voters near the center of the political spectrum, and generally avoiding potentially divisive ideological or programmatic stands.
- **Decentralization** of the state satisfied the demands for self-government of most regions of Spain – a minority within the Basque Country being the principal exception – thereby removing a potential obstacle to legitimation and consolidation of the new regime. But it also created a highly complex state structure in which regionalist and nationalist party leaders have activated the regional cleavage. In consequence, conflicts over the distribution of political authority and resources between center and periphery, as well as the emergence of distinctive regional party systems and sub-systems, have become distinctive features of the process of political decentralization.

The role of the mass public

Political leaders do not operate in a vacuum, however. In this chapter we will see that the positive outcome of the democratization process was, in part, a reflection of substantial changes in Spanish society that had taken place over the previous decades. Most importantly, by the late 1970s **economic development** had transformed the class structure of Spain, thereby reducing the potential for polarized conflict between class-based parties of the left and right. Indeed, ever since the first democratic election in 1977, the great majority of Spaniards have regarded themselves as moderate, with the largest bloc placing themselves just to the left of center on the ideological spectrum. We will also see that a profound process of **secularization**, coupled with a decision by Church leaders in the critical early stages of the democratic transition to avoid entanglements with specific parties, reduced the potential for the revival of a seriously disruptive religious cleavage.

The effects of these mass-level factors on politics are not, in themselves, direct or automatic. Their impact is dependent on how they interact with elites and institutions. Specifically, the attitudes and behavioral predilections of ordinary citizens set the context for the ways in which institutions operate and serve as the building blocks of partisan politics. Similarly, the strategies of and interactions among elites and partisan activists have a powerful impact in shaping citizen behavior.

Indeed, these interactions among elites and partisan institutions, and between ordinary citizens and actors at the "macro level" of the political system, can transform the societal context within which politics unfolds. At the national level, "the politics of consensus" reinforced the initial moderation of most Spaniards, and directly contributed to consolidation of the democratic regime and overwhelming support for its institutions and rules of the game. In the Basque Country, in contrast, the "dialectic of rocks, clubs, and tear gas" that we described in chapter 2 greatly polarized society, contributing to the progressive fragmentation of parties and secondary associations. As a result, a significant minority rejects the legitimacy of the current democratic regime and the state itself. In short, a self-reinforcing cycle of political violence and polarization helped to transform the very political culture of that region.

Aside from this partial regional exception, our overall conclusion is that a fully democratic political culture has been successfully established in all other sections of the Spanish population. This observation, in turn, raises an interesting and important question about citizen attitudes towards democracy in Spain: to what extent did nearly forty years of anti-democratic political socialization under the Franco regime instill anti-democratic attitudes in the Spanish population, and to what extent does that authoritarian interlude continue to cast a long shadow over citizen participation in Spain's current democracy?

■ Attitudes towards democracy

Over the course of nearly four decades, the Franco regime disseminated attitudes that were hostile towards democracy. It used its control of education and mass communications to articulate a loose cluster of ideas involving nationalism, patriotism, anti-liberalism, anti-communism, primordial conservatism, and a rejection of democracy.

The most widely used "civics textbook" of the time (*El hombre y la sociedad*), which was required reading in secondary education, explicitly rejected liberal democratic concepts of universal suffrage as a basis of regime legitimacy and as a method of elite recruitment. Universal suffrage was declared to be unacceptable because it included no provisions guaranteeing continued adherence to "natural law" and divine law. It was also rejected on the grounds that, according to the precepts of corporatist thought, it was inherently disruptive of social order, since political parties unnecessarily divided the nation and were dangerous. Support for the regime was to be based, instead, on its alleged roots in Spanish Catholic

Box 5.1

Organic corporatism and "representation"

The more extreme forms of corporatism used the organic metaphor of the human body (hence, "organic corporatism") to characterize society. This was a very useful concept for fascist authoritarian or totalitarian rulers in the 1930s and 1940s, since it clearly implied that there could be only one brain (hence, the "leadership principle"), and all of the other cells in the body were supposed to follow orders issued from that brain. There was to be no challenge to the leader, and no institutionalized contestation for power (e.g., through democratic elections). Accordingly, whatever "representation" of the people was allowed by the political system would be through the "natural organs" of society – through the occupationally based "syndicates" of the regime, through the single party of the regime (the National Movement), through such social institutions as the universities, and (after 1967) through representatives of families. Accordingly, "organic democracy" was very different from "electoral democracy," particularly since appointment to the "representative" institutions of the former could be and were determined "from above," while democratic elections entail selection by ordinary citizens.

civilization, the exceptional historical position of the "Caudillo" (see Glossary), and a corporatist form of "representation" through a system of so-called "organic democracy".

The failure of resocialization under the Franco regime

The Franco regime failed utterly in its efforts to re-socialize the Spanish population in a manner that could perpetuate the authoritarian system after the death of its founder. None of these corporatist/authoritarian values is embraced by any significant sectors of Spanish society today. It is even doubtful that they were taken seriously by more than a small handful of Spaniards by the 1970s. Instead, even the behavior of many of those who were responsible for disseminating these messages can be regarded as little more than "going through the motions."

The ineffectiveness of this socialization process is reflected in survey data gathered just before Franco's death. In the late 1960s and early 1970s, the decade before the death of Franco, only about 15% of the Spanish population actively identified with the Franco regime. Almost twice as many were opposed to the regime and, moreover, were active, informed, and interested in politics. Over half of the population – the "indifferent majority" – was passive, uninformed, and uninterested in politics. By the mid 1980s, however, the overwhelming majority of Spaniards fully embraced democracy and only a tiny minority had any lingering sympathies for authoritarianism. Nonetheless, passive political indifference became a durable characteristic of many Spaniards (as it is for many citizens in other stable democracies).

> ## Box 5.2
>
> *"Going through the motions"*
>
> Among those who occupied positions responsible for disseminating these anti-democratic, pro-Franco messages were Adolfo Suárez and Torcuato Fernández-Miranda, two of the last secretaries general of the National Movement – the "single party" that was supposed to drum up support for the regime. Suárez was also director general of the state's radio and television system, and Fernández-Miranda was appointed prime minister following the December 1973 assassination of his close friend Luis Carrero Blanco, as well as tutor for Franco's heir-apparent, Prince Juan Carlos. Moreover, Fernández-Miranda was the author of the "civics textbook" cited above, which was used throughout the education system for two decades. Nonetheless, Suárez and Fernández-Miranda were two of the three individuals (the other being King Juan Carlos) who played the most decisive roles in dismantling the Franco regime, with Suárez serving as prime minister and Fernández-Miranda as head of both the Cortes and the Council of the Realm – two institutions set in place by Franco to block a possible democratization process.

At the time of Franco's death, Spain's political culture could not be regarded as anti-democratic, but neither can we say that it was clearly favorable towards democracy. To be sure, by the early to mid 1970s large majorities of Spaniards preferred election over appointment for selecting public officials (82%), freedom of the press (74%), religious freedom (71%), and freedom of association for trade unions (58%). At the same time, however, only 37% of respondents in a 1973 survey favored freedom of association for political parties, while 52% agreed with the statement that "what we Spaniards need is discipline." As late as 1975, among those who favored a change of political regime, only 43% said that a liberal democracy would be desirable for Spain.

Support for democracy today

In contrast, support for democracy in Spain today is extraordinarily widespread, and is as strong as in long-established Western European democracies – indeed, stronger than in some. In our 2004 public opinion survey, 89% of our respondents selected democracy as the best form of government. By way of comparison, support for democracy was 85% among Greeks (as measured by that item in a 1996 public opinion survey), 78% among Americans (in 2004), 70% among South Africans (in 2004), 66% among Mexicans (in 2006), 64% among Chileans (in 1999), 58% among Hungarians (in 1998), and 55% among Taiwanese (in 2005) (see figure 5.1).

Once Spain's democratic regime was consolidated (around 1982 [see key term 1.2]), as can be seen in figure 5.1, democratic support remained extremely stable and has continued to strengthen, as the older cohorts (largely socialized under

Box 5.3

Why anti-democratic socialization failed

There are several reasons why efforts to resocialize Spaniards failed. (1) *Ideological incoherence*. There was little intellectual consistency in the regime's ideological message. Generalísimo Franco was not committed to any particular ideology. He had co-opted the Falange (a small fascist party) during the Civil War and used it through the early 1940s to drum up support for his regime only out of expediency. However, once **fascism** was definitively discredited by the mid 1940s, he sought to water down Falangist politics by drowning it within an eclectic coalition of various factions that supported the regime: non-ideological military officers and bureaucratic technocrats, Carlist Traditionalists and other conservative Catholics, upper-class landowners, and business elites, etc. (2) *Decreased repression*. The relaxation of repression during the regime's two final decades further weakened its ability to convey a consistent message to the population. Secret police penetrated only a few centers of active opposition (such as the Communist Party), which permitted deviant and occasionally rebellious subcultures to emerge, particularly in the universities and industrial zones. Within these subcultures, networks of face-to-face contacts served as conduits of opinions, attitudes, and values inconsistent with official propaganda. (3) *Exposure to affluent, democratic models*. Increased contact with the outside world in the 1960s following the end of autarky (see chapter 3) further weakened the regime's message, and exposed many Spaniards to conflicting points of view. Approximately 2 million Spanish workers temporarily migrated abroad, where they were exposed to open, free societies and stable, functioning democracies. Many more Spaniards encountered firsthand evidence – in the form of up to 40 million foreign tourists visiting Spain each year – that the regime's anti-liberal, anti-democratic propaganda did not ring true in an increasingly modern, urbanized, stable, prosperous, democratic Western Europe.

> **Fascism** is an extremist form of nationalism, rooted in organic corporatism (see Box 5.1) and overtly hostile to democracy. It is militaristic and aggressive, stresses "heroic violence" as a civic virtue, insists upon strict loyalty to a charismatic leader, and does not hesitate to use force to subordinate or eliminate its enemies.

the Franco regime and generally located among the "indifferent majority") are replaced by younger people whose **socialization** has taken place entirely under a democratic regime. What is most noteworthy is that fundamental support for democracy has been unwavering, while "satisfaction" with the performance of democracy has fluctuated substantially over time, largely in accord with the performance of the economy and of the incumbent government.

> **Political socialization** is the learning of political attitudes by individuals in a society. It takes place through both formal and informal processes. Formal political socialization involves the intentional teaching of political attitudes, through the schools, the media, etc. Informal socialization involves learning as a product of observation of political interactions, participation in political and politically relevant organizations, and passive internalization of the attitudes of respected authority figures, the most important being one's parents.

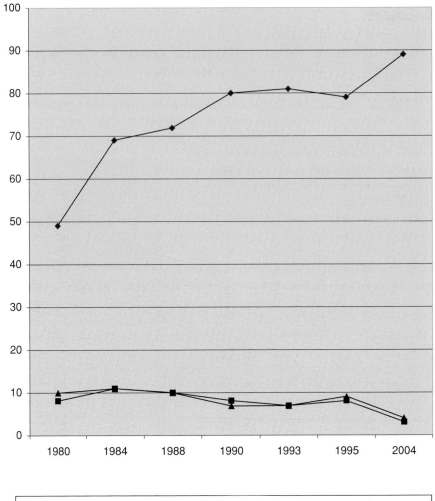

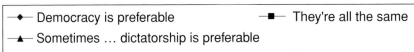

Figure 5.1 Support for democracy in Spain, 1980–2004[a]
[a] These represent responses to a questionnaire item in which respondents were asked to choose among the following alternative phrases: (1) "Democracy is preferable to any other form of government"; "Under some circumstances, an authoritarian regime, a dictatorship, is preferable to a democratic system"; and "For people like me, one regime is the same as another."
Sources: for 1980–95, Banco de Datos, CIS; for 2004, CNEP.

There are several reasons why support for democracy in Spain became so strong and widespread.

- **Socioeconomic modernization** and the spread of literacy. Numerous empirical studies have shown that higher levels of education and literacy have a big impact on political attitudes and behavior: deference to social and political elites gives way to expectations (if not demands) that citizens should have an active role in governance. In short, passive "subjects" (who could be manipulated by undemocratic patron–client relationships, as occurred in the late nineteenth and early twentieth centuries in Spain) become participating citizens.
- **Changes in the international environment** also help to explain change in the political culture. In contrast with the early 1930s, when fascism and Soviet communism were popular in some circles, those non-democratic alternatives are now totally discredited, and democracy is widely regarded as "the only game in town."
- **Elite support for democracy.** We contend that the pro-democratic stands taken by key political elites were also important – especially with regard to leaders of parties on the left and the right, whose support for democracy was not to be taken for granted.

Studies of democratization have also shown that democratic support is stronger in countries where elites in the former non-democratic regime had supported democratization. In the case of Spain, the leadership of Adolfo Suárez throughout the transition, as well as solid support for the constitution by Manuel Fraga, converted formerly pro-Franco sectors of Spanish society into democrats.

Box 5.4

Converting franquistas *into democrats*

One of the most important factors in forging and disseminating attitudes supportive of Spain's new democratic regime was the constructive role in the transition played by party leaders who had been prominent officials in the Franco regime. One of these was Adolfo Suárez, prime minister and leader of the UCD (see Box 5.2). Another was Manuel Fraga, who had served as Minister of Information and Tourism under Franco and in that capacity had introduced the Press Law of 1966, which made possible a partial liberalization of the regime. Fraga was founder and leader of Alianza Popular, the principal party on the right, initially dominated by several former ministers of the Franco regime. Fraga's decision to fully endorse the Spanish constitution in 1978 played a key role in convincing many Spaniards who had been supporters of the former regime that they should now support the new democracy. Accordingly, the main party of the right in Spain is not ambiguous in its support for democracy, and its followers are fully loyal to the democratic regime.

Similarly, the full embrace of democracy on the part of the PCE following its conversion into a Eurocommunist party (see Box 4.14) greatly strengthened left-wing support for democracy.

Democratic support, political discontent, and political dissatisfaction

The conceptual relationship between "satisfaction" with democracy in any given country (or its converse, "political discontent") and more fundamental support for democracy as the best form of government has given rise to considerable confusion and debate among scholars, journalists, and politicians. Some have argued that democratic support (a key dimension of regime legitimacy) is the product of satisfaction with the performance and outputs of democratic government over time. Accordingly, during the period 1980–2, Spanish journalists and opposition political leaders expressed concern over opinion polls showing a precipitous decline in satisfaction with the performance of democracy. They referred to this as *desencanto* (disenchantment), and argued that widespread discontent over the economic crisis and the irresponsible squabbling among the various factions of the governing UCD were posing a serious risk to the legitimacy of Spain's new democracy.

Fortunately, our analyses have found that political discontent and a fundamental lack of support for democracy are two entirely separable kinds of attitudes that are conceptually and empirically distinct from one another. First of all, the way in which these mass attitudes have evolved over time suggests that they are not at all the same thing.

- Fundamental support for democracy is relatively stable over time. As we saw in figure 5.1, it was low in the early years of the transition (with fewer than half of all Spaniards unequivocally supporting democracy as late as 1980) but increased steadily in the early 1980s and continued to strengthen over the following two decades to the extent that it exceeds similar levels of support in Great Britain today.
- In contrast, political discontent, or satisfaction with the performance of the incumbent government or with democracy more broadly, fluctuates substantially over time, and largely in accord with current economic and political circumstances (see figure 5.2).

These patterns strongly suggest that "democratic support" and "political discontent" are two different sets of attitudes, which are independent of each other, and that change over time is driven by different factors.

A third cluster of attitudes, in contrast, has proven to be remarkably durable over time. We refer to such orientations as *political disaffection*. These attitudes are often measured by responses to questionnaire statements like: "Politics is so complicated that people like me cannot understand what is happening"; "Politicians do not worry much about what people like me think"; and "People like me

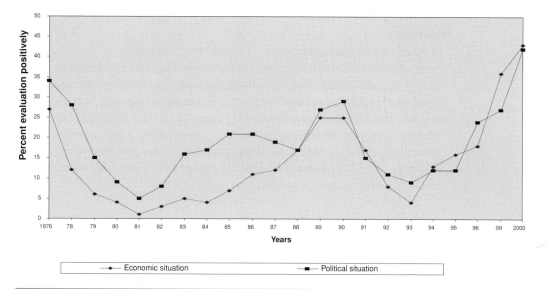

Figure 5.2 Satisfaction with the economy and the political situation of Spain, 1976–2000
Sources: For 1976–86, 1999, and 2000, Banco de Datos, CIS; and for 1987–96, Archivo de Datos, Demoscopia

do not have any influence over what the government does." Our analyses indicate that political disaffection is distinctly different from both political discontent (or dissatisfaction) and democratic support (related to regime legitimacy) with regard to both their causes and consequences, and their implications for the quality and the stability of democracy.

- A fundamental lack of support for democracy is strongly associated with votes for anti-system parties.
- Political discontent leads to a vote against the incumbent party; while
- political disaffection is conducive to withdrawal from politics and low levels of political interest and involvement. The politically disaffected tend to be uninterested in politics and the news, and tend to shun active involvement in most forms of democratic participation.

These three clusters of attitudes have entirely different implications for Spanish democracy. Widespread support for democracy is associated with the complete absence of anti-system parties at the national level, as we saw in the preceding chapter. This contrasts strongly with the numerous anti-system and semi-loyal parties in the Second Republic, and bodes well for the stability of the current regime. Political discontent, as we have seen, does not represent a serious threat to the survival of democracy. Accordingly, concerns in the early 1980s about *desencanto* were exaggerated. Instead, voting for an opposition party is

> ## Box 5.5
>
> *Dissatisfaction and the vote*
> As democratic theory would suggest, when voters are dissatisfied with the performance of the government, they should express their discontent by voting the ruling party out of office. The "direction of causality" of the link between dissatisfaction and the vote, however, is not clear. Opposition party supporters are strongly inclined to disapprove of the performance of the party in government. Accordingly, it may be prior support for opposition parties that determines one's satisfaction with the government's policies, rather than dissatisfaction with government policies leading to a vote for an opposition party.

exactly what democratic theory suggests that dissatisfied voters should do. However, disaffection has somewhat undermined the quality of democracy in Spain insofar as it has led substantial numbers of citizens to avoid active involvement in democratic politics.

The differing origins of three attitudes towards democracy

The principal cause of **political discontent** is poor performance by the government, especially with regard to the condition of the economy. A low level of **support for democracy** within a particular segment of the electorate is often the result of a hostile stand towards democratization by its political leaders, as we have argued. In Spain, once the leaders of all nationwide parties had demonstrated their firm support for democracy, their respective electoral clienteles also fully embraced the new democratic regime.

But **political disaffection**, we believe, is a product of early socialization towards politics, either overt and intentional or indirect and implicit.

- Many of those who hold attitudes shunning politics acquired them as the result of traumatic memories of the polarized Second Republic or the Civil War.
- Others may have become disdainful towards politics as a result of the intentional depoliticization of political communications under the Franco regime.

In contrast with totalitarian regimes – which seek to mold "the new man" or create a new "classless society" through regime-directed mass mobilization of the populace – the authoritarian system of General Franco had no such transformative desires. Indeed, historian Stanley Payne has written that "Franco asked nothing of his regime except that it should continue." Instead, citizens were expected to be passive and obedient rather than active and participatory, and while most aspects of social life were free from surveillance or manipulation by the state, all organizations designed for political mobilization (especially trade

Box 5.6

Totalitarian and authoritarian regimes

As defined by political scientist Juan Linz, *totalitarian* regimes (1) are dominated by a single ruler with virtually unlimited power and authority (like Hitler or Stalin), (2) have an elaborate and well-defined revolutionary ideology (like Nazism or Marxism-Leninism), and (3) demand active involvement of all citizens in support of the regime's revolutionary objectives. Those few secondary associations allowed to exist by totalitarian regimes are under its direct control or close supervision. There is no clear boundary between the public and private spheres of life.

Authoritarian systems (1) repress dissent, like totalitarian regimes, but their penetration into and domination of society is much less complete. (2) "Limited pluralism" is tolerated – that is, some secondary associations (particularly those generally favorable towards the regime or those deemed to be non-political) can function with considerable independence, and (3) the power of the leader or leaders is somewhat constrained. (4) Authoritarian regimes may either lack a coherent ideology altogether or embrace a loose cluster of values or attitudes (called a "mentality" by Linz). And (5) most of them expect passive obedience of citizens, rather than the carefully controlled active mobilization demanded by totalitarian systems.

unions and political parties) were vigorously suppressed throughout the life of the regime.

This strategy of demobilization and depoliticization was reinforced by the stupefyingly colorless nature of the news broadcast by government-run radio and television stations, and by restrictions of press coverage of political developments. For most people, by the early 1970s, repression was unnecessary: they were simply bored into passivity. This strategy also capitalized on traumatic memories of the Second Republic and the Civil War to discourage involvement in politics. The past was thereby manipulated in such a manner as to portray democratic politics as corrupt, divisive, and dangerous for ordinary citizens.

While these characteristics of the Franco regime help us to understand why many among the older generations have become disaffected from politics, they fail to account for the puzzling durability of such orientations, which contrasts completely with changes over time in levels of political discontent and democratic support. Instead, attitudes relating to disaffection have remained largely unchanged over the following three decades among Spaniards of all ages, suggesting that they may be transmitted from one generation to another. This continuity is quite remarkable given the social and economic changes witnessed since the late 1960s, and the political changes since the late 1970s. Disaffection appears to be the product of a long-standing process of "cultural accumulation," and has become a durable aspect of Spain's political culture. Accordingly, Spanish citizens are characterized by:

- a low level of interest in politics (with only about 4 to 6% of Spaniards describing themselves as "very interested," and another 15% "somewhat interested in politics" since the late 1980s);
- low exposure to political communications, especially through newspaper reading and discussion of politics with friends, neighbors, co-workers, and even family; only with regard to the frequency of watching television news broadcasts do Spaniards come close to the average among modern democratic societies;
- cynicism towards parties and politicians, although the majority of citizens regard parties as essential actors in democratic politics; and
- low levels of party identification – far fewer Spaniards feel close to or identify with a political party than is typical of Western democracies, with the percentage of Spaniards describing themselves as "very close" to one of the major nationwide parties actually declining from 32% to 23% between 1982 and 2004.

Negative attitudes are most widespread among the politically disaffected and appear to be rooted in long-term orientations that are not reflective of the actual behavior of parties and their leaders. Anti-party sentiments also appear to be most strongly held among those on the right and among practicing Catholics, among the older generations and the least educated, and among those who are least interested in and informed about politics. In short, they may be a legacy of depoliticization under the authoritarian regime of General Franco.

Nonetheless, it is important to reiterate that this cynicism towards parties and politicians is not also manifested in a fundamental lack of support for democracy or any widespread challenge to the legitimacy of the present regime. Neither has it led to the emergence of any electorally significant anti-system party in Spain.

■ Secondary associations

Low levels of psychological and behavioral involvement with politics in Spain may be part of a broader syndrome including many forms of civic engagement. Spain, together with East Germany, Moldavia, Romania, and Russia, occupies one of the bottom places among European countries in terms of involvement in secondary associations. Only 42% of Spaniards belong to an organization of any kind, 32% participate in their activities, 23% donate money, and 16% provide voluntary work. Far fewer Spaniards belong to secondary associations (trade unions, professional associations, cultural groups, etc.) than is typical of most established democracies. While membership in secondary associations appears to be declining in most advanced post-industrial societies, this level of civic engagement lags behind that of Italy (where 56% of citizens belonged to organized groups in 1996, and 43% in 2006), Japan (72% in 1993), and the United States (where fully 84% of citizens belonged to at least one secondary association in 1992, declining to 46% in 2004). Spain's level of organizational affiliation has increased only slightly since 1980, and does not vary substantially from one region to another.

The origins of this weakly developed civil society in Spain can be traced back over a century. Political scientist Juan Linz has argued that it can be attributed in part to the turbulence and discontinuities of the preceding two centuries of Spanish history, which disrupted the institutional development of organizations and norms of civic participation, reinforced by the demobilization of society under the Franco regime.

Among those types of organizations that are most commonly relevant to politics (except for political parties, which we will discuss later in this chapter), low levels of affiliation with trade unions and religious organizations are perhaps the most noteworthy.

- About 5% of respondents in surveys conducted in 2002 claimed to belong to labor unions, placing Spain, Greece, and Portugal in last place among European countries.
- Just 4% of Spaniards were members of religious associations in 2002.

While low affiliation levels must be regarded as in part a reflection of the general weakness of civil society in Spain, these two types of organizations are worthy of more extensive consideration.

Trade unions

Both of Spain's major parties of the left relied upon ties with substantial trade union organizations in the late 1970s and early 1980s. The Unión General de Trabajadores (UGT) had been linked to the Socialist Party since its founding in 1888 (just nine years after the party itself was established), and party–union ties were strong and close. The Comisiones Obreras (CCOO) emerged with the end of the Franco regime's corporate "syndicates" in the late 1960s. The decision to allow the direct election of shop stewards (*enlaces sindicales*) opened the way towards infiltration of the corporatist trade union structure by the clandestine PCE and several smaller leftist groups. Thus, paradoxically, Spain's predominantly communist trade union had its origins in the authoritarian system's own institutions (as also occurred in neighboring Portugal). Analysis of our 1979 survey data demonstrated that both parties received considerable electoral benefit from their ties with their respective union allies.

The decline of trade union membership

By the early 1990s, however, the ability of parties to count on trade unions as channels for electoral mobilization had diminished significantly. In part, this was the product of a precipitous decline in trade-union membership. Although

> ## Box 5.7
>
> *Ties between parties and unions in the 1970s*
> The links between the PSOE and its trade union ally, the UGT, were close and explicit in the late 1970s and early 1980s. Party members were required to join the UGT, the union's secretary general served on the executive committee of the party, and the trade union worked to mobilize its members in support of the PSOE during election campaigns. In 1979, this trade-union activity played an important role in channeling electoral support to the PSOE, as analysis of our survey data revealed. The relationship between the Communist Party and its allied trade union was neither so direct institutionally nor so deeply rooted historically, but it may have been even more effective electorally in the late 1970s. Given the ostensible non-partisanship of the Comisiones Obreras, the PCE had to be more subtle than the PSOE in its electoral mobilization of its trade union ally. No formal organizational ties existed between party and union, although domination of most of the provincial, regional, and national executive committees of the union by PCE members and supporters meant that the party could almost invariably count on the union for electoral support. Given the parliamentary weakness of the PCE (with only 23 deputies at its high point), the CCOO also played an important, independent political role in mobilizing extra-parliamentary opposition to the Socialist government during the 1980s.

this trend appears to have "bottomed out" in the mid 1980s and recovered somewhat throughout the 1990s, trade-union membership lags far behind that found in other Western European democracies.

- Only 17% of those in the labor force were members of trade unions in 2004. This is substantially less than the 71% union affiliation average found in Northern European countries and the 32% average for Central European countries, and far behind the levels of unionization found in Italy (35%), Greece (27%), and Portugal (24%).
- While these low levels of trade-union affiliation fit with the overall pattern of secondary association membership discussed above, they are also most likely the result of a peculiar institutional form of trade-unionism and labor relations in Spain.
- Over 80% of all workers in the year 2000 were represented in collective bargaining by trade-union representatives of their own choice, elected through formal balloting by workers within most firms.

What is unusual is that workers can vote for union representatives without actually belonging to the union. Accordingly, workers can receive the benefits of union representation (in collective bargaining with employers for increased wages and better working conditions) without having to pay union dues or contribute in other ways to these organizations. In short, low levels

Figure 5.3 Demonstration by striking transportation workers, Madrid, 2008

of union affiliation are to some extent the aggregate consequence of "free riding."

The disruption of party/union ties

The weakening of unions as mechanisms of electoral mobilization is also the product of important qualitative changes in Spanish labor relations during the 1980s. As part of a reaction against the allegedly "neoliberal" economic policies of the Socialist government (see Box 4.11), the bonds that linked the UGT to the PSOE became frayed and eventually snapped. These tensions led the UGT secretary general Nicolás Redondo to resign from the executive committee of the Socialist Party and abandon his seat in parliament, declaring his unalterable opposition to the policies of the González government. Party–union relations degenerated to such an extent that in December 1988 the UGT actively cooperated with other trade unions in organizing a general strike against the economic and social policies of the Socialist government. The UGT did not endorse the PSOE in the 1989 general election, and in May 1991, the UGT helped organize a series of nationwide transportation strikes (affecting trains, airplanes, and gasoline

stations) at least in part to embarrass the PSOE government on the eve of municipal elections. And in 1990, the PSOE eliminated from its statutes the requirement
that party members must also join the UGT.

Relations between the PCE and the Comisiones Obreras (CCOO) have been
less overtly contentious, but they, too, have undergone modification in response
to the Communist Party's conversion from what was (in the early 1980s) a traditional, working-class party into the organizational core of a broader coalition (Izquierda Unida, or "United Left"), which also includes feminist, ecological, and pacifist groups. Overall, this has led to a significant loosening
of the once collaborative relationship between the Communist Party and the
CCOO.

Increased collaboration between once rival unions

Following the breakdown of close links between the two major trade unions
and their respective political parties, the UGT and CCOO entered into close
collaboration, in particular with regard to developing strategies for labor negotiations and legislation introduced by successive Spanish governments. Taking
advantage of the new partisan independence of the two unions, and wishing
to enhance its image as a pragmatic, catch-all party, the Partido Popular under
prime minister José María Aznar launched legislative initiatives in 1997 that
included several reforms of the labor market. This led to a temporary renewal of
the earlier practice of "pacts" with business organizations, in which negotiation
and collaboration replaced the harsh confrontations of the previous decade. The
two unions did support the PSOE-IU coalition in the 2000 general election, but
they did so without explicitly calling upon their members to vote for the parties,
and without providing direct assistance during the campaign.

Following the PP government's shift to the right after its smashing election
victory in 2000, and now enjoying an absolute majority in parliament, the Aznar
government introduced tougher labor legislation. This quickly ended the brief
period of PP-union collaboration and triggered numerous protests and a successful general strike, jointly organized by CCOO and UGT. Poor relations with
the unions were further worsened by Aznar's decision to send Spanish troops
to Iraq. Here, again, the two unions collaborated in their opposition to these
policies.

The PSOE's return to power following its surprising election victory in 2004
led to an alteration of these party-union relations. The government of José
Luis Rodríguez Zapatero was keenly interested in reestablishing a collaborative
relationship with the two unions and succeeded in gaining their support for
fifteen agreements that brought about incremental reforms of the labor market.
This improvement in government-union relations was further reflected in a
reduction in the number of strikes to levels significantly below those of the
previous Aznar government, as well as the first tripartite pact (involving labor,
business, and government) since 1984. In the end, while the Socialist Party is no
longer tied institutionally to one of Spain's two major trade unions, neither is it

directly confronted by two formerly rival unions united in their efforts to bring
down a Socialist government.

Religious organizations

Religious-based organizations have been extraordinarily weak throughout the
democratic era, in terms of both their institutional presence in Spanish society,
and their impact on politics. Given the Franco regime's support for the Church
and its ancillary organizations, this is a somewhat surprising development. In
the 1960s, the various Catholic Action organizations had over 1 million members throughout Spain. Their organizational strength, one might have expected,
should have contributed to the development of a powerful Christian Democratic party (as one prominent political scientist predicted). By the time of the
transition to democracy, however, the strength of the Church had declined
precipitously.

- **Organizational decline.** In the late 1960s, the previous consensus over political, social, and economic values within these Catholic Action organizations
  broke down, bringing them into overt conflict with the Church hierarchy. As
  a result of this internal crisis, by 1972 total membership in Catholic Action
  had fallen to 100,000 – just one tenth of its size a decade earlier.
- **Secularization.** A dramatic secularization of Spanish society (which we will
  explore later in this chapter) had begun by the early years of the transition
  to democracy, further reducing the mobilization capacity of the Church and
  its importance as a reference point for making political decisions.
- **Non-partisanship of the Church.** The reduced partisan relevance of religious
  association membership was also profoundly affected by strategic decisions
  made by both religious and party leaders at key stages during the transition. The desire to avoid taking sides in a manner similar to that which had
  contributed to the outbreak of the Civil War in the 1930s led the Episcopal
  Conference (the council of bishops that makes major policy decisions) under
  Cardinal Tarancón to eschew partisan ties of any kind.
- **Party development strategies.** Party leaders also chose to avoid institutionalized links with the Church. This was particularly important with regard to
  the UCD: despite pressures from its Christian Democratic faction, it resisted
  the temptation to capitalize on its highly religious base of electoral support
  by forging any kinds of ties with the Church. Thus, unlike the Christian Democratic parties of West Germany and Italy in the postwar era, which depended
  heavily on religious organizations for infrastructural and "moral" support
  in the early stages of democratization, Spanish parties lacked associational
  links with the Church.

This is not to say that the religious cleavage had no effect on voting behavior. As
we shall see, religiosity was strongly linked to partisan preferences, especially
in the first few elections after the establishment of democracy.

Business and other organizations

A wide variety of other secondary associations exist in Spain, none of which have high levels of affiliation. In 2002, a survey of the Spanish electorate indicated that 14% of the population belonged to sport associations and another 4% to neighborhood associations, 6% were members of parent–teacher associations, 3% were affiliates of professional associations, and 8% belonged to cultural groups. Most other types of associations had lower levels of membership.

The potential political impact of these groups, however, as well as of the Church and trade unions, is not solely dependent on their size, and reaches beyond their own membership. These groups can serve as either positive or negative reference groups which citizens can take into consideration in making up their minds about political matters. This is particularly true of the "peak association" of Spanish business, the CEOE (Confederación Española de Organizaciones Empresariales [Spanish Confederation of Business Organizations]), which, even though its membership appears small as a percentage of the Spanish population, exerts enormous influence through its representation of virtually all the small, medium, and large business enterprises in Spain.

As an employers' organization, the CEOE links 2,000 individual trade associations grouped into 200 territorial units. Its substantial impact on public policy is due in part to its continuity of leadership (twenty-three years under a single president, José María Cuevas, from the CEOE's founding until his retirement), the consistency of its policy demands (reductions in employers' share of social security contributions, liberalization of the labor market, etc.), and its willingness to work with governments of all ideological orientations – under the UCD, the PSOE, and the PP. A parallel organization, the CEPYME (Confederación Española de la Pequeña y Mediana Empresa [Spanish Confederation of Small and Medium Businesses]), has also joined the CEOE and the major unions and the government for negotiations regarding the labor "pacts" discussed earlier in this chapter. Finally, while the CEOE and CEPYME have not hesitated to publicly express their policy preferences and opposition to specific government policies, neither have they overtly intervened in electoral politics. Their ostensible partisan neutrality is another factor that has enhanced their effectiveness as lobbying organizations.

Organizations as reference groups

As can be seen in table 5.1, the Church and business organizations have served more prominently as negative rather than positive reference groups for more citizens. As in many other countries, non-governmental organizations, ecological groups, and feminist organizations served as the most attractive organizations, despite their extraordinarily low levels of affiliation. Accordingly, they can influence voters by taking public stands on policy issues or electoral choices.

Table 5.1 "Which groups are closest to your opinions?," and "Which groups are most opposed to your opinions?," 1993

	Closest	Most opposed	Net impact
Trade unions	31%	28%	+3
The Church	29	34	−5
Feminist organizations	35	16	+19
Business associations	18	33	−15
Environmental groups	40	13	+27
Parent–teacher associations	25	13	+12
Neighborhood associations	25	14	+11

Source: Spanish CNEP survey, 1993 (www.cnep.ics.ul.pt).

The weakness of civil society

The policy impact of groups in Spanish society varies considerably depending on their overall levels of membership, their links to policy-makers, and their effectiveness in publicizing their policy demands. The low levels of organizational affiliation that characterize Spanish society, however, mean that citizen participation is not as well organized as in many other established democracies – as manifested in the frequency of public demonstrations and wildcat strikes as a means of expressing discontent. This weakness of what is commonly called "civil society" is a distinguishing characteristic of Spanish democracy. And we believe that it is, in part, a reflection of the relatively high levels of political disaffection that may have been a long-term inheritance from the Franco regime. Its clearest manifestation can be seen in similarly low levels of **political participation**. A 2002 European survey of "ways of attempting to bring about improvements or counteract deterioration in society" indicated that political

> **Political participation** refers to activities undertaken by ordinary citizens aiming at influencing some political outcomes. Its modes, or channels, include an extraordinary variety of forms, but they can usually be grouped into clusters of activities related to voting, political parties, contacting public officials (politicians, media, or public administration personnel), boycotting or consumption of given goods, and protest.

involvement in Spain is low, and that participation is undertaken by a small number of activists, who have at their disposition a wide repertoire for influencing political and social authorities. In this respect, Spain once again ranked near the bottom.

■ Social cleavages, ideology, and electoral behavior

Earlier in this chapter, we explored the impact of the Franco regime on democratic politics. We saw that, despite nearly four decades of anti-democratic propaganda, Spaniards in the first decade of the twenty-first century have attitudes fully supportive of democracy, to an even greater extent than is found in many older, established democratic systems. At the same time, we saw that there were some lasting imprints of the Franco authoritarian regime in the form of widespread attitudes of disaffection, which have led many Spaniards to feel somewhat distant if not alienated from daily involvement in democratic politics. We now turn our attention to the ways in which changes in Spanish society since the Second Republic have affected electoral behavior.

In chapter 1, we discussed the historical origins of several social cleavages that have had a substantial impact on political behavior in Spain over the centuries. Specifically, we argued that class and religious cleavages served as sources of disruptive and sometimes violent conflict in the past. The Spanish state-building process also gave rise to linguistic and cultural pluralism that, in turn, served as the basis for the emergence of nationalist movements that have challenged the Spanish state. Social cleavages serve as the underpinning of electoral behavior in many, if not all, democratic polities. To what extent have these cleavages been transformed over the course of the 20th century, and how have they influenced the nature of partisan competition in Spain's current democracy?

The class cleavage and politics

One of the most important aspects of any explanation of instability in the Second Republic is that the Spanish economy was generally undeveloped, giving Spain many social structural characteristics that had been superseded in Northern European countries by the end of the 19th century. Overall, in the context of Western Europe, Spain must be regarded as a "late modernizer." At the time the Second Republic was created, Spain was still an overwhelmingly agrarian and backward society, with nearly half of its labor force in the primary sector of the economy (agriculture, fishing, etc.). At that time the great bulk of the workforce in most other Western countries was employed in industry. Illiteracy was as widespread as it had been in other Western European countries in the mid nineteenth century. And economic inequality was extremely high, especially in the south, where latifundia (extremely large agricultural estates) were the principal form of land ownership (see key term 1.14).

Prospects for economic development were dealt a serious blow by the disruptions of the Civil War of the 1930s, as well as by the years of international isolation and famine that followed. Thus, living standards were no better in 1950 than they had been in the early 1930s.

Rapid socioeconomic modernization

Between 1960 and 1973, however, Spain's economy grew at an extraordinarily rapid rate – 7.3% per year in real terms, second only to that of Japan during the same period. The accompanying transformation of Spanish society was rapid and profound. Between 1960 and the mid 1970s, the percentage of the labor force active in agriculture fell from 40% to 23%. From a largely agrarian, traditional society, with low levels of per capita wealth, Spain was transformed into an overwhelmingly urban, mass-consumer society, with living standards comparable to those of other Western European countries. Indeed, by 1990, average life expectancy in Spain (76.6 years) was nearly three years longer than that of the average industrialized society, and nearly two years longer than that of the United States.

Between 1960 and 1989, Spaniards residing in towns with fewer than 10,000 inhabitants declined from 43% of the population to 15%, while the share of those living in cities larger than 100,000 increased from 15% to 42%. In the course of this massive wave of migration (which largely depopulated extensive rural areas), Spain became about as urban as the average Western European country. Among other things, this urbanization – in addition to a substantial decline in the birth rate and massive migration to expanding industrial zones in Catalonia, in the Basque Country, and around Madrid – also greatly reduced the number of landless peasants in the latifundist south. This shrank the rural proletariat that had contributed so much to the intensity of social conflict during the Second Republic, and thereby helped reduce the potential for polarized class conflict in those regions. Instead, a new industrial working class with few links to the organizations and the ideologies of the past emerged in the cities and, in the latter years of the Franco regime, began to share in the fruits of economic development.

Since the late 1960s, Spain's social structure has come to resemble those of other post-industrialized societies. Political scientist Juan Linz has observed that, in a period of less than two decades, Spain underwent as much social change as the United States over the course of six decades from 1880 to 1940.

- Spain has been converted into a society of urban middle classes typical of advanced capitalism, in which only about one third of workers can be classified as of the working class, and in which most workers are employed in the service sector of the economy.
- Once great inequalities (based on the existence of a large number of unskilled workers in industry and agriculture) have been substantially reduced, and the distribution of incomes in Spain has become much more typically European.
- Finally, the development of an incipient welfare state under the Franco regime contributed to the amelioration of poverty.

In the end, the old class cleavage line did not completely disappear, but it was certainly different from that which divided Spanish society during the Second Republic.

The political impact of modernity and affluence

In several ways, these socioeconomic changes have affected electoral behavior in Spain. First, the end of geographic isolation and illiteracy in most parts of Spain made possible genuinely free voting without the patron–client relationships and intimidation of the Restoration Monarchy (1876–1923) (see Box 1.6).

Secondly, socioeconomic development helped to soften some of the traditional cleavages that once deeply divided Spain. In particular, higher levels of affluence and reduced economic inequality meant that political ideologies calling for radical or revolutionary socioeconomic change had substantially less appeal. To be sure, these changes in the socioeconomic context of democratic politics do not guarantee that party leaders will moderate their electoral claims in this manner. The socialist PSOE and communist PCE, however, were influenced by electoral strategists who were keenly aware of the political implications of these social changes, and the parties adjusted their electoral appeals accordingly. They realized that an exclusive emphasis on attracting votes from a shrinking working class would culminate in defeat at the polls, and broadened their electoral target groups accordingly. This contributed to the ideological reorientation discussed in the preceding chapter, especially the conversion of the PCE to Eurocommunism, and of the PSOE into a moderate, center-left, catch-all party.

The nature of the relationship between social class and electoral behavior can be seen in table 5.2, which shows how much of the vote for each major party is explained by social class and religion. The Socialist and Communist parties received a disproportionate share of the votes cast by skilled and unskilled workers, while Alianza Popular initially drew most of its electoral support from the upper-middle and upper social strata. But the most important point is that, except in the mid 1980s, the two principal parties (UCD and PSOE in 1979, and PP and PSOE in 1993 and 2004) went to great lengths to cross over the class barrier and attract a mixed base of electoral support. This was particularly true of the UCD (not included in this table in order to increase comparability of these findings over time), which emphasized inter-class electoral appeals in both the 1977 and 1979 elections. At the same time, the PSOE has always been successful in drawing electoral support from the middle class. The replacement of the overtly "inter-classist" UCD in 1982 by the more conservative AP led to a short-term increase in class polarization, but by the 1990s, even the Partido Popular (following its conversion from Alianza Popular) was successful in reaching across class barriers.

In short, while the class cleavage has had a significant influence on electoral behavior, it did not do so in the polarizing manner that destabilized the Second Republic. Moreover, continuing socioeconomic development and increases in affluence, combined with electoral appeals that intentionally downplay class differences, have led to a steady decline in the electoral impact of social class.

The religious cleavage

A second divisive cleavage whose origins we examined in chapter 1 involved deeply divided opinions concerning the proper role of religion and the Church in Spanish society and politics. To a considerable degree, the demise of the Second Republic was the product of a conflict between a substantial portion of

Table 5.2 Percentages of variance in the vote explained by class and religious variables[a]

	PCE/IU	PSOE	AP/PP	Overall R^2
Class				
1982	**	.18	.23	.178
1993	.09	.13	.14	.126
2004	.03	.06	.06	.061
Religion				
1982	**	.23	.22	.235
1993	.14	.07	.09	.085
2004	.21	.10	.11	.104
Class + religion				
1982	.55	.41	.45	.413
1993	.23	.20	.23	.211
2004	.24	.16	.17	.165

** There were too few PCE voters in our sample to produce statistically significant findings for class variables alone. Accordingly, it was not possible to produce reliable estimates of the separate contributions of class and religion.

[a] These numbers represent the "percentage of variance explained" by each of these social cleavages. They are Nagelkerke R^2 statistics resulting from the inclusion, first, of the "class" variables (producing the statistics for "Class"), then adding the "religiosity" variable to the previous group of independent variables (producing the statistics for "Class + religion"). "Religion" was calculated by subtracting the percentage of variance explained by class from the total of class + religion. The figures for each party used as a dependent variable in the equation the vote for that party vs. statewide party/ies on the other side of the left–right cleavage (e.g., for the PSOE vs. the PP). The "Overall R^2" figure used the vote for the PP vs. the parties of the left (PSOE and PCE/IU). Class variables include self-employed vs. working for others, income (or, if that variable produced too many cases of missing data, the interviewer's assessment of the quality of the respondent's housing), and occupational status. Religion was measured by frequency of church attendance (in 2004) or self-description as "very good Catholic," "practicing Catholic," "not-very-practicing Catholic," "non-practicing Catholic," "agnostic," "indifferent," "atheist," or "believer in another religion."

the population with markedly anticlerical views, and a religious sector of society that challenged the legitimacy of that regime. Under Franco, the Church was restored to its privileged position in Spanish society, and, in turn, it initially gave strong support to the authoritarian regime. These earlier periods were marked by a heavy politicization of religion.

The role of religion in Spanish society and politics began to change in the early 1970s. Church officials initiated the depoliticization of religion by distancing themselves from Franco's regime. They further facilitated depoliticization by not explicitly supporting political parties during the crucial first election in 1977.

At the start of the transition to democracy, however, there were widespread concerns that a revival of religious conflict might greatly complicate the processes of political change. Religiosity was very strongly correlated with and reinforced by left–right ideological orientations, and this was clearly reflected in electoral preferences as well. As we will see, religious Spaniards overwhelmingly supported parties of the right and center, while the communist electorate was disproportionately non-religious or atheist. Since potentially explosive issues such as the separation of Church and state, legalization of divorce and abortion, and the status of the religious sector of the education system had to be dealt with in the process of establishing a new regime, it was feared that religious conflict might reemerge.

Restraint on religious issues

The disruptive potential of the religious cleavage, however, was not realized. Both religious and political elites studiously chose to avoid conflict of this kind. As noted in chapter 1, party elites successfully resolved potentially divisive religious issues in the constitution by committing themselves to seeking democratic consensus through moderation and restraint. In making concessions over these issues, party elites may have abandoned the defense of their traditional electoral clienteles' preferences, but they also made an enormous contribution to the consolidation of Spanish democracy. And over the following two decades, the leaders of the two major parties (even after AP had replaced the UCD as the main party to the right of centre) avoided conflictual positions on religious issues.

The one exception involved relations between the state and the private (overwhelmingly religious) sector of elementary and secondary education. Annual budget battles and revisions in the statutes regulating the education system inevitably pitted defenders of the religious sector of education against Socialist governments, whose ministers of education increased state oversight of private schools that receive state funds. For the most part, however, these policy debates had little impact on public opinion until the end of the twentieth century. Even the PSOE government's liberalization of abortion rights in 1985 did not provoke harsh and protracted opposition from the leaders of Alianza Popular.

Religiosity and the vote

Nonetheless, despite the fact that all major parties sought to avoid religious conflict, and despite the fact that the Church took no overt stand in partisan politics, religiosity emerged from the very first elections as a powerful determinant of the vote. As can be seen in table 5.2, religiosity clearly divided the political left and right, particularly in 1982 and in the 1977 and 1979 elections (not included in this table). We suspect that this electoral manifestation of the religious cleavage is the product of "historical memories" of anticlerical socialist and communist parties in the Second Republic and the Civil War.

With the passage of time and the consistent avoidance of religious issues by the major parties, however, religiosity declined significantly as a politically relevant cleavage. In the 1993 election it exerted only a modest influence on the decision to vote for the PSOE or the PP. Overall, the strength of the religious factor declined by two thirds in just over a decade. While, as we shall argue, this was mainly a result of the restraint exercised by party elites and religious leaders, it was also a product of secularization of Spanish society and the diminished role of organized religion in everyday life.

Secularization

In the 1970s and early 1980s, the nature of the religious cleavage itself underwent a profound transformation as a result of the long-term process of secularization.

- In 1970, 64% of those interviewed in a public-opinion survey described themselves as "very good Catholics" or "practicing Catholics." Just 14 years later, only 29% of Spaniards described themselves in these terms.
- During this same time period, the segment of the Spanish population who described themselves as "non-practicing," "indifferent," or "atheist" increased from 12% to 38%.
- Since that time, little additional change has taken place. In 2002, for example, 32% of Spaniards described themselves as "very good Catholic" or "practicing Catholic," while 37% regarded themselves as non-practicing, indifferent, or atheist.

By the end of this process, Spain had become a much more secular country than the United States. This must be regarded as a dramatic development, particularly since as late as the mid-1970s Catholicism was the official state religion and obligatory religious instruction was required throughout the public education system from kindergarten to university level.

The net consequence of this secularization process and the avoidance of polarizing behavior by political elites is that religiosity had ceased to be a divisive force in electoral politics by the 1993 election.

Re-polarization

As we saw in the previous chapter, however, the sharp turn to the right and the explicit embrace of religious issues by the Partido Popular government of José María Aznar after its 2000 electoral victory substantially reactivated the religious cleavage as a determinant of the vote in Spain. And during the 2004–8 legislature, tensions were further increased by the establishment of a close relationship between the PP and conservative sectors of the Church hierarchy, who opposed various policies adopted by the government of Rodríguez Zapatero. This culminated in the convoking of mass demonstrations against the government, as well as an abandonment of the three-decades-old partisan neutrality of the Spanish Catholic Church: for the first time in the new democratic era, the

Episcopal Conference of the Church released a statement calling for Catholics to cast ballots in the 2008 election in opposition to the PSOE government's alleged destruction of democracy, the disintegration of the family, and the breakdown of national unity. It remains to be seen whether this will become an enduring characteristic of Spanish politics or is merely a short-term aberration.

Ideological moderation

As we saw in chapter 4, political parties in Spain are often seen as competing on a left–right continuum (more commonly referred to in the United States as pitting liberal parties against more conservative parties). While the precise meaning of "left" and "right" is complex, multidimensional (involving religion, individualism, economic stands, attitudes towards law and order, etc.), and varies from country to country and over time, it is a very common device that helps voters simplify political life and and interpret several characteristics of parties and their programs. It also helps them to choose among parties because they can select which party is closest to them on the left–right continuum. Seen from this perspective, electoral choice is the joint product of how voters place themselves on the left–right continuum in conjunction with how they assess the position of each political party.

One extremely important determinant of the overall lack of polarization of the Spanish party system is that the vast majority of Spanish voters have been consistently moderate. As can be seen in figure 5.4, the largest bloc of voters is located just to the left of center on the left–right scale. This distribution has remained remarkably stable throughout three decades of Spanish democracy: the mean self-placement of voters between 1979 and 2004 has ranged between 4.5 and 4.8 (with 5.5 representing the exact center of the scale). And only a small and shrinking minority place themselves in positions 1 or 2, on the left, or 9 or 10, on the right: a combined total of 15% in 1979, 14% in 1982, 12% in 1986, 11% in 1993 and 2000, and just 9% in 2004.

It is particularly noteworthy that there is no significant "extreme right" segment of the Spanish electorate or party system (in contrast with the substantial share of the vote that has been cast for Le Pen's National Front in France or Haider's Freedom Party in Austria). At no point between 1979 and 2004 did more than 4% of respondents place themselves in positions 9 or 10 on the left–right continuum, and by 2004 this had fallen to just 2%. We are tempted to speculate that four decades of Franquist authoritarianism has completely discredited the extreme right in Spain, in effect "inoculating" Spanish voters against the appeals of such parties.

Insofar as party leaders correctly perceive the distribution of public opinion as moderate, and insofar as they want to maximize their respective shares of the vote in order to win elections, they should respond by moderating their images, their ideologies, and their programmatic stands. To a considerable degree, this "Downsian" calculation of how to maximize votes underpins the "centripetal"

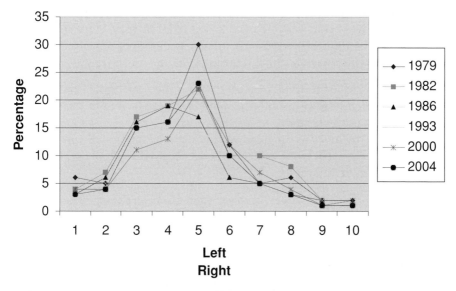

Figure 5.4 Self-placement of Spanish votes on the left–right continuum[a]
[a] It should be noted that the way this questionnaire item was administered in the 1979 survey produced a much lower number of "don't know" and "no answer" responses than was typical of the other surveys.
Sources: For 1979, Richard Gunther, Giacomo Sani, and Goldie Shabad, *Spain After Franco* (Berkeley: University of California Press, 1986), DATA survey; for 2004, CNEP Spanish post-election survey (www.cnep.ics.ul.pt); for all other years, Banco de Datos, CIS

Box 5.8

The "Downsian" modal voter theorem

In *An Economic Theory of Democracy*, Anthony Downs arrayed voters on a policy preference continuum (similar to their placement on our more generic left–right scale). Each candidate for office could also be placed at a specific point on that scale in accord with his/her stand on that particular policy issue. In Downsian analyses of electoral behavior, voters will select the candidate who is closest to their respective issue positions. (When applied to positioning on the left–right continuum, this has become known as the "least distance" model of voting.) In anticipation of this pattern of electoral choice by voters, "rational, vote-maximizing" candidates will reposition themselves (in terms of public statements, policy pronouncements, and general public image) closer to the "median voter" in order to pick up the largest share of the popular vote.

dynamics of electoral competition in Spain, as discussed in the previous chapter. Accordingly, the positions of the two major parties in Spain since 1982 (when the AP replaced the UCD as the largest party to the right of center) conform perfectly with this theorem through the mid 1990s:

- the mean placement of the socialist PSOE on the 10-point left–right continuum marched steadily towards the center, from 3.6 in 1982 to 3.8 in 1986, to 4.5 in 1993 and 1996; and
- voters saw the AP/PP as progressively more moderate, from 8.5 in 1982 and 1985, to 7.9 in 1993, to 7.4 in 2000 (when it received an absolute majority in the Congress of Deputies).

As noted in the previous chapter, however, there has been a slight re-polarization of the Spanish party system since 2000. The image of the PSOE shifted from 4.5 in 1993, to 4.3 in 2000 (when it entered into an ill-fated electoral alliance with Izquierda Unida and the Communist Party), and to 4.1 in 2004, while the public's average placement of the PP moved from 7.4 in 2000 to 7.6 in 2004. The net result is that the ideological space separating the PP from the PSOE widened from 3.1 to 3.5 points on the left–right scale from 2000 to 2004.

Determinants of polarization: a summary overview

These changes in patterns of electoral behavior in Spain over the past three decades make it clear that important characteristics of partisan competition such as the degree of polarization are determined by several factors in interaction with one another. Among the more important factors are:

- the social structure, and the general attitudes of voters;
- the types of political parties; and
- the behavior of political elites.

To be sure, the *long-term social-structural characteristics* of societies are potentially important, but their actual association with political conflict and the nature of the party system is not automatic, by any means. Social change (such as socioeconomic modernization and secularization) can reduce the potential for conflict along class and religious lines by softening social divisions and moderating the attitudes of voters. Whether partisan conflicts are mitigated or exacerbated, however, is determined by other factors, most notably by what sorts of parties emerge and how their leaders behave.

The *types of parties* in a party system have a significant impact on the intensity of conflict. Other things being equal, catch-all parties are by their nature predisposed to downplay the potential for divisive conflict in their efforts to attract a broad array of different voters. Conversely, parties that are more ideological or programmatic (like the AP/PP) or that appeal to particular social groups (like the working-class PSOE in the Second Republic) can deepen cleavages and sharpen political conflict.

The *behavior of political elites* and how they deal with potential political cleavages is partly constrained by the nature of the parties within which they operate. Leaders can act with considerable autonomy in these matters. They can try to increase or decrease the degree of polarization in a given election, and they can try to reform or transform their party to make it more or less centrist or extreme. In other words, leaders can try to push their parties further to the left or the right or towards the center, so widening or narrowing the gaps between the parties, and increasing or decreasing the political conflict between social groups.

In the case of Spain following the death of Franco, these factors helped to soften lines of socioeconomic cleavage and reduce levels of political conflict.

- Socioeconomic modernization, increased affluence, and the expansion of the middle class helped to reduce class polarization.
- Secularization and, especially, the decision by both party and Church leaders to avoid the politicization of religion throughout the transition to and consolidation of democracy helped to defuse the potential for conflict along religious lines.
- These socioeconomic and cultural changes, in combination with a desire to avoid rekindling the divisions of the past, culminated in a moderate, center left distribution of public opinion.
- The adoption of "catch-all" electoral strategies, combined with the great restraint exercised by party leaders in the interest of stabilizing the new democracy, further reinforced this moderation.

The result was that by the mid to late 1990s the dynamics of partisan conflict and competition had become quite moderate. Alternation in government between parties of the center left (with roots in the Second Republic) and the center right (whose founders were prominent in the Franco regime) posed no threat to the stability of Spanish democracy. The partial re-polarization of the system since 2000 is a puzzling anomaly that clearly demonstrates the important independent role played by political elites.

■ Attitudes and electoral behavior in regional party systems: nationalism and regionalism

In this final section of our exploration of basic characteristics of mass-level attitudes and behavioral norms relevant to politics, we turn our attention to three aspects of the regional cleavage in Spanish politics. In some respects, they lie at the core of distinctive regional party systems or sub-systems, as well as differing political trajectories followed by some regions (particularly the Basque Country). They are:

- preferences regarding the form of the state and the current *Estado de las autonomías*;
- national identities; and
- attitudes towards political violence and ETA in the Basque Country.

By no means do these three factors capture the great cultural differences and rich traditions of the various parts of Spain – whose musical expressions range from flamenco in the south to bagpipes in the north – but they do tap the most powerful determinants of political behavior that differentiate one region from another.

Attitudinal support for the Estado de las autonomías

A generation after the initial decisions to decentralize the Spanish state and to establish seventeen autonomous regional governments, a certain consensus seems to have emerged that generally supports the current institutional structure. Among the Spanish population as a whole, as the data in table 5.3 reveal, only small minorities support the formerly centralized state structure, on the one hand, or independence for one's region, on the other. Just 9% of Spaniards favor a centralized state, while only 6% would allow regions to become independent. Eighty-four percent of respondents in a 2005 nationwide poll favor either the current level of autonomy or more regional autonomy within the framework of the Spanish state.

Partisanship and attitudes towards the state

This poll also reveals that attitudes vary between the regions, and even more dramatically among supporters of statewide vs. regional-nationalist parties. By far the highest percentage favoring complete independence for their region are the Basques, 32% of whom support that option. This is almost identical to the percentage favoring a higher level of autonomy within the Spanish state – even though it is one of the most decentralized in Europe. What is most striking is the divergence within that region among supporters of statewide parties as compared with regional nationalist parties. Only 1% of socialist voters in the Basque region favor independence as an option. In sharp contrast, over 90% of HB voters and 63% of EA supporters prefer outright independence, with 44% of PNV voters. While the differences between the statewide and the nationalist parties within this region are quite dramatic, there are also important differences among the nationalist parties (as described in the preceding chapter).

In Catalonia, as well, it is noteworthy that over 1 in 5 favor independence for the region, and over three quarters of ERC supporters prefer independence. Again, patterns in mass-level attitudes closely mirror the stands of party leaders. As noted in the previous chapter, over the past two decades the regional branch of the PSOE has been dominated by Catalan nationalists whose origins can be traced to the two branches of the PSC that merged with the PSOE in 1978. Accordingly, fully 13% of the socialist electorate in that region endorses independence from Spain – very much higher than the level of such support among their socialist counterparts in the Basque region.

As we saw in the preceding chapter, despite its distinctive language and culture, Galicia has lacked a tradition of support for independence from Spain.

Table 5.3 Preferences for different forms of state, 2005[a] (in horizontal percentages)

Community/ party		Preferences				Vote (%) in last regional elections[b]
	Centralized state	Autonomy as at present	More autonomy	Independence	(N)	
Basque Country	**2**	**28**	**37**	**32**	(523)	
IU	–	18	55	27	(11)	3.8
PSOE	5	46	47	1	(74)	11.3
PP	11	81	7	–	(27)	4.2
EHAK	–	–	–	–	(21)	7.1
EA	–	–	37	63	(19)	–
PNV	–	10	45	44	(106)	24.0[2]
Aralar						2.6
Catalonia	**5**	**24**	**50**	**21**	(889)	
IC	4	16	54	26	(50)	5.2
PSOE	4	23	60	13	(347)	29.8
PP	8	57	33	2	(63)	5.2
ERC	–	1	23	76	(103)	13.6
CiU	6	16	55	23	(103)	16.2
Galicia	**7**	**66**	**24**	**3**	(581)	
IU	–	62	35	–	(8)	0.8
PSOE	6	58	35	2	(58)	29.5
PP	13	78	9	–	(130)	20.8
BNG	–	40	44	16	(50)	13.5
Andalucía	**7**	**72**	**20**	**2**	(867)	
IU	6	59	27	9	(34)	
PSOE	4	71	23	1	(354)	
PP	12	77	12	–	(172)	
Spain	**9**	**58**	**26**	**6**	(4,910)	

[a] Rows may not add up to 100 because "don't know" and "no answer" have not been included. *Party* is party voted for in the general election of 2004.
[b] In 2006 in Catalonia, in 2008 in Andalucía, in 2005 in Galicia, and in 2005 in the Basque Country.
Source: Banco de Datos, CIS.

This is clearly reflected in the attitudes of Galego voters (just 3% of whom favor that option), and even among those who supported the Galego nationalist BNG.

In short, the various regions of Spain differ substantially with regard to their preferred state structure. But more dramatic is the divergence of preferences among supporters of statewide Spanish parties and regional nationalist parties within each region. These orientations lie at the core of the regional cleavage, and have served as the basis of political conflicts since the late 1970s. The fact that popular support for independence closely parallels the formal platform positions taken by these parties provides *prima facie* evidence of the extent to which political elites have been able to mold and channel mass-level political attitudes since the early 1980s.

National identities

To what extent do regions and supporters of parties within the autonomous communities vary with regard to their national and regional identities? To answer this question we must first recognize that people who have lived together for centuries – intermingling, intermarrying, and sharing a common culture in addition to their distinctive cultures and languages – do not necessarily see the world in the simple terms of "us vs. them," as some conceptions of national identity might suggest. Instead, people in multinational societies can have multiple, overlapping identities. Moreover, while national identities may not be completely malleable, they certainly can be modified, reduced, or intensified. The emphasis given to one national identity (e.g., Basque) over the other (Spanish) can vary over time, depending upon specific processes and circumstances, and in response to framing by political and/or intellectual elites. And in the case of some regions with their own distinctive languages and cultural traditions (such as Galicia and Valencia), no regionally based national identity has emerged, and no demands for the creation of a separate nation-state have ever been articulated by any politically significant sector of the population; instead, most inhabitants regard themselves as residing within a region that is an integral part of a Spanish nation. More generally, individuals sharing a primordial characteristic (e.g., speaking the regional language) may not feel politically identified with a nationalist cause; conversely, some of those not sharing those primordial characteristics may very well choose to identify themselves with a region's nationalist aspirations.

Moreover, national identities can be held with varying degrees of intensity, allowing political elites some room for maneuver in developing and implementing their political strategies. Indeed, nationalist political elites may have a strong incentive (e.g., in terms of broadening their basis of electoral support) to extend their definitions of nationality and their appeals for political support beyond those sectors of the population sharing a particular primordial characteristic. In the Basque case, for example, we saw that the initial definition of the Basque nation was primordial ("race," as defined by PNV founder Sabino Arana) and rigidly limited to those descending from ethnically pure families. Over the years, however, Basque nationalist political elites have progressively broadened their definition of their target community to include descendants of Spanish immigrants (once dismissed as *maketos*). As a result, many of those who have supported the most extreme nationalist group, ETA, have purely Spanish family names, such as Pedro García López or Manuela Rodríguez.

Any attempt to understand politics and the party systems in Catalonia, Galicia, and the Basque Country must take into account a wide range of factors,

the virtual disappearance of political violence that had occasionally erupted during the transition to democracy. The only notable and tragic exception is, of course, the Basque terrorist organization ETA, which has been responsible for over 3,000 violent acts, including over 50 kidnappings, almost 800 murders, and many more cases of extortion, blackmail, and intimidation. The persistence of its terrorist activities (albeit at a much reduced level compared with the late 1970s and early 1980s) indicates that ETA has managed to create both a complex social movement and a political subculture within which violence has been justified and supported. The movement's main purpose has been to mobilize popular support for the terrorists and recruit new members willing to use violence in pursuit of independence from Spain.

Violence has been a key feature of the Basque polity since the early 1970s. It is uncertain whether it will disappear in the near future or continue at its current low intensity. ETA has created a dense network of anti-democratic social movements in the Basque Country, some of which are willing to undertake mafia-like activities and use violence to intimidate or attack the organization's political adversaries. While few people are actively engaged in such activities, their success (and even the continued existence of ETA) depends on the ambivalent attitude towards violence of many more in the population and some leaders of moderate parties, who frame these events within a context allegedly pitting the Spanish state against the "Basque people." Accordingly, they participate in the "Basque conflict" as "patriots" or "idealists," rather than as criminals, although this is sometimes accompanied by ambiguous assertions that "We agree with their goals, but not with their methods."

Such ambivalent attitudes were often found among many leaders of the relatively moderate PNV and EA since the early 1970s. These views stand in sharp contrast with those of the Spanish electorate as a whole, which rejects violence of whatever origin. One of the most encouraging recent trends in this respect is that public opinion in the Basque Country has become progressively less supportive and more negative toward ETA terrorism. As can be seen in table 5.6, in 1978 about half of the Basque electorate saw ETA activists as "patriots" and "idealists," and only 7% as "criminals." In the late 1970s, few Basques regarded ETA as "terrorists" or "madmen," opting instead for the ambiguous term of "manipulated." Three decades later, as ever larger numbers of Basque citizens became wearied with the disruption of political and social life by ETA terrorism, over half had come to regard ETA militants as "madmen," "terrorists," "criminals," or "murderers," while just 23% considered them to be "patriots" or "idealists."

Not surprisingly, attitudes towards ETA and its use of violence are strongly correlated with one's partisan preference. "Total rejection" of ETA and its violent tactics are strongest among supporters of the statewide or Spanish parties (87% among PP voters and 74% among socialists, with 65% among supporters of IU), but a solid majority (56%) of PNV voters by 1993 had also come to adopt that view. In sharp contrast, only 1% of HB supporters "totally" rejected ETA and its violence. This great attitudinal chasm has led to the political isolation of HB.

Table 5.6 Images of ETA activists in the Basque Country, 1978–2007[a] (in percentages)

Image	1978	1993	1999	2004	2007
Patriots	13	9	13	4	4
Idealists	35	13	36	20	19
Manipulated/fanatics[a]	33	25	11	13	6
Madmen/terrorists[a]	11	14	23	39	36
Criminals/assassins[a]	7	21	8	17	18
No answer	1	18	9	7	17
(N)	(1,140)	(629)	(1,400)	(1,800)	(1,200)

[a] The second term has been included since 1996.

Sources: For 1978, Juan J. Linz *et al.*, *Conflicto en Euskadi* (Madrid: Espasa-Calpe, 1986), 628; and for 1993–2007, *Euskobarómetro*, Departamento de Ciencia Política y de la Administración, Universidad del País Vasco.

Figure 5.5 Massive demonstration in the Plaza de Colón, Madrid, against ETA terrorism, 1997

This isolation, however, has been softened by the existence of some ambivalence among one fifth of PNV voters and one third of those for EA, who (in 1996) saw ETA activists as idealists. More importantly, it has been undermined by the ambiguous statements made by some moderate Basque nationalist leaders calling on the Spanish state to negotiate with ETA to resolve the so-called "Basque problem." This reflects a semi-loyal stance towards Spain's democratic institutions and its constitution, coupled with a belief in independence for the Basque Country. In this sense, the proclamation of a ceasefire by ETA in 1998 helped to narrow the gap between ETA and HB (then called Euskal Herritarrok), on the one hand, and the more "mainstream" EA and PNV, on the other. All of these nationalist parties signed a pact (the Estella Pact, named after the site of this conference) calling for independence from Spain and the integration of Navarra and the French Basque provinces into a new Basque nation-state. In effect, this meant that, in exchange for ETA's suspension of terrorist violence, the moderate nationalist parties would support the creation of an independent Basque state.

In turn, this agreement radically transformed the atmosphere of cooperation between moderate nationalist and statewide parties in a number of PNV-PSOE regional coalition governments (which governed the Basque Country from 1986 until 1998) and anti-terrorist policies (agreed in the so-called Ajuria Enea Pact, signed in 1989 by all parties except HB). After the regional elections of 1998, EH signed an agreement to provide external support for the minority coalition PNV-EA government, which then contributed to electoral gains for Basque nationalist parties in the regional elections of October 1998 and in the local elections of June 1999. The end result was a widening and deepening of the regional cleavage, and increasing polarization between nationalist parties and statewide parties in both the Basque Country and the Spanish parliament. In 1999, ETA ended its 400-day truce and renewed its terrorist campaign, killing several politicians, businessmen, judges, and military and police officials.

In 2006, ETA proclaimed another truce. This occurred at a time of organizational weakness following an effective police effort that led to the arrest and conviction of several of its leaders. ETA's political wing had also been damaged in the aftermath of the Spanish parliament's passage in 2002 (by an 87% majority) of a new Political Parties Law and the outlawing of Batasuna by the Supreme Court. Several of its allied social movements were also banned and prosecuted. In contrast with the previous period, however, the PSOE government's policies were fiercely criticized in parliament by the opposition PP. This was the first time since the establishment of the new democratic regime that a government's anti-terrorism policies had been used by a rival statewide party for partisan purposes.

ETA's second truce ended with the killing of two people in December 2006. By this time, however, other Basque nationalists were less supportive of ETA. This erosion of the group's image, coupled with its organizational weakness and the arrest of several of its leaders, suggested that its ability to continue its campaign of terrorist violence may have been substantially reduced.

■ Summary

In this chapter, we have examined Spain's changing social structure and the ways in which this has influenced citizen attitudes regarding democratic consolidation and electoral competition. We have seen that:

- Despite forty years of anti-democratic political socialization under the Franco regime, support for democracy is actually more widespread and stronger than in many long-established West European democracies. This helps to explain the complete absence of anti-system parties at the statewide level, as well as the stability of Spanish democracy since the early 1980s.
- However, political disaffection (which may be an inheritance from the Franco regime) has reinforced Spain's long tradition of weak secondary associations.
- Socioeconomic development since 1960 has softened the class cleavage, contributing to the adoption of "catch-all" electoral strategies by the principal party of the left, the PSOE.
- Secularization has diminished the role of the Church in Spanish life, while the avoidance of links between parties and religious organizations has helped to depoliticize the religious cleavage. Religiosity, a strong determinant of the vote in the 1970s and early 1980s, had declined substantially by the end of the twentieth century. The re-politicization of religion by some party leaders since 2000 has partially revived this cleavage.
- Spaniards have remained remarkably moderate in their attitudes since the first democratic elections. This has served as an incentive for party leaders to further moderate their stands, thereby contributing to predominantly center-seeking drives in the national-level party system.
- The multilingual, multicultural diversity of Spain, and the distinct political traditions of some of its regions, have led to the emergence of complex national identities. To the extent that these are overlapping and inclusionary (as is the case for most Catalans), these national identities are compatible with peaceful coexistence within the decentralized structure of the *Estado de las autonomías*. Mutually exclusive national identities, particularly when political violence is regarded as acceptable, help to explain the polarization and instability of the Basque Country, especially in the 1970s and 1980s.
- Political elites play decisive roles in molding those identities and related political attitudes, however, and over the decades there has been an increase in the percentage of the population in both Catalonia and the Basque Country adopting multiple, overlapping, non-exclusionary national identities and supporting the decentralized structure of the Spanish state.

■ Further reading

Astudillo, Javier, *Los recursos del socialismo: las cambiantes relaciones entre el PSOE y la UGT (1982–1993)*, doctoral thesis, Instituto Juan March de Estudios e Investigaciones, Madrid, 1998

Fishman, Robert, *Working-class Organization and the Return to Democracy in Spain* (Ithaca: Cornell University Press, 1990)

García de Polavieja, Javier, "¿Qué es el voto de clase? Los mecanismos del voto de clase en España," in *Zona Abierta*, 96–7 (2001), 173–213

Gunther, Richard, and José Ramón Montero, "The Anchors of Partisanship: A Comparative Analysis of Voting Behavior in Four Southern European Democracies," in P. Nikiforos Diamandouros and Richard Gunther, eds., *Parties, Politics, and Democracy in the New Southern Europe* (Baltimore: Johns Hopkins University Press, 2001)

Gunther, Richard, José Ramón Montero, and Joan Botella, "A New Political Culture," in Gunther, Montero, and Botella, *Democracy in Modern Spain* (New Haven: Yale University Press, 2004)

Gunther, Richard, José Ramón Montero, and Mariano Torcal, "Democracy and Intermediation: Some Attitudinal and Behavioral Dimensions," in Richard Gunther, José Ramón Montero, and Hans-Jürgen Puhle, eds., *Democracy, Intermediation, and Voting on Four Continents* (Oxford: Oxford University Press, 2007)

Linz, Juan J., *Obras Escogidas*, vol. II: *Nación, estado y lengua*, ed. José Ramón Montero and Thomas Jeffrey Myley (Madrid: Centro de Estudios Políticos y Constitucionales, 2008)

Martínez, Robert, *Business and Democracy in Spain* (Westport: Praeger, 1993)

Montero, José Ramón, and Kerman Calvo, "An Elusive Cleavage? Religiosity and Party Choice in Spain" in David Broughton and Hans-Martien ten Napel, eds., *Religion and Mass Electoral Behaviour in Europe* (London: Routledge, 2000)

Montero, José Ramón, Joan Font, and Mariano Torcal, eds., *Ciudadanos, asociaciones y participación en España* (Madrid: Centro de Investigaciones Sociológicas, 2006)

van Deth, Jan, José Ramón Montero, and Anders Westholm, eds., *Citizenship and Involvement in European Democracies: A Comparative Analysis* (London: Routledge, 2007)

■ Websites

www.ugt.es	Unión General de Trabajadores
www.ccoo.es	Comisiones Obreras
www.cnt.es	Confederación Nacional del Trabajo
www.ceoe.es	Confederación Española de Organizaciones Empresariales
www.cis.es	Centro de Investigaciones Sociológicas
www.observatoriosocial.org	Observatorio Social

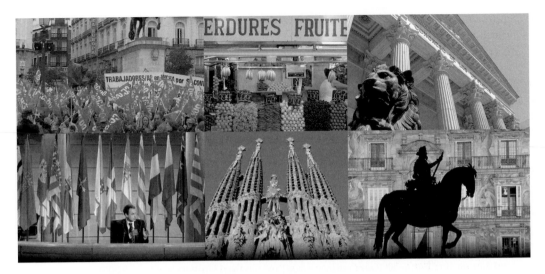

6   Public policies and decision-making processes

Public policy is what government and politics are all about. The policies that are formulated and implemented by governments – with regard to taxation, education, social welfare, public works, etc. – often represent the most important points of contact between government and the people. In democratic systems, these are the goods and services that are delivered to citizens in response to their preferences and demands.

An examination of public policy processes and outputs in Spain can provide particularly valuable insights into the extent to which different types of political regimes do, in actual practice, have a significant impact on the responsiveness of government to its citizens. This is because the regime that existed prior to 1977 was an authoritarian system that explicitly rejected the notion of citizen participation in governmental decision-making, while the current political system is, like all democracies, supposed to provide institutional channels of access to policy-makers. Thus, a comparison of policy processes and outputs before and after the transition to democracy will enable us to address a key question: does politics really matter with regard to the impact of government on most peoples' lives? How and to what extent does democracy help to make government more responsive to the wishes of the people?

In this chapter, we will seek answers to these questions by

- comparing the distinguishing features of policy outputs under the Franco regime with those of the current democracy; and

- analyzing policy-making processes under both political systems to see exactly how the type of political regime can affect the flow of goods and services to citizens.

We will find that democracy does, indeed, have an important impact both on the capacity of citizens to convey their policy preferences to decision-makers, and on the type and volume of government services delivered to those citizens. In short, examining public policy processes and outputs in Spain over the period since the late 1960s helps us to understand the extent to which democracy affects the performance of government institutions.

One of the specific functions of representative democracy is to present policy options to voters in the form of alternative party programs and competing promises made by candidates for office. To what extent have Spain's governing parties since the transition to democracy (the center-right UCD, the center-left PSOE, and the right to center-right PP) differed in the policies they have implemented while in office? Accordingly, in this chapter we will also

- examine the public policy priorities of Spain's democratic governments; and
- analyze the various factors (both domestic and international) that led to the adoption of these policies.

Finally, an examination of the publicly stated policy preferences of the various parties enables us to look forward, insofar as those programmatic commitments are most likely to emerge as the issues over which partisan politics will be fought in the coming years. We will therefore conclude this chapter with

- an overview of the ideological and programmatic commitments of the major Spanish parties, as well as the stands they have taken in their electoral manifestoes or party platforms.

The Franco regime and the impact of democracy on public policy

One of the basic purposes of representative democracy is to give citizens some control over public policy by allowing them to choose among candidates for office those who are most likely to defend their interests, and by providing channels of access through which they can express their policy preferences to office-holders. Authoritarian regimes, in contrast, do not provide such institutionalized mechanisms for the expression of the public will. Recruitment and political accountability primarily reflect the concerns of the dictator or the ruling elite, and do not flow from below – from the citizenry. And in many single-party regimes, the only channels for contact between citizens and the government are those created by and under the control of the ruling elite, and these rarely, if ever, provide equal access to citizens from all sectors of society.

The Franco regime, as we saw in chapter 1, made no pretense of representing the general public in the government's principal decision-making arenas. All significant political appointments were from above, either directly or indirectly under the control of the dictator, Francisco Franco. In making those decisions, moreover, the Franquist elite restricted recruitment to those individuals with conservative values, who were drawn disproportionately from the upper socioeconomic strata of Spanish society, and from the ranks of those groups that had supported Franco's seizure of power – especially religious conservatives who were strongly Spanish nationalist in their political values.

To what extent did this restrictive recruitment of decision-making elites affect the formulation of public policy? Did ordinary citizens, especially those in sectors of society that had opposed Franco in the Civil War, have any means of expressing their policy preferences or pushing for the adoption of policies that would benefit them? A detailed study of decision-making processes and outputs during the final years of the Franco regime (1973–5) was undertaken by one of the authors of this volume with the specific objective of addressing these questions. It involved over 300 hours of interviews with policy-makers inside Franco's state administration, as well as taxation and expenditure data concerning the most important characteristics of public policy outputs. A subsequent series of interviews with government elites who were elected following the establishment of the current democracy, conducted by that same author, has made it possible systematically to compare the processes by which major decisions were made, as well as any changes in policy outputs that may have resulted.

These studies provide further evidence that democracy does, indeed, make a big difference. The policy-making process under the authoritarian regime was under the control of elites who were not accountable to the citizenry and whose policy preferences departed substantially from those of most Spanish citizens (as their electoral preferences would later reveal). With regard to **interest articulation**, policy processes were closed to outside influences, except for demands made by individuals from social strata generally supportive of the regime regarding specific investment projects or other particularistic "payoffs." As a result, the outputs of government were highly disadvantageous to ordinary citizens from modest socioeconomic backgrounds. In addition, since government expenditure policies emerged as the product of a disjointed series of bilateral negotiations between the finance ministry and other departments of the state administration, and since the Council of Ministers felt little sense of collective responsibility for budgetary policies, the "**interest aggregation**" function was inadequately performed.

Interest articulation Among the input or "process functions" conceptualized by political scientist Gabriel Almond is interest articulation. This is the public expression of demands by citizens for specific government services or other narrowly defined policy outputs.

Interest aggregation Almond described this function as one in which specific demands by individual citizens or groups are combined into more comprehensive and coherent policy programs which would appeal to broader sectors of society.

Table 6.1 Tax revenues as a percentage of gross domestic product, 1975

Country	
Norway	44.9
Sweden	43.4
Netherlands	42.9
Luxembourg	42.8
Belgium	41.8
Denmark	41.4
Austria	38.6
Finland	37.7
France	36.9
West Germany	36.0
United Kingdom	35.5
OECD average	**32.7**
Canada	32.4
New Zealand	31.1
Ireland	30.0
Switzerland	29.6
United States	29.0
Australia	27.5
Italy	26.2
Greece	25.5
Portugal	24.7
Japan	20.9
Spain	**19.5**
Turkey	16.0

Source: OECD, *Revenue Statistics of the OECD Member Countries, 1965–1994* (Paris: OECD, 1995), 73.

Policy outputs under the Franco regime

Throughout the final years of the Franco regime, Spain differed substantially from other Western industrialized societies with regard to several important public policy outputs. In 1975, for example,

• its overall level of taxation was the lowest of any country in Western Europe, and it trailed all the other OECD member states except the much less economically developed Turkey.

As can be seen in table 6.1, less than 20% of Spain's GDP flowed to all levels of government in Spain – a level substantially below the OECD average of 32.7%.

As a result of the small volume of revenues flowing to the state during the final years of the Franquist era, in combination with the adoption of conservative balanced budgets, Spain lagged far behind other industrialized societies in the provision of basic services. In 1975,

- only 9.9% of Spain's GDP was devoted to the provision of social services, as compared with the European Community (now European Union) average of 24%.

Indeed, some basic services were at "Third World" levels.

Education

In 1964, Spanish state spending on education as a share of GDP was less than one third of education expenditure levels in Germany, France, and Austria, and less than one quarter of those of the United Kingdom, the Netherlands, and Belgium. Spanish rates of enrollment in higher education in 1967 were as low as impoverished, socioeconomically undeveloped countries such as Upper Volta (now Burkina Faso), Togo, and Paraguay. And with regard to all levels of education,

- Spain's low level of public expenditure on education (as a percentage of GNP) in 1965 placed it in a tie with Angola, in 122nd place out of 131 countries included in an important published study.

A significant reform of the education system was initiated in 1970, but despite this policy change Spain's education system remained underdeveloped and drastically underfunded.

- By 1973, public education expenditures stood at just 2.1% of GDP – a level far behind education spending in other Western European societies (which ranged between 4.2% and 7%).

National defense and the transportation infrastructure

There were other striking examples of the low levels of state budget spending under the Franco regime, including national defense. In 1973, the Spanish government was spending less (as a percentage of GDP) on defense than any other European country except Luxembourg. The country's road system was also sadly deficient. Indeed, it was not until the 1980s that the capital city, Madrid, was connected with the rest of Western Europe by a multi-lane highway.

The exceptional status of social security

The only partial exception to this pattern of extraordinarily low public spending involved the social security system. The origins of this social protection system can be traced to decisions taken decades prior to the coming to power of General Franco, but some important programs were initiated under the authoritarian regime itself. The social security system administered old-age pensions

Box 6.1

Social spending and socioeconomic development

Much of the scholarly debate in the field of comparative public policy has focused on the extent to which government policies are determined by political factors, on the one hand, or by the socioeconomic context within which policies are developed and implemented, on the other. The latter argument includes several components, the most important of which involves poverty and the inability of governments in poor countries to raise a volume of revenues necessary to establish government programs. Succinctly stated, unless a certain threshold of development has been surpassed, revenue scarcity will make it impossible for governments to adopt and implement social welfare policies of the kind and volume commonly found in advanced post-industrial societies.

(first established in 1919), maternity services (1926), occupational injury insurance (1938), disability insurance (1939), and health insurance (1942). This sector of government activity deviates from the extremely conservative expenditure decisions that characterize the rest of the state budget insofar as

• social security spending regularly increased, from 4.2% of GDP in 1965 to 9.2% in 1975.

It should be noted that these levels were still considerably below those found in other Western industrialized societies, but the fact that they were allowed to increase so substantially represents a significant departure from the conservative spending policies discussed above. As we shall see, this is because they were made largely outside of the state administration's budgetary process.

Socioeconomic development and social spending

Why did Spain lag behind other Western countries in the provision of public services? One finding from the comparative public policy literature is that, on a global scale and over the long term, the level of government spending is strongly correlated with socioeconomic development. This is particularly true with regard to social spending: poor countries cannot afford well-developed social welfare systems, while most rich countries generously provide a wide variety of social services. Thus, to some extent the low levels of government spending under the Franco regime can be attributed to the lagging effects of Spain's late industrialization.

But this economic "historical legacy" argument provides, at best, only a partial explanation of these unusual characteristics. By the final stages of the Franco regime in the mid 1970s, Spain had become the world's 10th ranking industrial power, and its per capita GDP in 1973 ($6,945 in Purchasing Power Parity International 1985 Dollars) placed it among the world's 30 richest countries

> ## Box 6.2
>
> *The income-distributive impact of taxes*
> Taxes have important implications with regard to the distribution of wealth among various social strata. "Progressive taxes" (such as estate taxes, luxury taxes, and most income taxes) impose a heavier burden of taxation on the rich than on the poor – that is, the rich pay a larger percentage of their income to the state than do the poor. "Regressive taxes" (such as sales taxes, value-added taxes, and most social security taxes), in contrast, tax the poor on a higher percentage of their income than the rich. Even though all consumers pay the same percentage of the cost of each purchase in VAT and sales taxes, since the poor "consume" a higher percentage of their total incomes than do the rich (who typically save substantial portions of their incomes, thereby exempting them from the payment of these regressive taxes), the poor pay a higher percentage of their incomes than do the rich through these kinds of regressive taxes.

(number 21, if oil sheikdoms are excluded). Nonetheless, as we saw in table 6.1, Spain's overall level of taxation and spending in 1975 was significantly below levels of poorer countries like Ireland, Greece, and Portugal.

- Not only was increasingly affluent Spain not catching up with its Western European counterparts, but between 1965 and 1975 tax revenues (not including social security taxes) actually declined as a share of GDP.

In short, by the mid 1970s Spain had become a relatively affluent, socioeconomically developed society, so its extraordinarily low levels of public spending and taxation could no longer be regarded as a consequence of lagging socioeconomic development.

The taxation system and inadequate public expenditures

Instead, the immediate cause of these unusual characteristics was a taxation system that generated an insufficient volume of revenues. In addition, it was also grossly unfair in its distribution of the tax burden. One study of the actual distribution of the tax burden under this taxation system revealed that in the early 1970s

- upper-income Spaniards paid 50% less in taxation as a percentage of their income than did those in the poorest economic categories.

Thus, the question that must be addressed is: why was this inadequate, regressive, and evasion-prone taxation system allowed to continue? Interviews with high-ranking officials inside the state administration under General Franco indicated that this inefficient and unfair taxation system, and the resulting scarcity of revenues for basic government services, were products of unusual characteristics of economic decision-making processes and the configuration of political forces within this authoritarian system.

Policy-making processes under the Franco regime

One important aspect of the Franco regime that contributed to these unusual patterns of public expenditure or outputs involved the recruitment of government ministers. Conservative fiscal policies were almost guaranteed by the recruitment to office only of persons with conservative political values, and upper- and upper-middle-class social backgrounds. Accordingly, they were generally predisposed to adopt conservative expenditure policies and maintain a regressive taxation system that would preserve the existing inegalitarian distribution of wealth in Spanish society.

This did not mean that government ministers did not request increased budgets for their various departments. Indeed, the annual budgetary role of all government ministers except the Minister of Finance was to advocate higher levels of spending for their respective programs. And in some cases, spending on a handful of programs did increase significantly.

The overall conservatism of these public expenditure policies, however, was substantially reinforced by an unusual characteristic of decision-making under the Franco regime, namely:

- these policies were determined almost exclusively through private, bilateral negotiations between the top-ranking officials in the finance ministry and officials in the various ministerial departments.

Unlike decision-making in most parliamentary democracies, the Council of Ministers never attempted to systematically control the budgetary priorities of the state. Its role was effectively limited to the perfunctory ratification of decisions made in the course of the preceding series of bilateral negotiations between the finance minister and the various spending ministers. Accordingly, it was not possible for a group of spending ministers to "gang up" on the finance minister to bring about a higher level of spending on government services.

Those other ministers had no incentive to support the spending claims of one of their colleagues.

- Unlike in democratic systems, where the government is collectively accountable to the general public, ministers in Franco's governments were accountable as individuals only to the dictator himself.

Accordingly, there was no collective sense of responsibility for the government's overall expenditure and taxation policies. Instead, each spending minister was interested only in increasing his own department's budget, and, given the privileged position of the finance minister in the decision-making process, a spending minister had no means of exerting external pressure on the finance minister to accede to his demands.

Box 6.3

"Spending advocates" and "guardians of the public purse"

It is difficult, if not impossible, for a single individual to deal with the enormity and complexity of the millions of individual decisions that go into formulating a government budget. For this reason, in traditional "incremental" budgeting systems, the budget emerges as the end product of a series of negotiations between individuals playing the roles of "spending advocates" and "guardians of the public purse." The process begins at relatively low levels within each sub-unit of each ministerial department, with the head of that unit (a section chief, for example, playing the role of spending advocate) proposing a budget for the forthcoming year that includes a "base" amount (usually that unit's budget from the previous year) plus an "increment" (an increase above that base level). Negotiations between the section chief and his/her superior (e.g., a director general) focus on the spending advocate's justification of the requested increase. If the director general (playing the role of guardian of the public purse in this early stage in the budgetary process) agrees to the spending increase, then it will be included in his/her budget request along with all similar budget allocations for the sections that make up the *Dirección General* (DG). Then that director general will switch roles, and will subsequently serve as an advocate for the budget proposal of his/her DG, with the minister or his/her undersecretary serving as guardian of the public purse. Again, negotiations between the director general and the undersecretary or minister of the department will focus on the incremental increase requested. If the minister approves of the incremental increases requested by a DG, they will be included in the department's overall budget request. Now it is the turn of the minister to play the role of spending advocate on behalf of his/her department's budget request in negotiations with the finance minister or his/her undersecretary. The finance minister plays the role of guardian of the public purse in bilateral negotiations with each of the "spending ministers" in the state administration. In Franco's Spain, the finance minister's approval of a department's budget (accepting some proposed spending increases, but rejecting most) was usually the final stage in the budgetary process. Budgeting in most democratic systems, however, often involves appeals by a spending minister of a negative decision by the finance minister to the prime minister or the cabinet.

Also unlike democratic regimes, where voters and organized groups outside of the state administration can mobilize their supporters and exert pressure on the government on behalf of certain government programs,

- no institutional bodies outside of the Council of Ministers played significant roles in these decision-making processes.

The Cortes (the authoritarian regime's quasi-parliament) did not modify the government's budget bill or its economic development plan. The National Movement (the regime's single official party) had by the early 1970s become a lifeless bureaucratic hulk that government officials generally ignored. Private-sector interest groups were involved with regard to certain kinds of economic policy decisions, but these did not involve the broad outlines of the government's expenditure priorities. Instead, they involved lower-order decisions regarding individual investment projects, subsidies paid to private firms, the geographical location of various projects, and other economic decisions that affected the narrow interests of specific groups. In short, these contacts involved the articulation of interests of specific groups, rather than aggregated interests or the higher-order priorities of government policy.

In the absence of institutionalized channels of access for most citizens (except for those in the upper social strata who used their personal connections to articulate their demands),

- only sporadic outbursts of protest demonstrations effectively influenced government spending decisions.

However, these mass mobilizations (such as labor unrest in the late 1950s and early 1960s, and the student mobilizations of the late 1960s) were usually spasmodic and limited in scope, and they posed serious risks to the personal well-being of the protesters. Moreover, they sometimes produced a backlash reaction by the government that was contrary to the demands of protesters, such as the increased police repression and declaration of a state of emergency in the Basque Country following protests in the late 1960s.

Sporadic intervention by Franco

General Franco and his closest collaborator (*de facto* prime minister Luis Carrero Blanco) very rarely intervened in the making of economic policy decisions, and when they did, it was because an economic policy decision directly affected something they regarded as lying near the very core of the regime itself. Certain kinds of issues, however, were of great concern to Franco, and thus effectively constituted reserve policy areas. These included:

- matters of public order;
- Church–state relations;
- the Armed Forces; and
- the character of the regime's basic institutions and, in particular, the selection of his successor.

The most important example of Franco's direct intervention in budgetary matters involved a tax reform proposal presented to the Council of Ministers in 1973. This bill had been prepared by technocrats in the ministry of finance and the economic development planning office, who saw that the infrastructural weakness of Spanish society was impeding economic development. They called for a modest tax increase, elimination of many features of the tax system that made tax evasion a "national sport" (as described by one government official), and a less regressive structure of taxation. However, Carrero Blanco regarded this tax reform proposal as "socialist," and urged Franco to reject it.

Box 6.4

"Enchufes"

"Here I am, trying to do a technical study of a dilapidated building in Madrid, and a friend of mine phones and says, 'Listen, my brother-in-law and his wife have been living in that building for forty years. If you tear it down, they'll have no place to go.' Well, I don't care whose brother-in-law lives in that building; if I were to declare it structurally sound, and it later collapses, it would be my neck!"

"I'm sorry about arriving late [for dinner] this evening. It's because I've been engaged in this mysterious affair with Pilar Franco [the Generalísimo's sister]. Last week I started getting messages from my maid and my secretary, saying that Pilar Franco had called and wanted to talk to me. Well, that began a week-long hassle of trying to get in touch with her, without success. I even made an appointment with her secretary, setting up a time when I should phone her. But when I called, her maid told me she had just gone to the beauty parlor to get ready for the wedding [of Franco's granddaughter] at the Pardo Palace. So I gave up. While I was getting dressed to come over here tonight, I got a phone call – from Pilar Franco, calling from Salamanca. It was a harrowing experience – the Spanish telephone system was up to its old tricks again, so the whole thing degenerated into a scene from a Jerry Lewis movie: we spent the first five minutes shouting, "Hello, who is this?" at each other over a terrible connection. But finally the line cleared up."

"Well, what did she want?" I asked impatiently.

"She said, 'Listen, I've got a cousin who lives in that building you're thinking about tearing down, and she . . .'"

"How did you respond to that request?"

"All I could tell her is that I had just resigned from the study. I couldn't take all this pressure any more!"

[Excerpt from a dinner conversation between one of the authors and a housing ministry official, January 1974.]

"Enchufes" are personal "connections" that are used by an individual seeking to lobby a government decision-maker concerning a particular project. Since decision-makers are more likely to respond positively to a request from someone they know, rather than a total stranger, lobbyists would commonly use a mutual friend, family member, co-worker, etc., as an intermediary in articulating this demand. Under the Franco regime, such personal networks were largely restricted to the upper socioeconomic strata, which was also the social position of most government decision-makers.

The term *enchufe* literally means "electric plug" or connection through which "the juice" would flow.

- The dictator responded by dismissing the entire government. He replaced it with ministers who were unwilling to push for the enactment of this tax-reform proposal.

In addition, the proposal was classified as a "decision pending before the Council of Ministers," and was therefore kept secret from the general public. There can be no clearer evidence of the impact of authoritarianism on public policy than this dramatic intervention by Spain's dictator.

Government officials interviewed in 1974 and 1975 interpreted this intervention as motivated by the belief that the proposed reforms might alienate the professional and middle classes whose support for the regime had been "bought with low tax rates"; that the proposal was inconsistent with Franco's conservative values and anti-leftist political orientation; and that this proposal might give rise to conflict or at least dissatisfaction among those groups making up the regime's supportive coalition.

The consequences of Franco's intervention in opposing tax reform were far-reaching: the June 1973 ministerial turnover and the suppression of the four-volume finance ministry report effectively killed all prospects for tax reform for the duration of the Franquist regime and imposed severe constraints on the evolution of the entire public sector. As a result, the provision of basic government services remained inadequate until after the death of the dictator and the transition to democracy.

The policy consequences of right-wing authoritarianism

These distinguishing features of Spanish public policy processes and outputs under the Franco regime were systematic by-products of important features of the authoritarian system itself. To be sure, personalism, departmental fragmentation of policy jurisdictions, and powerful finance ministers are by no means unique to Franco's Spain; but these features assumed an inordinate importance under that regime due to the absence of other kinds of factors relevant to policy formulation that are universally found in democratic systems.

In democracies, the function of interest aggregation is greatly enhanced through electoral competition. Elections directly involve the building of coalitions, either prior to the election (as in the United States) or after the election (as in multi-party parliamentary systems), and coalition-building is by its very nature an interest-aggregating process. In formulating electoral appeals – in bidding competitively for electoral or parliamentary support – politicians aggregate the interests of an ever broader range of social groups. These incentives were absent under the Franco regime.

Ministers were responsible not to a mass electorate, with disparate interests and conflicting goals, but to a single individual who did not care about most economic policies most of the time, but did intervene heavy-handedly when he thought that his core concerns were involved. Above all, this entailed the protection of the basic characteristics of his regime. Moreover, the virtually exclusive recruitment of government officials from the upper social strata (especially from the upper levels of the *clases medias*, described in chapter 1) predisposed the policy-making process towards the adoption of conservative budgetary policies that would not alter the inegalitarian distribution of income in Spanish society.

As we noted earlier, the only exception to this pattern was the social security system, which allowed expenditures to increase significantly in the 1960s and early 1970s. The main reason social security spending increased is that this sector of government was completely outside of the regular budget process, thereby immune from cuts imposed by the minister of finance, and it was financed through contributions by workers themselves and their employers. Accordingly, this source of revenues did not imply any income redistribution that might have threatened the economic privileges of the upper socioeconomic strata that dominated the state administration itself.

■ Policy-making under the current democratic regime

Following the death of Franco and the dismantling of his regime, policy processes and outputs in Spain changed substantially. With the removal of the conservative constraints imposed from above, Spanish public policies and decision-making practices progressively converged on patterns more typical of established democracies in advanced post-industrial societies.

One dramatic symbol of the change in policy-making processes could be seen just four months following the first democratic election, in negotiations over the "Pacts of the Moncloa," which committed the government to a series of progressive policy reforms in exchange for restraint by labor unions regarding strike activity and potentially inflationary wage demands. This event is widely regarded as one of the most important symbolic acts of the transition to democracy, insofar as leaders of the Socialist and Communist parties (the latter just legalized earlier that same year) were invited to the prime minister's residence (the Moncloa Palace) for face-to-face negotiations over a wide variety of social and economic policies.

The broad inter-party negotiations over the Pacts of the Moncloa were primarily a manifestation of "the politics of consensus" and particular demands of the transition to democracy. However, regular decision-making processes under the more "majoritarian" style of government which followed enactment of the new constitution also differ markedly from policy-making under Franco.

In contrast with the Franquist regime, *"central" political figures are key players in establishing the broad outlines of government policies.* In all of the governments of Adolfo Suárez, Leopoldo Calvo Sotelo, Felipe González, José María Aznar, and José Luis Rodríguez Zapatero, the prime minister and/or his close collaborators exerted direct control over the establishment of expenditure priorities. Finance ministers continued to conduct private bilateral negotiations with individual spending ministers in the final and decisive phases of the budgetary process, but by no means were they as autonomous in performing this role as they had been under Franco. Accordingly, higher-order spending priorities were explicitly established by the central political figures and did not emerge as the *de facto* product of a series of bilateral bargains struck with the finance minister.

Also in contrast with the Franquist era, when ministers were held accountable, as individuals, only to the head of state, *policy-making in the democratic era is based upon a much keener awareness of the collective responsibility* of the government to society and the electorate. This has led to a much more effective aggregation of interests – a function that was very poorly performed under the previous authoritarian system. Government ministers are more conscious of the need to appeal to the moderately progressive majority of the Spanish electorate, and, accordingly, to formulate policies oriented towards maximizing the production of "collective goods," as compared with a much greater emphasis on rewarding entrenched economic elites that characterize the Franquist era.

With regard to direct participation in the policy process, *groups outside the state administration* (which had no institutionalized role in establishing governmental spending priorities under Franco) *have consistently exerted influence*, and at times have had direct and decisive leverage on the setting of policy. The general passivity of the Cortes under Franco has given way to the much more active involvement of parliament, for example, although the specific nature of its legislative involvement has varied from one phase of democratic government to another (as will be described below). And on several occasions, representatives of opposition political parties, trade unions, and big business have been brought into face-to-face negotiations over socioeconomic "pacts." However, contrary to assertions by some observers that these pacts should place Spain in the category of "neocorporatist regimes," we contend that the predominantly majoritarian style of governance (as described in chapter 2) and the weakness of interest groups in Spain preclude such a designation. Pressure groups lack the permanent channels of consultation with the state that characterize neocorporatist countries like Sweden and the Netherlands. This is not to say that the major trade unions or business associations do not play a significant role in the policy process. They engage in a great deal of particularistic lobbying, sometimes have sufficient power to block government policy proposals (such as various efforts to reform labor relations, as described later in this chapter), and on occasion resort to mass mobilization when they believe their vital interests are at state. But overall, interest groups do not exert systematic influence on the government as a whole.

Only one of the distinguishing characteristics of Franquist policy-making has continued into the democratic era: *government ministers are still largely autonomous in setting policies that fall within the jurisdictions of their respective departments.* Only when highly controversial issues erupt (such as over legalization of divorce, the tight-money policies of PSOE finance ministers, the "industrial reconversion" program, four of the five organic laws regulating the education system, intervention in the war in Iraq, and various efforts to liberalize the labor market) does a broader array of social forces (party, secondary organizations, and, sometimes, mass mobilizations) exert significant influence on the relevant government

Box 6.5

Socioeconomic pacts

In some respects, the corporatist legacy of the Franco regime has had some beneficial effects, insofar as it established norms and expectations underpinning "pacts" among business, labor, and government representatives. These agreements dealt with salaries, the length of the working day, productivity, working conditions, public investment, fiscal incentives for businesses concerning labor contracts, and some specific policy commitments by the government. These agreements have made positive contributions in reducing the number of strikes, controlling inflationary wage demands, and regulating working conditions. They have also contributed to the development of a culture of constructive negotiations between labor and management.

This series of negotiations began with the Pacts of the Moncloa in October 1977, which included direct participation by the UCD government and representatives of other parties, the unions, and the CEOE. In 1979, the CEOE and UGT signed the *Acuerdo Básico Interconfederal*, to which the CCOO subscribed in 1981 under the new name, *Acuerdo Marco Interconfederal*. With the coming to power of the PSOE in 1982, the CEOE joined the two major unions in signing the *Acuerdo Nacional de Empleo*. The next big agreement, the *Acuerdo Interconfederal* of 1984, involved only labor and management (CCOO, UGT and CEOE). The PSOE government returned to these negotiations in 1986, reaching agreement with labor and management over the *Acuerdo Económico y Social*. Following a gap of over a decade, the 1997 *Acuerdo Interconfederal para la Estabilidad en el Empleo* involved the CEOE and the unions (under the auspices of the Aznar government). Finally, in 2006 the Zapatero government negotiated with business and labor organizations over the *Acuerdo para la Mejora del Crecimiento y del Empleo Estable*.

minister. The Council of Ministers would only deal with disputes between ministers that involved issues affecting more than one departmental jurisdiction, or that were brought to the Council by a minister who regarded one of his or her policy proposals to be of such political transcendence as to require broad ministerial deliberation. It is likely that this high level of ministerial autonomy is a product of the extent to which decision-making authority is concentrated in the Council of Ministers, in combination with the general weakness of parliament as an independent policy-making body (as in the case of the British House of Commons, and in contrast with the broad dispersion of powers found in the US Congress).

The Committee of Undersecretaries

A key participant in the legislative process is the Committee of Undersecretaries, composed of the second-ranking officials of all ministries, and whose weekly meetings are chaired by **the Minister of the Presidencia del Gobierno**, who would sometimes also be designated as a Vice President of the Government. This committee has the authority to introduce minor amendments in the text of proposed legislation. If no ministry objects to the text of the proposal, it is placed on the "green list" (*índice verde*) and ratified in the subsequent meeting of the Council of Ministers without debate. If,

on the other hand, deliberations within the Committee of Undersecretaries do not produce a supportive consensus, the matter is put on the "red list" (*índice rojo*) for more extensive discussion in the Council of Ministers, where the prime minister would ultimately resolve the dispute. Deliberation over economic or budgetary matters by the Council of Ministers is rare; normally, the cabinet restricts its plenary sessions to more purely political questions. And never are budgetary disputes resolved through a vote in the Council; the prime minister himself usually arbitrates to produce a resolution of the conflicting preferences of government ministers.

■ Differences among phases of policy-making

While these general characteristics of decision-making have been shared by all of Spain's governments since the restoration of democracy, there are some minor differences from one phase of Spain's post-Franco democratic history to another.

Phase one (1977–1982)

In the first phase of policy-making in the democratic era,

- UCD minority governments, lacking a parliamentary majority, engaged in *ad hoc* negotiations with representatives of other parties in the Congress of Deputies in order to enact legislation.

Sometimes they would move to the left, negotiating with the PSOE for its support, while, on other occasions, they would seek the votes needed to pass legislation from regional parties (especially the Catalan CiU) or from the more conservative AP.

At the same time, the UCD as a party did not play a direct role in the establishment of budgetary priorities (unlike the influential policy research offices of the Conservative and Labour parties in Great Britain). However, intra-party politics did have an impact on many occasions whenever a particular faction demanded specific ministerial posts or policy concessions that would benefit its private-sector allies. This had the unfortunate consequence of reinforcing the jurisdictional fragmentation that had been inherited from the Franquist regime, as well as raising the stakes in factional conflicts within the party.

Among the UCD governments of 1979–82 there was a significant difference with regard to the extent of the prime minister's involvement in the budgetary process. Adolfo Suárez was often preoccupied with matters of "high politics," particularly concerning the tasks associated with completing the transition to the new regime (including negotiations with Basques and Catalans over their respective statutes of regional autonomy in mid 1979). Accordingly,

- Suárez devolved most responsibility for budget policy to a vice president, who was a close collaborator and political ally.

The decision-making style of Leopoldo Calvo Sotelo was significantly different. Calvo Sotelo succeeded Fernando Abril as vice president for economic affairs in September 1980, and served as prime minister from February 1981 through November 1982.

- Calvo Sotelo enjoyed involvement in economic and budgetary matters so much that he continued to play the role of chief budget-policy-maker even after he became prime minister, rather than delegating this responsibility to a vice president.

While this certainly represented a difference in style from that of his immediate predecessor, it makes even clearer the sharp break from the non-involvement on the part of the Franquist regime's central political figures, when the finance minister and (with regard to the development planning process) the commissioner for economic development planning were left to negotiate such priorities largely on their own.

Phase two (1982–1993)

A substantial modification of these economic decision-making processes occurred following the 1982 election. The first three Socialist governments of Felipe González (1982–6, 1986–9, and, to a markedly lesser extent, of 1989–93), were supported by an absolute majority in the Congress of Deputies, and therefore did not need to negotiate with other parliamentary parties in order to pass legislation. Moreover, the democratic regime was consolidated by this time, so the government was not constrained by the same reluctance to undertake controversial policy reforms as were the previous UCD governments. Thus, in contrast with the broad inter-party consultations of the "politics of consensus," and with the shifting, *ad hoc* coalition-building procedures that characterized the period immediately following enactment of the democratic constitution,

- more majoritarian decision-making norms were adopted, and the government's sense of political security enabled it to adopt bold and unpopular economic restructuring policies, such as the "industrial reconversion" program (which we describe later in this chapter). Input into the legislative process from opposition parties reached its lowest level during the 1982–6 legislature.

- A second distinctive feature of budgetary processes under the Socialist governments of Felipe González was the dominant priority-setting role of the prime minister.

González was heavily involved in establishing general priorities at the beginning of each budget cycle, and he often directly intervened at the end. Moreover, consideration of legislative proposals in the Committee of Undersecretaries was tightly controlled by González's powerful ally, Vice President Alfonso Guerra. The cumulative impact of frequent interventions by González over the course of more than a decade was to leave his imprint on the spending and taxation policies of the Spanish state. In particular, the emergence of education and infrastructural development as the government's top priorities were reflections of his own personal policy preferences.

- Another distinguishing characteristic of the PSOE government was the influence of the party.

Often, in disputes between spending ministers and the finance minister, the programmatic commitments of the party were invoked in frequently successful efforts to secure additional funds for a particular sector of government activity. In addition, the executive committee of the party would sometimes discuss the budgetary priorities that were emerging from negotiations within the government, and would support the budgetary requests of a spending minister. In general, the existence of a relatively homogeneous party executive, which (unlike the faction-ridden UCD) was able to reach consensus on key aspects of public policy, represented an important asset for spending ministers in their annual battles with the finance minister.

Phase three (1993–2000)

The coming to power of the PP in 1996 put an end to fourteen years of Socialist government. However, the basic features of the decision-making processes under the first Aznar government (1996–2000) had actually been established under the last González government (1993–6). What the two had in common was the absence of a parliamentary majority. Accordingly, these single-party minority governments depended on the support of other parties in parliament to pass their legislation. But unlike the minority UCD governments of 1977–82, which negotiated *ad hoc* agreements with parties of both left and right in efforts to secure legislative majorities,

- both the PSOE government of 1993–6 and the PP government of 1996–2000 formed durable legislative alliances in order to pass their legislation.

In neither case, however, did the smaller parties in these agreements occupy ministerial posts in a coalition government.

In the case of Felipe González's final government, this took the form of a legislative alliance with Convergència i Unió. The importance of the CiU during this period was so substantial that its party leader, Jordi Pujol, was commonly referred to in the press as the *de facto* vice president of the government – even though, as President of the Generalitat (the Catalan regional government) he did not even hold a seat in the Spanish parliament.

The narrowness of the PP's electoral victory in 1996 made it impossible to sustain a minority government with just the votes of the Catalan CiU. Prime minister José María Aznar therefore established a formal parliamentary agreement that included the Basque Nationalist Party and Coalición Canaria, as well as the CiU. Taking into consideration the relatively small size of the PP delegation in the Congress, the government's record of enacting 89% of its proposed legislation is a remarkable achievement. Indeed among all legislative sessions since the reestablishment of democracy, only the legislative success rate of the Socialist government of 1982–6 (which was supported by an absolute majority in parliament) exceeds that figure.

- However, this alliance with centrist and regional parties made it necessary for the PP to renounce part of its legislative program in order to gain their support, and to shift most policies towards the center.

Convergence criteria Before they could abandon their separate national currencies and adopt the euro, EU member states had to meet a number of economic and fiscal-policy objectives. These were intended to maintain price stability following admission of new members to the euro zone. These "convergence criteria" included limits on the level of annual budget deficits, on rates of monetary inflation, on long-term interest rates, and on the size of the standing public debt.

The moderation of policies adopted by this minority government was also reinforced by the constraining influence of the European Union. In its efforts to join the monetary union, the Spanish government was compelled to adopt policies meeting the "**convergence criteria**" imposed by the EU.

With regard to the decision-making style of these PP governments,

- prime minister Aznar exerted close control over the formulation of policy in a manner more typical of a majority single-party government than of a minority government.

He dominated the party, assigned its most powerful leaders to the key posts of Minister of the Presidencia del Gobierno and the Minister of Economics and Finance, and located the Office of the Budget within the Moncloa Palace itself. Aznar personally participated in the establishment of broad policy priorities and in the passing of a tax cut in 1999. His domination of the policy process over a period of eight years was made possible by a high level of party discipline in parliament (unlike the faction-ridden UCD), and a new climate of dialogue that he had established with the trade unions, as well as by the weakness of the opposition PSOE. The Socialist Party could mount only a weak parliamentary opposition, despite having almost as many seats as the PP in the 1996–2000 parliament, and it was soon embroiled in a complicated and conflictual process of selecting a new leader (see chapter 4).

Phase four (2000–2004)

The Aznar government adopted a more markedly majoritarian style following its electoral victory in the 2000 elections. Having secured an absolute parliamentary majority, it was no longer necessary to form a governing alliance with the moderate regional-nationalist parties and restrain policy options in accord with their more centrist ideological stance. A more majoritarian decision-making style and more polarizing, right-wing policies characterized this period.

In particular, beginning in 2002, relations between the government and the principal party of opposition became much more confrontational. To some extent, this coincided with the Aznar government's decision to send troops to Iraq as part of George Bush's "coalition of the willing," despite the intense opposition of the overwhelming majority of the Spanish public. A substantial increase in polarization also resulted from PP policy initiatives regarding Church–state relations (including restoration of obligatory religious instruction in all public and private secondary schools, substantial increases in state subsidies to the Church, and restrictions on scientific research involving such matters as stem cells), as well as economic issues. The latter led to confrontations with trade unions (including a general strike in June 2002), and even with the CEOE (the umbrella organization for big business) over a new law on unemployment insurance.

Finally, in an effort to reduce expenditure in order to make possible another tax cut, there were substantial reductions in spending on infrastructural development, on education and science, and on social welfare programs. In short,

- the Aznar government of 2000–4 adopted a more sharply polarizing and majoritarian style of governance, and
- implemented policies that reversed the convergence of Spanish public expenditures on the European Union norm – an evolutionary process dating back to the very earliest stages of the transition to democracy.

While Spain's governments have conformed to the "majoritarian model" in all phases except that of the "politics of consensus," this confrontational style represented a significant departure from the tolerance and mutual respect that had characterized inter-party relations in previous decades.

Phase five (2004–)

The surprising return to government of the PSOE in 2004 initiated a fifth distinct phase in policy-making. In some respects, continuity with the previous four phases was noteworthy, and provided further evidence of the substantial and systematic differences between decision-making processes under the Franco regime and in the current democracy. Perhaps most importantly,

- the role in determining higher-order policy priorities (i.e., aggregated interests) played by the party, its leader, and his closest collaborators underlines the importance of the regime's "central" political actors and institutions.

This central involvement in policy-making and coordination systematically differentiates the democratic era from policy processes under the Franquist regime.

Continuity with phase four could also be seen in the simultaneous service of the secretary general of the governing party as prime minister, two of whose closest confidants closely supervise the development and implementation of policy. The first Vice President of the Government (who is also minister of the Presidency and spokesperson of the government [*Portavoz del Gobierno*]) presides over the Committee of Undersecretaries, whose policy-making role and procedures were described earlier in this chapter. And the appointment of the minister of economy and finance as second vice president of the government also reinforces the prime minister's ability to coordinate economic and budget policies.

There are some ways in which phase five of decision-making differs from its predecessors. In the absence of a parliamentary majority, the first PSOE government under José Luis Rodríguez Zapatero (2004–8) depended on the parliamentary support of several smaller parties. In some respects, this was consistent with the previously established pattern in which those parties would support the single-party minority government without receiving ministerial posts in the government. But it differed from previous practices in one important respect: unlike the UCD's shifting, *ad hoc* agreements with other parties in support of its legislative proposals that characterized phase one, and unlike the durable alliances with centrist regional parties in phase three,

- the first Zapatero government depended on parliamentary support from parties of the left – Izquierda Unida (the coalition that includes the PCE), and two left-wing Catalan parties, Esquerra Republicana de Catalunya and Iniciativa per Catalunya (which includes the Catalan Communist Party).

This pushed the "center of gravity" of the policy-process decidedly to the left, in sharp contrast with the moderating influences of parliamentary alliances between 1993 and 2000: in phase three, the Socialist government of Felipe González had to adopt more moderate policies in order to satisfy its partner, the center-right Convergència i Unió; and the first Aznar government was restrained by its parliamentary alliance with its more centrist regional allies.

A second characteristic of this phase has been referred to as

- *la política de la crispación* (the closest translation being "the politics of rancor").

As we saw in chapter 4, unprecedentedly rancorous conflict has characterized the strategy of opposition implemented by the second largest party, the Partido Popular, towards the Zapatero government, particularly with regard to the government's territorial policies (i.e., relations between the central and regional governments) and its counter-terrorism strategy. In both of these policy areas, parliamentary criticism has been characterized by vitriolic language and efforts to undercut the legitimacy of the PSOE government by systematically questioning its motives, particularly by accusing it of undermining the national unity of Spain and caving in to ETA. These kinds of accusations, combined with PP-organized protest demonstrations involving hundreds of thousands of persons, not only represent an abandonment of the non-partisan consensus against ETA that had characterized government–opposition relations over the previous two and a half decades, but they also shattered the norms of restraint and mutual respect that had characterized inter-party relations in the earlier years of Spain's post-Franco democracy.

It remains to be seen whether a change in the composition of the parliamentary alliance supporting the second Zapatero government following the electoral collapse of Izquierda Unida in 2008 will shift the center of gravity of policy-making back towards the center, and whether this will contribute to a reduction of polarization between the PSOE and the Partido Popular.

▪ Public policy outputs of the democratic regime

As we saw earlier in this chapter, governments under the Franco regime adopted extremely conservative fiscal policies in the 1960s and early 1970s, maintained an inadequate and regressive taxation system, and starved the public sector of revenues that would have made it possible to provide public services at levels more typical of economically advanced societies. We argued that these policy outputs were the systematic consequences of authoritarianism, which prevented citizens from effectively demanding basic government services and some redistribution of wealth in this inegalitarian society, and which allowed individuals drawn exclusively from the upper and upper-middle classes to use their control over the policy process to protect their economic interests. The Franco regime's corporatism also left a substantial economic legacy in the form of a massive structure of subsidized para-state or nationalized industries, as well as a labor market that was regarded as undesirable by both workers and management. The Franco regime also embraced a reactionary, traditionalist version of Catholicism that outlawed divorce and abortion, and denied civil and economic rights to women and homosexuals. Finally, the state under the Franco regime was rigidly centralized.

To what extent has change in these public policy outputs taken place since the establishment of a democratic regime in 1977? Overall, as we shall see, the transformation of Spain's public policies has been massive. In many respects, these changes in policy outputs represent a multifaceted effort to "undo the excesses of *franquismo*" that had made Spain notably "exceptional" within Western Europe.

What is remarkable is that the broad outlines of these policies were shared by all of the governments of the post-Franco era, with some slight nuances. Unlike the United States, for example, there was no deep chasm separating parties of the left or right concerning social welfare: while the UCD and PSOE governments increased spending on social protection programs, and PP governments somewhat reduced those expenditures, no major politician in any party has ever pledged to "end welfare as we know it" (as President Bill Clinton and Congressional Republicans did in the mid 1990s). Similarly, both socialist and

Table 6.2 Tax revenues as a percentage of gross domestic product, 1965–2006

Year	All tax revenues as % of GDP		All tax revenues except social security as % of GDP	
	Spain	OECD average	Spain	OECD average
1965	14.7%	25.8%	10.5%	21.1%
1970	16.3	28.3	10.2	22.8
1975	18.8	30.5	9.9	23.7
1977	20.7	32.2		
1980	23.1	32.1	11.9	24.7
1982	24.6	33.3		
1985	27.8	33.9	16.3	25.9
1987	31.4	35.0		
1990	33.2	35.1	21.4	26.8
1995	32.8	36.1	20.5	26.7
2000	35.2	37.4	22.3	27.9
2005	35.8	36.2	23.8	26.5
2006	36.7 (provisional)			

more conservative PP governments regarded liberalization of the industrial sector and the labor market as important policy objectives. And decentralization of the state proceeded under UCD, PSOE, and PP governments alike.

Nonetheless, there were differences in the policy priorities of these parties and governments under their leadership that significantly influenced the volume and structure of policy outputs. Differences between the programs of the PSOE and PP became increasingly sharper after 2000, and will most likely help to structure partisan competition and policy-making priorities in the future.

Taxes

One early sign of this change was immediate and dramatic. In the summer of 1977, less than two months after Spain's first democratic elections in nearly four decades, the tax reform proposals rejected in 1973 were enacted by an "emergency decree" issued by Spain's first post-Franco democratic government. These were followed by a number of other tax reforms, enacted through more conventional legislative processes. The overall effect was to massively expand the volume of resources flowing to the state, and bring Spain into much closer alignment with the levels of taxation found in other OECD countries (that is, other advanced Western economies). As can be seen in table 6.2,

- tax revenues increased from just 14.7% of GDP in 1965 (which was just over half of the OECD average at that time) to 36.7% in 2006.

By that time, Spain had caught up with the average among OECD member countries.

Similarly, changes in the structure of the taxation system greatly reduced its regressivity. In 1970, only 11.5% of total tax revenues (amounting to just 1.9% of GDP) was generated through the progressive income tax. Most of the other sources of tax revenues imposed a heavier burden on the poor than on the rich. By 1995, however, more than twice that share of tax revenues (23.6%, or 9.4% of GDP) came from the income tax. Moreover, other tax reforms increased the top marginal rate of taxation for the wealthiest Spaniards, cut taxes paid by the poor, and eliminated tax loopholes benefiting the rich, making the taxation system much more progressive than it had been under Franco. This provides clear evidence that

- the advent of democracy made it possible for the majority of the population to effectively demand and receive greater fairness in taxation.

Alternation in power between parties representing different social strata and different sets of economic interests (another manifestation of the impact of democracy), however, also left its mark on the structure of taxation.

- The replacement in government of the Socialist Party by the more conservative Partido Popular in 1996 resulted in significant movement away from these income-redistributive tax policies.

By the 2000 fiscal year, the share of total tax revenues derived from the income tax had fallen back to 18.7%. While the tax cuts enacted by the Aznar government favored the upper socioeconomic strata, we should not forget that even under this conservative government democratic Spain was more committed to economic equality through fair taxation than any government under the Franco regime.

The Aznar government's tax cuts, first implemented in 1999, did have a marked impact on the size of the state budget and the ability to finance government services. These tax cuts were part of a neoliberal philosophy stressing greater reliance on market forces and a reduced role of government. Spending on all major categories of government activity, as we shall see, declined as a percentage of GDP. These trends were accelerated following the PP's securing of an absolute majority in parliament in 2000: the overall volume of public expenditures fell from 45% in 1995 to 39.9% by 2001.

The Aznar government did not, however, reverse the preceding PSOE governments' efforts to reduce the burden of regressive social security taxes. Under the Franco regime, the social security system had been allowed to increase, in part because it derived its revenues from regressive taxes on workers, as well as from direct contributions by employers. By 1975, nearly 48% of all government revenues were derived from social security taxes. Beginning under the UCD governments, but especially under the governments of Felipe González and the PSOE, efforts were made to reduce the burden of social security taxation by funding social security expenditures out of general revenues. In 1977, only 3.6% of the social security system's revenues came from state-budget transfers; by the last year of UCD governance (1982), this had risen to 14.9%; but by 1994, fully 34.8% of the social security system's revenues came from the general revenue fund, whose burden of taxation was much more progressive. Accordingly, social security revenues declined from 48% of total tax revenues in the last year of the Franco regime to 36% in 1995. And this trend continued under Aznar's more conservative PP governments. Social security revenues further declined to 34.9% of all taxes collected by the Spanish state by 2000, and to 33.6% in 2005 under the Zapatero government.

Finally, integration within the European Union has had a substantial impact on the structure of taxation in Spain. Like all other EU members, Spain was required to introduce a **value-added tax (VAT)**. Nonetheless, the income-redistributive effect of this regressive "European tax" was more than offset by the impact of the change of regime: where 40.8% of total tax revenues were derived from regressive taxes on goods and services in 1965, by 2005 this share of total revenues had fallen to 28.0% – below the OECD average of 31.9%.

> The **value-added tax (VAT)** (*impuesto sobre el valor añadido*, or *IVA*). Value-added taxes are like sales taxes insofar as they are ultimately paid by consumers at the time an item or service is purchased. Like sales taxes, they are regressive: even though all consumers pay the same percentage tax on purchases, the wealthy save substantial amounts of their incomes, and the amount saved is exempt from this taxation, while for the poor, whose marginal propensity to consume is usually close to 100%, this tax is imposed on a larger portion of total income. VAT is different from a sales tax, however, insofar as it is imposed on the "value added" at each stage in the production process: for an automobile, for example, this would include mining, the forging and stamping of steel parts, their assembly into a car, and the mark-up in price by the retail sales agency. (Also see Box 3.5.)

Government spending

One extremely negative consequence of the taxation system under Franco was that the state was starved of funds needed to provide basic government services. As we have seen, however, a series of changes in that system was initiated by the UCD governments of 1977–82, and continued under the PSOE governments of 1982–96. This made it possible for spending on social services and the economy's physical infrastructure to increase from previously Third World levels and converge on those typical of other advanced countries.

Another major structural change that followed the end of the Franco regime is the decentralization of the state. While nearly all taxes are still collected by the Spanish state administration, a steadily increasing share of government expenditures is under the control of the autonomous communities – from 0% in 1978 (before the establishment of the first of the CCAA) to 14% in 1985, to 23% in 1995, to 35% in 2005.

Education

As can be seen in table 6.3, the pitifully low levels of spending on education throughout the 1950s and 1960s had been raised somewhat as a consequence of the General Education Law in 1970, but education expenditures in the final year of the Franquist era still placed Spain in last place among industrialized societies.

Table 6.3 The evolution of Spanish public expenditures, 1953–2001

| Year | Percentage of gross domestic product spent on ... | | | |
	Education	Defense	Social protection	State capital investments
1953	0.7	2.6	—	—
1963/4	1.5	2.1	—	2.1
1970/3	2.1 (1973)	1.5 (1973)	9.5 (1970)	2.7 (1970)
1975	2.2	1.7	12.1	2.7
1980	3.3	2.0	18.1	1.9
1985/6	3.6 (1985)	2.0 (1985)	19.5 (1986)	3.7 (1985)
1989/90	4.1 (1990)	1.8 (1990)	20.1 (1989)	4.9 (1990)
1991/2	4.3	1.6	22.5	5.2 (1992)
1995	4.5	1.4	20.4	6.1
1997	4.4	1.3	19.6	4.9
1999	4.4	1.2	19.0	5.4
2001	4.3	1.2	18.9	5.1

Sources: 1970 and 1975 social protection data from Juan Velarde, *El tercer viraje de la Seguridad Social en España y América* (Madrid: Instituto de Estudios Económicos, 1990), 109; social protection data 1980–92 from Gregorio Rodríguez Cabrero, "Políticas de rentas," in Miguel Juárez, ed., *V Informe sociológico sobre la situación social en España* (Madrid: Fundación FOESSA, 1994), 1449; social protection data for 1994 from OECD, 2002 (www.OECD.org/xls/M00029000/M0002983); education and defense expenditures 1953–75, from Richard Gunther, *Public Policy in a No-Party State* (Berkeley: University of California Press, 1980), 50, 62, and 68; education 1994, *Anuario El País 1995*, 117; education 1990 and 1995 from OECD, 2002 (www.OECD.org/xls/M00022000/M00022095); defense spending 1990, 1992, and 1994 from SIPRI (Stockholm International Peace Research Institute), 2002, http://first.sipri.org/non_first/result_milex.php; other education and defense data, Rodríguez Cabrero "Políticas de rentas," 1458; capital investment data for 1953–90 from Julio Alcaide Inchausti, "Tendencias macroeconómicas," in Salustiano del Campo, ed., *Tendencias sociales en España (1960-1990)* (Bilbao: Fundación BBV, 1994), 72, and for 1992 from José María Maravall, *Los resultados de la democracia* (Madrid: Alianza Editorial, 1995), 112. All data after 1995 are from Ministerio de Hacienda, *Actuación económica y financiera de las Administraciones Públicas* (Madrid: IGAE, Ministerio de Hacienda, 2002), 92–5 and 113–32. (Social protection includes health expenditures, and capital investments include both gross fixed capital formation and other capital expenditures, such as aid to investment.)

This was quickly and dramatically altered after the transition to democracy. The Moncloa Pacts (discussed above) included a commitment to increase education spending, and under the UCD government of Adolfo Suárez the share of GDP devoted to public education increased by half. Under the PSOE governments of the 1980s (whose top expenditure priority was the development of the social and physical infrastructure),

* education spending in Spain caught up with levels typical of other Western democracies.

These greater expenditures resulted in spectacular increases in enrollment rates in secondary and higher education. Between 1982 and 1994, the percentage of young persons aged 14 and 15 who were enrolled in school increased from

76.9% to 99.7%, while enrollment rates among those aged 16 and 17 increased from 57.3% to 78%. Similarly, the number of university students more than doubled, from 640,000 in 1979 to nearly 1.4 million in 1994, making Spain's university enrollment rate (37% of those aged 20 to 24 in 1993) one of the highest in Europe. By the late 1980s it could be said that

- the Spanish education system, in little more than a decade, had been transformed from the most poorly developed in the industrialized world to one that (at least in quantitative terms) exceeded most other Western European countries, and this impressive status has been maintained since then.

Another important change in the education system involves the profound decentralization of the state. In accord with the 1978 constitution and the autonomy statutes of Catalonia, the Basque Country, Galicia, Andalucía and the Valencian Community, regional governments assumed full jurisdiction over education policy in the 1980s. In the late 1990s, the remaining autonomous communities also took control over education, making it one of the most profoundly decentralized sectors of government. As a result, the functions of Spain's ministry of education and science have been sharply limited. Administrative coordination of education in Spain is performed by a Sectoral Conference on Education, composed of the *consejeros* (ministers) of the various regional governments and the Spanish minister of education, whose function is basically consultative.

Similarly, other changes in expenditure policies clearly differed from those of the Franco regime, but they also reflected the distinct policy priorities of Spain's democratic governments, as well as the impact of some significant aspects of the international and domestic environment.

Social protection

The primary concern of UCD prime minister Adolfo Suárez was the establishment and consolidation of Spanish democracy. Unfortunately, the death of Francisco Franco corresponded almost exactly with the onset of two deep, worldwide recessions, triggered by the "oil crises" of 1973–5 and 1979–81. This had clear implications for the government's expenditure policies. Soaring increases in unemployment rates (which rose from less than 3% in 1973 to over 20% of the labor force in the early 1980s) introduced socioeconomic stresses into an already demanding domestic political environment. In order to help mitigate social tensions as potential sources of increased political conflict within the precarious new democratic system,

- the Suárez government gave high priority to social protection programs regarding health, old age, maternity, disability and unemployment.

As can be seen in table 6.3, government spending on these programs increased by half (in terms of the share of GDP committed to these expenditures) between 1975 and 1980. In short, the special requirements of the transition to democracy

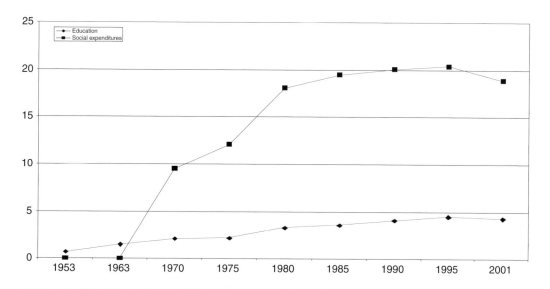

Figure 6.1 Social expenditures in Spain, 1953–2001[a]
[a] "Social expenditures" does not include spending through the social security system.
Source: Carles Boix, "Spain: Development, Democracy, and Equity," prepared for the World Development Report Background Papers (2006), 46.

implied that the government should immediately increase social protection expenditures.

It is noteworthy that spending on these programs quickly reached a "plateau" of around 20% of GDP (as can be seen clearly in figure 6.1). Their share of GDP has increased marginally in some years (in response to economic recessions) and decreased in others, but the major adjustment of social protection expenditures occurred during the crucial stages of the transition to and consolidation of democracy.

The conservative budget policies and commitments to tax cuts of the Aznar governments, however, did have a substantial negative impact on social protection spending. As table 6.3 reveals, state budget expenditures on social protection declined from 20.4% of GDP in 1995 to 18.9%. The net effect of these cuts was to further diminish Spain's ranking among EU countries in terms of social spending. After two decades during which Spanish public policy outputs were converging on those of other advanced Western European countries, the gap separating Spain from the average level of social spending among EU countries significantly widened: in 1993, Spain was less than 5 percentage points below the EU average of 28.8% of GDP devoted to social programs; by 2002, it lagged by more than 7 percentage points.

This situation has changed since the return to power of the PSOE in 2004. The Zapatero government has established new social policies and increased spending on established programs. Its policy agenda has combined orthodox economics with redistributive social policies, thereby reversing the decline of social protection spending under the previous Aznar governments. Further reinforcing its social democratic programmatic predilections is pressure from the PSOE's left-wing allies in parliament – Izquierda Unida and the two Catalan parties, IC and ERC.

In a manner similar to education policy, responsibility for and resources in support of many social protection programs have been devolved to the autonomous communities, although the laws governing these transfers maintain a collaborative role for the central government. Since the partisan make-up of the CCAA governments varies from region to region, the evolution of these social policies also varies. These include health, old-age protection, family services, disability policies, and consumer protection.

Infrastructural investments

One of the reasons why important government ministers in the Franco regime (including the minister of finance and the commissioner for economic development planning) proposed the aforementioned tax reform in 1973 is that they understood how the inadequacy of the country's infrastructure was impeding economic growth. Roads, ports, airports, etc., were all seriously deficient, and were limiting the economy's ability to expand. Blockage of their tax reform proposal by Franco and Carrero Blanco, however, put all plans for significant improvements on hold.

The demise of the Franco regime and the emergency tax reforms of 1977 seemed to remove obstacles to substantial infrastructural development. Indeed, some of the would-be reformers from the Franco regime who had worked on the abortive 1973 tax reform proposal served as ministers or high-ranking state administration officials in the UCD governments of 1977 and 1979. They had hoped that they might finally be allowed to proceed with their economic development plans. Unfortunately, the UCD governments were prevented from doing so by the deep recessions that afflicted Spain in the late 1970s and early 1980s.

Economic downturns both restricted the flow of tax revenues to the state and (as explained above) required high levels of expenditures on social protection programs, especially unemployment insurance payments. The net result was that state spending on capital investments was crowded out of the budget, and actually declined as a percentage of GDP from 2.7% in 1975 to 1.9% in 1980. This erosion of infrastructural spending thus reflected the impact of constraints originating in the economic environment, rather than ideological or programmatic preferences of the UCD. But in light of the high priority given by prime minister Suárez to the consolidation of democracy (which, in turn, dictated substantial increases in social protection spending), there was little choice but to postpone the modernization of the economy and its infrastructure.

By the time the PSOE government came to power in late 1982, one constraint on policy-making had been removed and a powerful new incentive to modernize Spain's economy had emerged from the international environment: Spain's democratic regime was by now largely consolidated, while the anticipated entry of Spain into the European Community (now European Union) meant that economic reform would have to be given top priority. Particularly important was development of Spain's social and physical infrastructure. As we saw above, one key component of these reforms was the full development of the education system, since increased competitiveness of the Spanish economy required a better-educated labor force.

A second aspect of the PSOE government's economic development strategy was the massive increase in investment in the country's physical infrastructure. As the data in table 6.3 reveal,

- the level of state capital investments nearly doubled as a share of GDP between 1980 and 1985, and nearly tripled by 1992.

This made possible a huge improvement in the country's transportation system. What had been (along with that of Portugal) one of the worst highway systems in Western Europe in the early 1980s was transformed by the mid 1990s into one of the best, with multi-lane expressways linking virtually all the regions of Spain. This not only removed "bottlenecks" that had slowed down economic activity, but also stimulated the domestic economy and encouraged a substantial increase in private-sector and foreign capital investments in Spain between 1985 and 1990. The overall level of capital investment increased from 19.5% to 24.4% during this 5-year period.

While it is not possible to directly attribute subsequent economic growth to these infrastructural investments, it is noteworthy that

- during the period 1985–90 Spain experienced a significantly faster rate of economic growth (4.5%) than the average for EC member countries (3.1%), and its 5.6% growth rate in 1987 was the highest in Western Europe.

Even though the PSOE's approach to economic development has been called a "supply-side" strategy, it differs markedly from the kinds of policy prescriptions of "supply-side" economists in the United States, who hold as an article of faith the belief that economic growth is the direct result of tax cuts and minimal government interference with the market economy. Instead, the "social-democratic supply-side" strategy of the PSOE involved an active role of the state with regard to a number of policy areas. It sought to increase the competitiveness of the Spanish economy principally through government investment in the economy's infrastructure, and through "rationalizing" the industrial sector by undoing the excesses of corporatism and making firms more efficient (as described in the following discussion of "industrial reconversion"). Under the PSOE, government expenditures increased from 38% of GDP in 1982 to 45% in 1995, at the same time that high levels of economic growth transformed Spain into an affluent and modern country. The impressive success of the PSOE's economic development strategy calls into question the simplistic assertion that economic growth requires low taxes and minimal government involvement.

As part of its effort to reverse the growth of government spending,

- infrastructural investments were substantially reduced under the PP governments of José María Aznar.

This spending cut was partially offset by the increased flow of investment funds from the European Union's Cohesion Fund (which played an extremely important role in the development of the national highway system) and by development programs of the expanding CCAA governments. With the highway network nearing completion, the Aznar government concentrated its infrastructural spending on two ambitious new programs – the National Hydraulic Plan and the development of a high-speed rail network.

The Zapatero government developed its own Strategic Program for Infrastructure and Transportation (*Programa Estratégico de Infraestructuras y Transporte – PEIT*), whose annual expenditures initially amounted to about 1.5% of GDP. This plan channeled substantial investments back to the highway system, with the objective of increasing the extent of freeways and toll expressways from 9,000 km to 15,000 km. It would develop "horizontal" highway links (e.g., directly linking Catalonia with Galicia), thereby reducing dependency on the "radial" network that had Madrid as its center. It would also continue the development of Spain's high-speed rail network.

"Industrial reconversion"

A major thrust of the economic reforms stimulated by the anticipated entry of Spain into the European Community (which took place on January 1, 1986) involved the imposition of market discipline upon the sizable and inefficient sector of para-state industries inherited from the Franco regime.

For several reasons, maintenance of this legacy of the corporatist past could not continue. First, the inefficiency of many of these industries may have been tolerable during the period of autarky in the 1950s (when Spain's isolation from the rest of Western Europe meant that these firms faced no foreign competition), but

- there was little doubt of their inability to compete with more efficient producers based in other EC countries after tariff barriers were removed.

Second, many of those firms were so inefficient that they had to be subsidized by the Spanish government. However,

- government subsidy payments to industrial firms would have violated EC (now EU) policy, since they would have given those firms an unfair competitive advantage within the EC Customs Union.
- Finally, subsidy payments to inefficient "rust belt" industries, producing goods for which there was little market demand, represented a drain on the government's revenues, depriving other, more worthy, government programs of scarce resources.

Accordingly, the first PSOE government under the leadership of Felipe González boldly adopted an "industrial reconversion" program intended to modernize the Spanish economy and prepare it for the rigors of competition within the EC.

- Tens of thousands of redundant employees of para-state firms were laid off (particularly in the steel and shipbuilding industries), inefficient plants were closed down, and some firms (including the automobile manufacturer, SEAT) were sold to the private sector.

This was not the same kind of "neoliberal" program of privatizations as Margaret Thatcher was implementing in Britain at the same time, nor was it of the kind that the PP government of José María Aznar would undertake in the late 1990s. It was never intended to transfer the bulk of nationalized industries to private hands. Instead, its goal was to improve the efficiency of those industries, focusing the activities of para-state firms on key sectors within which they might enjoy a competitive advantage. As a result, the scope of privatization was limited.

Nonetheless, the closing of steel and shipbuilding plants (particularly in Valencia and Galicia) provoked bitter and sometimes violent protests by laid-off workers, and drove a wedge between the PSOE government and its allied socialist trade union, the UGT. In combination with the González government's restrictive monetary policy, these policies gave rise to intense conflict between the PSOE and its former union ally, eventually leading to a breakdown in this century-long collaborative relationship (as we saw in the previous chapter).

Why did a *socialist* government engage in this bold program of closing or trimming down nationalized or para-state industries, while the preceding center-right UCD government refused to do so, despite the urging of many economists and economic elites that supported the party? One reason is that by late 1982,

- democracy was largely consolidated in Spain, and it was possible for the political system to survive even in the face of intense labor unrest.

Indeed, out of concern over the disruptive potential posed by social unrest that might have resulted from the bankruptcy of inefficient para-state firms in the late 1970s, the UCD government actually *increased* the nationalization and subsidization of firms during its tenure in office.

Secondly,

- the González government of 1982–6 was supported by an absolute majority of Socialist deputies and senators in the Cortes, and faced no credible electoral threat from another party.

In contrast, the minority UCD governments lacked the votes necessary to move these policies forward, and would have faced fierce opposition from the Socialist and Communist parties in parliament had it chosen to do so.

Finally,

- the González governments were deeply committed to economic moderniza-tion and European integration, and the policy-makers who formulated these policies were firm believers in the virtues of competition within a "social market economy."

A different approach to reorganizing the para-state sector was adopted by the Aznar government immediately after coming to power in 1996. In some respects, this program of deregulation and "rationalization" of para-state industries represented a continuation of policies initiated under the PSOE governments. As had been the case under the previous PSOE governments, the ministerial posts most directly relevant to these policies were under the control of the most neoliberal sector of the government.

- But the PP gave much heavier emphasis to outright privatization of these firms.

Between 1996 and 2000, nearly $30 billion in fixed capital was transferred to the private sector, generating "windfall" income that amounted to nearly 1% of GDP in each of those years. These one-time revenues, in combination with the termination of subsidies to the 47 privatized firms, reduced budget deficits, and helped Spain meet the "convergence criteria" imposed by the EU as a precondition for becoming a founding member of the euro zone. But the sale of public assets to private-sector investors was also intended to serve a domestic political purpose. In addition to advancing the neoliberal ideology that the party increasingly embraced following its conversion from the post-Franquist Alianza Popular, the party sought to expand its "natural" electoral base by making stock ownership more widespread, thereby swelling the ranks of the property-owning middle and upper-middle classes.

With regard to deregulation,

- market liberalization was pushed most aggressively in the energy and telecommunications sectors, and initial steps were also taken with regard to air and rail transportation.

In contrast, there was little change with regard to deregulation of more politically sensitive sectors, like housing, public transportation, professional associations (many of which had a restrictive "guild" mentality), pharmaceuticals, mining, and steel-making. Overall, liberalization was not pursued in a consistent or even coherent matter, as reflected in the reintroduction of regulations and price controls in response to inflationary outbreaks, and in heavy state investments in key para-state firms (such as Repsol, the petroleum firm, or Telefónica, the burgeoning giant that has subsequently established a worldwide communications empire) just prior to privatization. Indeed, there was substantial government intervention in an effort to create "national champion" firms by designating certain individuals (many of whom were personal friends of Aznar) as managers and establishing a stable core of supportive stockholders.

The Zapatero government reversed this latter policy by eliminating the partisan nature of appointments to the governing boards of public and para-state firms, although it allowed directors appointed by the previous PP government to retain their positions. It also streamlined the bureaucracies of these enterprises. Its 2004 Plan for Energizing the Economy (later subsumed within the National Reform Program of 2005)

- significantly reduced government regulation of the economy and encouraged greater competition in the private sector.

These two objectives of the Reform Program were successfully implemented, but a third component intended to increase productivity has had little impact. The most important deregulation initiatives involved the telecommunications, audiovisual, electrical, and postal sectors. At the same time, new regulations concerning social and environmental protection were set in place. Finally, the accountability of government to citizens was enhanced by increasing access to government data.

Labor policy

Another legacy of the Franco regime was a corporatist structure of labor relations. While the state-corporatist *sindicatos* were completely liquidated in the early stages of the transition to democracy, a number of policies and behavioral norms have carried over into the current democratic era with decidedly negative implications, both with regard to the competitiveness of the Spanish economy, and with regard to unequal access to stable employment and the benefits of the social welfare system.

The authoritarian regime outlawed strikes, but it also imposed a rigid set of constraints on employers with regard to the job security of their workers. Heavy-handed government regulation took the place of collective bargaining and the market mechanism, with a detrimental impact on both workers and their employers. The latter lost flexibility with regard to the deployment of labor (forcing employers to retain workers in posts where they were no longer needed), while the job security granted to workers came at the cost of artificially low wages.

The transition to democracy led to prompt legalization of the right to strike and greatly enhanced collective bargaining between workers and employers. This substantially benefited workers, but these political developments did not include a substantial relaxation of job security guarantees, which employers had hoped for.

Full-time Spanish workers are guaranteed 45 days of severance pay for each year they were employed, up to a maximum of 42 months. Thus, an employer wishing to terminate a worker who had held a job for 6 years would have to pay over one full year in severance payments, over two years of pay for a 12-year employee, etc.

- This creates a structure of incentives that perpetuates serious rigidities in the labor market, which employers believe undercut the efficiency of their firms and their ability to compete in international markets.

It also introduces serious distortions into Spain's social welfare system. Unemployment insurance and retirement pensions are tied to employment through the social security system. Since employers have to pay substantial amounts into that system for each "permanent" employee, and since they cannot get rid of redundant or incompetent "permanent" workers without paying enormous severance settlements, they are reluctant to hire new full-time workers. Instead,

- a common practice is to hire new "temporary" workers, under so-called "precarious contracts," then fire them just short of the 6 months on the job that would have entitled them to "permanent" status and all of the resulting social welfare benefits that come with employment.

The result of this practice is an exceptionally high level of unemployment and job insecurity among young people, who would be bounced from one "temporary" job to another – all without the social protection benefits received by "permanent" workers. A common response to the resulting poverty and insecurity of young people, in combination with the soaring cost of housing in Spain, is that a stunningly high percentage of young people continue to live in their parents' homes.

- In 1997, 90% of males aged 19–24, and 60% of males aged 25–9, still lived with their parents, and these percentages had increased steadily over the previous two decades.

Efforts to reform this system have been successfully opposed by organized labor, whose members, not surprisingly, were overwhelmingly full-time employees who benefited from this system. In the course of labor–management negotiations relevant to the various socioeconomic "pacts" (see Box 6.5), unions have promised fewer strikes, non-inflationary wage demands, and a new culture of negotiation and mutual confidence to employers, but in return for retaining these job security guarantees. The result has been the maintenance of rigidities in the labor market, especially with regard to the terms of dismissal, as well as salary "leveling" irrespective of productivity gains or the profitability of the various sectors of the economy. Efforts by Spanish governments (particularly in 1997, under the PP, and 2006, under the PSOE) to alter these restrictive policies failed to have much of an impact, and powerful unions (despite their low membership levels) have preserved the privileged legal status of their members.

To some degree, this represents a predictable failure of democracy.

- The winners in these struggles have been the well-organized, politically powerful labor unions.
- The losers, in contrast, lack political resources.

Unemployed young people, women entering the workplace for the first time, and immigrants are not represented by powerful or influential interest groups; they tend to be unorganized and leaderless; and because they tend not to vote regularly (or not at all, as is the case with the immigrant population), they have little power in the electoral arena. Accordingly, they have little voice and no political resources to employ in the policy-making process. Governments, therefore, have little incentive to undertake bold measures to address these problems, since the principal beneficiaries are sectors of society that do not vote regularly, while their reform efforts could alienate powerful unions and their members. In 2006, for example, the PSOE government chose to address these problems through "consensual" negotiations with the unions and employers over a new "pact" (the *Acuerdo para la Mejora del Crecimiento y del Empleo Estable* [Agreement for the Improvement of Growth and Stable Employment]), rather than the more "majoritarian" (and politically risky) approach of introducing new legislation in parliament. While the resulting agreement includes some modest incremental adjustments of existing policies (providing incentives for employers to make "temporary" positions permanent, for example), the requirement to pay 45 days of severance pay for each year worked remains untouched.

The persistence of these labor-market rigidities with regard to permanent workers, juxtaposed against a sizable segment of the labor force beset with extreme job insecurity, have given Spain an odd macroeconomic profile that distinguishes it (in a highly undesirable way) from that of the average European Union country:

- The level of "temporary" employment is much higher in Spain than else-where; 34% of workers are employed under "precarious" temporary contracts, and in agriculture, construction, and the hotel industry, these levels are between 44% and 61% of all employees.
- Female participation in the labor force and female employment are much lower than in the rest of Europe.
- Youth unemployment is a serious problem.
- And the massive increase in immigration since the last couple of years of the twentieth century has created a sizable and growing underclass of poor, temporary workers without the social protection benefits that accrue to other citizens.

Indeed, the very success of the dynamic Spanish economy has created a social (and potentially political) problem: job creation in Spain accounts for one third of all new employment that took place in the European Union in the mid 1990s, and this has served as a powerful magnet attracting immigrants from North Africa, Sub-Saharan Africa, and Eastern Europe. Spain – a country that had "exported surplus population" to Latin America and Western Europe for centuries – has, since 2000, had one of the highest rates of immigration in the world, and, in absolute numbers, is second only to the United States in terms of the number of people migrating into the country. The impact of these population shifts is huge: in 1996, only 1.4% of the population were immigrants; by 2007, this figure had risen to 9.9% of the population. Clearly, the exclusion of this rapidly expanding sector of the population from full, fair participation in the labor market and the social security system cannot continue indefinitely without serious social and political consequences.

Not surprisingly, immigration has become a significant political issue. Given Spain's proximity to North Africa and its enormous coastline, Spanish governments have been unable to control the entry of undocumented immigrants into the country. While no major party took a strong stand on this issue prior to 2005, the expansion of immigrants' access to social protection benefits by the PSOE government in that year triggered strong opposition by the Partido Popular. Immigration has been a divisive political issue ever since.

■ The policy agenda: the future lines of partisan conflict?

To what extent does politics matter? More specifically, how much difference does it make which party governs a country? Cynical citizens might be tempted to conclude that it makes no difference – that politics has little impact on the daily lives of citizens since governments all adopt the same policies irrespective of their partisan coloration. Our response to these questions is more nuanced: with regard to most sectors of public policy, the positions taken by parties (both in opposition and in government) differ significantly.

In this concluding section, we shall examine the policy proposals of the major Spanish parties in the 2004 and 2008 election campaigns. One of the key functions of democratic politics is to present to the voters real political alternatives, not only in terms of the individuals competing over formation of the next government, but also with regard to the promises they make to voters. In some political systems, or at least in some elections, this function is not performed very well, insofar as candidates are allowed to speak in vacuous generalities or raise "red herring" issues that are designed to conceal their real intentions. In others, however, parties and candidates clearly announce their plans, and present to voters alternative policy agendas that they promise to enact if they should be elected to office. In general, Spain falls into this latter category.

Earlier in this chapter, we saw that there were systematic differences among Spain's governing parties that were reflective of their respective programmatic commitments. The UCD governments were most concerned with the tasks of establishing and consolidating the new democratic regime. Accordingly, preserving "social peace" through expanding social protection policies and reducing the regressivity of the taxation system were both given high priority. The PSOE governments under Felipe González, in contrast, were able to focus their attention on economic modernization, and stressed development of the educational and physical infrastructure of the economy. At the same time, as a social democratic party, they maintained the social welfare safety net that had been built up under UCD governments, and they enacted further reforms of the tax system. And the PP governments under José María Aznar, consistent with their more conservative ideological orientation, enacted a number of tax cuts (with regressive redistributive impact) and reduced spending on social programs, in addition to efforts to enhance the role of religion in Spanish society and its education system. All of these structural changes in Spanish public expenditures were predictable manifestations of their fundamental ideological and programmatic commitments. In accord with democratic theory, they provide evidence that public policy outputs have been adjusted in line with the preferences of the electorate.

Other major changes are not rooted in long-standing ideological or programmatic differences, but nonetheless demonstrate how policies have responded to the wishes of the electorate. With regard to foreign policy, for example, the 2002 decision by the conservative government of José María Aznar to ally itself with the United States in the invasion and occupation of Iraq represented a major break from Spain's previous European orientation. This policy shift was opposed by the overwhelming majority of Spanish public opinion, as well as by the PSOE opposition under José Luis Rodríguez Zapatero. When the Zapatero government came to power in 2004, one of its first acts was to fulfil its electoral promise by reversing this policy, removing Spanish troops from Iraq, and, more broadly, loosening its ties with the Bush administration. Policy differences between the two parties on this important issue were clearly perceived by Spanish voters in 2004, and had an important impact on their voting decisions; and the parties acted in accord with the wishes of their respective electorates.

Another sharp difference between the two major parties in that same election involved what Americans would call "family values," and was not rooted in the traditional ideological orientations of the two major Spanish parties. Zapatero and other PSOE candidates in the 2004 election promised to expand the rights of homosexuals. The change in the Civil Code by the Zapatero government, shortly after the election, to legalize marriage between homosexuals represented, to say the least, a radical shift away from the traditionalist religious orientation of the Franco regime, and even set Spain apart from other European countries at that time. Such a policy change would have been inconceivable under the conservative Partido Popular.

What about the parties' most recent commitments to future policy changes, as reflected in the election manifestoes (or party platforms) presented to voters in the March 2008 election campaign? These party platforms not only present a roadmap for the likely course of public policy following the election of a new government, but, more broadly, they give some indication of the areas over which parties disagree, thereby representing an outline of the lines of partisan conflict for coming years. They also serve as an important instrument for holding governments accountable for their performance in government, since they help voters determine if the governing party had actually "delivered" what it had promised the electorate prior to assuming its mandate.

While the major parties' electoral programs shared some common themes (such as calls for reforms that would enhance the competitiveness of the Spanish economy, and for tighter immigration controls), they also included some sharply divergent stands. In general, these appeared to confirm the PP's shift to the right with regard to a number of important dimensions of policy and political conflict – including foreign policy (along the lines discussed above), the fight against ETA terrorism, redistributive fiscal and social welfare policies, Church–state relations, and the structure of the state.

The failure of negotiations between ETA and the Zapatero government during the March–December 2006 "truce" ended the multi-party *Pacto por las Libertades y contra el Terrorismo* (Pact for Freedom and Against Terrorism), and initiated a period in which counter-terrorism policies would be the objects of partisan conflict. While the PSOE election platform was silent on the issue of future dialogue with ETA, the PP, on the one hand, continued to attack the PSOE's previous policy, while Izquierda Unida, on the other hand, called for dialogue and criticized the government's counter-terrorism policies as violations of fundamental individual liberties. These opposing stands clearly reflected an abandonment of the inter-party consensus against ETA among nationwide parties, and suggested that partisan conflict over this matter would continue in the future.

Unprecedented budgetary surpluses amassed under the Zapatero government stimulated a plethora of promises to expand publicly funded welfare programs. In this respect, the PSOE and PP staked out opposing stands with regard to fiscal and budget policies, with the Zapatero government departing markedly from Aznar's policies of cutting social spending in order to make possible tax cuts (which disproportionately benefited upper-income Spaniards). An erosion of economic conditions in early 2008 (triggered by the financial crisis and collapse of the housing market in the United States) provided an opening for the PP to criticize the PSOE's economic performance. It also appeared to give credibility to the PP's attack on Spain's educational system, on the grounds that it was failing to meet the needs of a modern economy.

A revival of a politicized religious cleavage was the most noteworthy development of the 2008 election campaign. On one side, the PSOE and IU called for a national debate over the *Ley Orgánica de Libertad Religiosa* (the Organic Law on Religious Freedom), passed three decades earlier to promote and enhance the non-denominational character of the Spanish state. Closely linked to this were support from the two parties of the left for expanded abortion rights and a reduction in state financial support for the Catholic Church. The PP and the Church hierarchy adopted sharply conflicting stands in opposition to these proposals. Indeed, the Episcopal Conference of the Church overtly criticized the policies and overall stance of the PSOE government, and called for religious Spaniards to vote accordingly. This was the first instance of overtly partisan intervention by the Church in a Spanish election since the Second Republic, suggesting that the religious cleavage – dormant for nearly three decades – had been revived.

Finally, the territorial structure of the state pitted the Partido Popular against most nationwide and regional parties. It pledged to enact a law formalizing key policy jurisdictions as "inalienable" responsibilities of the central government. The PSOE, in contrast, favored additional reforms of autonomy statutes along the lines of the legislation it had negotiated with Catalonia in 2006. But the CiU called for still more transfers of governmental authority, the creation of a Catalan court of cassation (court of appeals), and direct representation in European Union institutions. Finally, the PNV called for a referendum on Basque self-determination as the only vehicle for resolving its historical conflicts with the Spanish state.

In the aggregate, these diverging partisan stands clearly indicated that Spanish politics had become substantially more polarized than it had been, not only during the transition and the "era of consensus," but also in comparison with the 1990s. While many lament the increasing rancor among opposing political leaders that has accompanied this polarization, others have noted that the clarification of policy differences and a greater willingness to confront them head-on can also be interpreted as behavior characteristic of a consolidated democratic system.

■ Summary

In this chapter, we have examined public policy outputs and policy-making processes in Spain since the late 1960s – that is, under both the authoritarian Franco regime and the current democratic system. This has enabled us to address a crucial question in political science: *does democracy matter?* We have uncovered plentiful evidence that it does.

- Despite the fact that by the early 1970s Spain had become relatively affluent and modern, the public policy outputs of Franquist governments more closely resembled those of poor Third World countries than of advanced industrialized societies.
- In sharp contrast, in nearly all policy areas (including taxation, education, social welfare, and infrastructural development), democratic Spain's policy outputs have converged on levels characteristic of affluent Western European countries.

We have argued that the distinguishing characteristics of these policy outputs are systematic products of the basic nature of authoritarian and democratic political regimes.

- Democracies establish institutional channels through which the policy preferences of the majority (such as demands for government services and a fair system of taxation) can prevail over the self-interests of privileged classes. Conversely, an authoritarian political regime rooted in those privileged classes can repress demands for redistribution and adopt policies in their own self-interest.
- Democratic regimes hold governments collectively responsible for the policies they adopt, so central political figures (prime ministers and the cabinet) and governing parties intervene in policy-making in support of "aggregated interests" that will appeal to the majority of the electorate. In the authoritarian regime of General Franco, however, the dictator was largely uninterested in most policy matters, and, since government ministers were held accountable as individuals for the performance of their departments, there was little intervention by central political figures in systematically setting the policy

priorities of the government. The "interest aggregation" function was poorly and sporadically performed in this fragmented policy process.

A key function of democratic systems is to present to voters alternative policies from which they can choose at election time. Indeed, in Spain there are significant differences between parties of the left and right in this respect, although all of these democratic governments adopted and implemented policies that were closer to the Western European mainstream than did the governments of the Franquist regime.

- The centrist UCD governments (1977–82) and the Socialist governments of Felipe González (1982–96) expanded social services, rapidly developed the education system, and adopted more progressive forms of taxation. The González governments also "rationalized" the economy by reforming corporatist para-state industries, and modernized the infrastructure (especially through highway construction).
- The conservative Partido Popular governments of José María Aznar (especially the majority government of 2000–4) reduced the public sector's reliance on progressive taxes, cut back on social services, and privatized a number of industries.
- When the support of small parties was necessary to sustain a minority government in office, they influenced the direction of public policy. Moderate regional parties pulled both the Socialist PSOE government of 1993–6 and the conservative PP government of 1996–2000 towards the center of the left–right continuum, while the PSOE government of José Luis Rodríguez Zapatero was encouraged to adopt more leftist policies by the left-wing parties on which it depended for parliamentary support.

In short, democracy works in Spain as it is supposed to work.

■ Further reading

Boix, Carles, *Political Parties, Growth and Equality: Conservative and Social Democratic Economic Strategies in the World Economy* (Cambridge: Cambridge University Press, 1998)

Encarnación, Omar, "Social Concertation in Democratic and Market Transitions: Comparative Lessons from Spain," *Comparative Political Studies*, 20 (1997), 387–419

Gibson, Heather D., *Economic Transformation, Democratization, and Integration into the European Union* (Basingstoke: Palgrave, 2001)

Gomà, Ricard, and Joan Subirats, eds., *Políticas públicas en España: contenidos, redes de actores y niveles de gobierno* (Barcelona: Ariel, 1998)

Grau, Mireia, and Araceli Mateos, eds., *Análisis de políticas públicas en España: enfoques y casos* (Valencia: Tirant lo Blanch, 2002)

Gunther, Richard, *Public Policy in a No-Party State: Spanish Planning and Budgeting in the Twilight of the Franquist Era* (Berkeley: University of California Press, 1980)

Gunther, Richard, P. Nikiforos Diamandouros, and Dimitri A. Sotiropoulos, *Democracy and the State in the New Southern Europe* (Oxford: Oxford University Press, 2006)

Gunther, Richard, José Ramón Montero, and Joan Botella, "Public Policy and Decision Making: From Dictatorship to Democracy," in Gunther, Montero, and Botella, *Democracy in Modern Spain* (New Haven: Yale University Press, 2004)

Hamann, Kerstin, "Spain: Changing Party–Group Relations in a New Democracy," in Clive Thomas, ed., *Political Parties and Interest Groups* (Boulder and London: Lynne Rienner, 2001)

Maravall, José María, *Regimes and Markets: Democratization and Economic Change in Southern and Eastern Europe* (Oxford: Oxford University Press, 1997)

■ Websites

www.bde.es   Banco de España
www.ine.es   Instituto Nacional de Estadística

Glossary of key terms

A priori **judicial review** allows a group of legislators to appeal the constitutionality of a new law to the Constitutional Court even prior to its coming into effect. Much more common is *a posteriori* review, in which the court makes a "corrective" decision regarding cases brought to it involving disputes over the constitutionality of a law only after it has been enacted.

Absolute majority vs. plurality. Some parliamentary decisions require an "absolute majority" for passage, that is, the bill must be supported by at least 50% + 1 of all members of the Congress of Deputies. Others can be enacted only by "qualified majorities" of two-thirds or three-fifths, particularly for the appointment of some counter-majoritarian bodies. And still other bills or policy decisions need only a simple majority of those voting, even though that would amount to only a plurality of members rather than an absolute majority.

Abstract and concrete review. Some judicial systems (such as that in the United States) limit rulings on the constitutionality of the law to specific cases which are appealed to the courts. In Spain, the Constitutional Court engages in both concrete review and abstract review, where a ruling can be issued even when no specific case is appealed to the courts.

Anarchism, of the variety which most strongly influenced European politics in the late nineteenth and early twentieth centuries, is a political ideology that rejects all forms of authority, especially that of the state, but also the authority of religious leaders and property-owning elites. As classically stated by the Russian Mikhail Bakunin (1814–76), "all exercise of authority perverts; all submission to authority humiliates." Accordingly, anarchists were strongly anticlerical, favored abolition of the state, and demanded replacement of private ownership of the means of production with communal ownership.

Anarcho-syndicalism. Anarcho-syndicalists share with anarchists a hostility towards the state, organized religion, and private ownership of the means of production. They differed, however, in that they believed that the abolition of these forms of authority relationships could be brought about only through the organized efforts of workers under the leadership of an anarcho-syndicalist trade union, and through polarization of politics and labor relations which would bring about a "general strike" that would paralyze the economy and bring the state to its knees.

Backbenchers are members of parliament who hold no ministerial or sub-ministerial appointments and are not heads of committees or officially designated legislative leaders. This term was coined in Britain, where government ministers and members of the "shadow cabinet" occupy the front benches in the House of Commons.

Cabinet durability. The length of time that a particular cabinet government remains in office is called "cabinet durability." It can be measured in different ways. One is based on the replacement of individual ministers. It is this measure that produces the 101-day lifespan of the average government during the Second Republic. If we were to use the replacement of the prime minister as the indicator of a change of government, the average cabinet durability between April 14, 1931, and the outbreak of the Civil War on July 19, 1936, would be just over 5 months.

A *Caudillo* is a charismatic figure who dramatically appears on the scene to restore order and provide leadership following a time of chaos. El Cid (who conquered and expelled the Moors from Valencia in the eleventh century) was the very model of a *caudillo*. Francisco Franco claimed the title of *caudillo*, even though he was short and squat, spoke with a high-pitched voice, and looked somewhat silly when bedecked with the paraphernalia of a conquering military hero.

Centrifugal vs. centripetal drives in party systems. Party systems characterized by polarized pluralism have, as the name implies, "centrifugal" tendencies, resulting from each party's pursuit of voters from the more extreme ends of the political spectrum. When most parties appeal primarily to voters near the center of the left–right continuum, the drives inherent in partisan competition are "centripetal," the aggregate result of which is that they adopt more moderate stands that would appeal to centrist voters.

Chancellor democracy. This term is commonly used to denote parliamentary systems in which the prime minister is explicitly designated by the constitution as having the primary role in decision-making and policy implementation regarding the government's foreign and domestic policies. It was originally coined in the late 1950s to describe the dominant role of the prime minister ("chancellor," in the German system) Konrad Adenauer.

"Clientelism" is a form of political loyalty based upon an exchange of favors between a "patron" (typically a local notable or leader of a party faction) and a "client," who, in return, pledges his loyalty and support to his superior in this sociopolitical network.

Comunidades autónomas (CCAA). The autonomy statutes enacted over the 5 years following ratification of the constitution established regional governments for each of the 17 "autonomous communities" thereby created. CCAA are the most powerful government bodies below the national level, followed by municipal government institutions (*ayuntamientos*). Provincial governments (*diputaciones provinciales*) have sharply limited authority.

The Congress of Deputies. The Congreso de los Diputados is the "lower house" of the Spanish parliament (Cortes Generales). The Senate is the "upper house," but nevertheless it is quite weak.

Consolidated democracy. A consolidated democracy is a political regime which is fully democratic (see "Democracy"), whose key political institutions are regarded as legitimate by all politically significant groups, which accept and adhere to democratic "rules of the game."

Convergence criteria. Before they could abandon their separate national currencies and adopt the euro, EU member states had to meet a number of economic and fiscal-policy objectives. These were intended to maintain price stability following admission of new members to the euro zone. These "convergence criteria" included limits on the level of annual budget deficits, on rates of monetary inflation, on long-term interest rates, and on the size of the standing public debt.

The Cortes. The two houses of Spain's present-day parliament (the Congress of Deputies and the Senate) are collectively referred to as the Cortes Generales. The historical origins of this representative body can be traced back to chambers of medieval "estates" (including the aristocracy, clergy, and local notables) which claimed varying levels of authority *vis-à-vis* the Crown. The two most important of these were the Cortes of Castile and the Cortes of Aragón.

Democracy. A democracy is a political system whose leaders are elected in competitive multi-party and multi-candidate processes in which opposition parties have a fair chance of electing representatives to legislative bodies and attaining executive power. These elections must be held at regular intervals, and must allow all members of the political community to express their preferences through the use of basic freedoms of association, information, and communication.

The d'Hondt formula is a procedure for allocating seats among parties within each electoral district. It is a "highest averages" method that divides the number of votes by a series of divisors reflecting the number of seats awarded to each party on the previous round of seat allocation (in contrast with "largest remainder" methods that award seats in accord with numerical quotas surpassed by each party, and then allocate the remaining seats in accord with votes "left over" after the quotas have been taken into consideration). Compared with "largest remainder" systems, the d'Hondt formula has a slight majoritarian bias in its representation of parties in parliament.

Electoral volatility. The magnitude of shifts in the popular vote from one election to the next is referred to as electoral volatility.

The *Estado de las autonomías.* Spain's quasi-federal system, called the *Estado de las autonomías* (state of the autonomies), was established in a piecemeal fashion through the granting of autonomy statutes to each of seventeen Spanish regions, called *comunidades autónomas* (autonomous communities). These give somewhat differing levels of autonomy to each region, representing a departure from the more uniform devolution of political authority to states in most federal systems.

ETA ("Basque Homeland and Liberty," or, in the Basque language, Euskadi ta Askatasuna, founded in 1959) is a clandestine terrorist organization seeking to bring about the secession of four Spanish provinces (Álava, Guipúzcoa, Navarra, and Vizcaya) and three French *départements* (Basse Navarre, Labourd, and Soule) as a newly independent Basque nation-state. Beginning in the late 1960s, in support of those demands, ETA launched a campaign of terrorist violence that, over the following four decades, claimed the lives of over 800 persons.

Fascism is an extremist form of nationalism, rooted in organic corporatism (see Box 5.1) and overtly hostile to democracy. It is militaristic and aggressive, stresses "heroic violence" as a civic virtue, insists upon strict loyalty to a charismatic leader, and does not hesitate to use force to subordinate or eliminate its enemies.

Feudalism is a geographically decentralized sociopolitical order in which the strongest political authority is possessed by aristocrats who own massive tracts of land (and, in the case of serfdom, the peasants residing on it) and function as the principal law-makers, law-enforcers, and law-adjudicators. While they are nominally subservient to a monarch, the king's authority is sharply limited, most commonly consisting of the right to call upon the aristocracy to provide military services temporarily in time of war.

"First past the post" electoral systems. Single-member-district electoral systems are of two types. One of them (as practiced in France and the state of Louisiana) requires that a candidate must receive an absolute majority of votes to be elected. If not, a runoff election is held one or two weeks later among the top candidates, in which the candidate receiving the largest number of votes (absolute majority or plurality) is elected. In Britain and other American states, the candidate receiving the most votes (even if it falls short of 50% of all votes cast) is elected, and there is no need for a runoff. These are commonly referred to as "first past the post" electoral systems.

Fueros were charters of privileges and some self-government rights that were granted to regions, towns, and medieval corporate entities (e.g., the Church). The expansion of the powers of the centralized Castilian state over the following centuries involved the weakening and (in several instances) the abrogation of *fueros* in all regions except Navarra and the Basque province of Álava.

The **Generalitat** is the name of the regional government of Catalonia both today and in the 1930s.

Iberia includes the mainland parts of Spain (that is, all except the North African territories of Ceuta and Melilla) and Portugal (except for the Azores and Madeira islands). It is bounded on the north by the Bay of Biscay and the Pyrenees, on the west by the Atlantic Ocean, on the east by the Mediterranean, and on the south by the Straits of Gibraltar.

Interest aggregation political scientist Gabriel Almond described this function as one in which specific demands by individual citizens or groups are combined into more comprehensive and coherent policy programs which would appeal to broader sectors of society.

Interest articulation. Among the input or "process functions" conceptualized by Almond is interest articulation. This is the public expression of demands by citizens for specific government services or other narrowly defined policy outputs.

Latifundia (a Latin term meaning "broad estates") are huge agricultural properties. The term was first used to describe the slave-worked estates that characterized southern Italy under the Roman Empire, but is now commonly used in reference to such properties in Southern Europe and Latin America.

The left–right continuum. Over more than a century of democratic politics in Western Europe, parties have often been referred to as of the "left," "right," or "center." The left–right continuum is a simplifying device that captures several aspects of political ideology or party program. While the meaning of left and right has evolved over time, and varies from country to country, in the early twenty-first century parties of the "right" have tended to be more religious, opposed to taxes and government spending, favorable towards the socioeconomic status quo, and strongly in favor of "law and order." Parties of the "left" have tended to favor individual freedoms and protection of civil liberties, and a more egalitarian distribution of income, and have been non-religious or sometimes anticlerical.

Legitimacy of a state or political regime entails acceptance of and respect for its norms and institutions by the people. In Spain, continuation of a centralized state that denied self-government rights to historic regions (especially the Basque Country and Catalonia) would have been regarded as unacceptable, and its government authority would have been challenged by significant sectors of the population.

Liberalism emerged in the late eighteenth century in reaction against several aspects of Western European society during the era of absolutism. It stressed the autonomy and dignity of the individual in several domains of social and political life. It demanded more equal civil liberties in contrast with aristocratic privilege, religious freedom rather than subservience to an established state religion, and individual initiative and the free market instead of state-dominated mercantilist economies, and, eventually, it led to democracy in lieu of monarchical authoritarianism. In Spain and some other Western European countries (e.g., France), protracted conflict with the Church infused anticlerical sentiments into "continental" versions of liberalism, but American and English liberalism was largely devoid of hostility towards the church or religion in general. It should be noted that in the United States the term "liberalism" took on entirely new meanings in the twentieth century.

Majoritarian biases in electoral laws. Consistent with the definition of the concepts of "majoritarianism" and "consensualism" set forth in chapter 2, consensual electoral laws are those which allocate parliamentary seats to parties strictly in accord with the percentages of the popular vote they received in the preceding election. Majoritarian electoral laws, in contrast, are those which systematically over-represent the largest party (or, as in Spain, the two largest parties), while under-representing smaller parties or denying them parliamentary representation altogether. They "magnify" electoral pluralities, sometimes to the extent of "manufacturing" an absolute majority in parliament for a party that received less than half of the popular votes cast.

The Ministry of the Presidencia del Gobierno. While the official title of the Spanish prime minister is Presidente del Gobierno (President of the Government), another minister is appointed to preside over the office of the Presidencia del Gobierno, whose principal task is to coordinate policy implementation by the various ministerial departments that govern Spain.

Organic laws are those which establish or modify core governmental institutions or fundamental individual rights. They must be ratified by an absolute majority of all members of parliament, rather than by a "simple majority" of those voting on the measure. As noted in article 81 of the constitution, legislation pertaining to the statutes of regional autonomy, the electoral law, and basic civil rights are examples of subjects that must be dealt with as organic laws requiring absolute majority support.

Party systems are typically categorized in terms of the number of parties with significant representation in parliament, usually distinguishing among 2-party systems, moderately pluralistic systems (with between 3 and about 6 parties), and highly fragmented party systems (with 7 or more parties having significant parliamentary representation). Party systems involve the number of parties with significant parliamentary representation, their patterns of competition and cooperation, and their capacity to form durable governments.

Plurinational states are those that include populations identifying themselves as belonging to more than one national group. In some instances, the minority-national group will identify with both the majority-national group (in this case, Spanish) and the regional-national group (e.g., Catalan). In other instances, however, the two national identities are regarded as incompatible with each other. The latter situation may culminate in an effort to secede from the plurinational state and form a separate, homogeneous nation-state.

Political participation refers to activities undertaken by ordinary citizens aiming at influencing some political outcomes. Its modes, or channels, include an extraordinary variety of forms, but they can usually be grouped into clusters of activities related to voting, political parties, contacting public officials (politicians, media, or public administration personnel), boycotting or consumption of given goods, and protest.

Political socialization is the learning of political attitudes by individuals in a society. It takes place through both formal and informal processes. Formal political socialization involves the intentional teaching of political attitudes, through schools, the media, etc. Informal socialization involves learning as a product of observation of political interactions, participation in political and politically relevant organizations, and passive internalization of the attitudes of respected authority figures, the most important being one's parents.

A **predominant party system** (as described by political scientist Giovanni Sartori) is one in which one party "outdistances all the others," that is, it obtains a share of seats that is sufficient to form a government supported by an absolute majority or a large plurality in parliament over at least three successive elections, and in which the second largest party receives at least 10 percentage points fewer votes. This is a system within which there is democratic competition, but without electoral competitiveness.

Pronunciamientos are rebellions against the national government by military officers. In some instances they may take the form of a *coup d'état*, although in most instances the rebellion is not followed by an attempt by the rebel officers to form a national government of their own; instead, they may be limited to demands for a change of the government, policies, or even constitution of the national government.

Social cleavages. Cleavages are deep and persistent differences in society where (1) objective social differences (class, religion, race, language, or region) are aligned with (2) subjective awareness of these differences (different cultures, ideologies, and orientations), and are (3) organized by political parties, groups, or movements. Cleavages are often the basis of political conflict.

The state is a set of sovereign governmental institutions which controls a well-defined, contiguous territory, which imposes a single legal code over all persons residing in that territory, and which ultimately or potentially possesses a monopoly over the right to use force to implement that legal code.

State-building in the Middle Ages involved two processes. One is the acquisition of territory (typically by war or marriage), and the other involves the establishment of a common set of government institutions and laws.

Supranational institutions are those in which member states have transferred some real decision-making authority to a higher level of government that can make decisions that are binding on all member states by "qualified majority voting," rather than unanimity. The European Commission is an example of a supranational institution.

Value-added tax (VAT) (*impuesto sobre valor añadido*, or *IVA*). Value-added taxes are like sales taxes insofar as they are ultimately paid by consumers at the time an item or service is purchased. Like sales taxes, they are regressive: even though all consumers pay the same percentage of tax on purchases, the wealthy save substantial amounts of their incomes, and the amount saved is exempt from this taxation, while for the poor, whose marginal propensity to consume is usually close to 100%, this tax is imposed on a larger portion of total income. VAT is different from a sales tax, however, insofar as it is imposed on the "value added" at each stage in the production process: for an automobile, for example, this would include mining, the forging and stamping of steel parts, their assembly into a car, and the mark-up in price by the retail sales agency. (Also see Box 3.5.)

Index